FAITH DISCIPLESHIP
Growing as a
FAITH Leader
FACILITATOR GUIDE

Mark H. Anderson
Greg Miller

LifeWay Press
Nashville, Tennessee

© Copyright 2003 • LifeWay Press
All rights reserved

No part of this book may be reproduced or transmitted in any form or by any means, electronic or mechanical, including photocopying and recording, or by any information storage or retrieval system, except as may be expressly permitted in writing by the publisher. Requests for permission should be addressed in writing to LifeWay Press; One LifeWay Plaza; Nashville, TN 37234-0175.

ISBN 0-6330-9332-7

Dewey Decimal Classification: 268.1
Subject Headings: SUNDAY SCHOOL—ADMINISTRATION \ LEADERSHIP \ EVANGELISTIC WORK

Cover photograph © copyright 2003 Carr Clifton Photography.

Old Testament Scripture quotations are from the Holy Bible,
New International Version © copyright 1973, 1978, 1984 by International Bible Society.

New Testament Scripture quotations are from the *Holman Christian Standard Bible*®,
copyright © 1999, 2000, 2001, 2002, 2003 by Holman Bible Publishers. Used by permission.

Scripture quotations marked NKJV are from the *New King James Version*,
© 1979, 1980, 1982, Thomas Nelson, Inc., Publishers. Used by permission.

We believe that the Bible has God for its author; salvation for its end; and truth, without any mixture of error, for its matter and that all Scripture is totally true and trustworthy. The 2000 statement of *The Baptist Faith and Message* is our doctrinal guideline.

The FAITH Sunday School Evangelism Strategy® is an evangelistic venture
of **LifeWay Christian Resources** of the Southern Baptist Convention
and is endorsed by the North American Mission Board.
For information about FAITH, visit our Web site at *www.lifeway.com*.

FAITH churches may obtain additional copies of this book by writing
to LifeWay Church Resources Customer Service; One LifeWay Plaza;
Nashville, TN 37234-0113; by calling toll free (800) 458-2772;
by faxing (615) 251-5933; or by e-mailing *customerservice@lifeway.com*.

Printed in the United States of America

Leadership and Adult Publishing
LifeWay Church Resources
One LifeWay Plaza
Nashville, TN 37234-0175

Contents

The Writers 4

Expression of Commitment 5

Introduction 6

FAITH Visit Outline 8

FAITH Participation Card 10

Session 1   *Growing as a FAITH Leader*: An Orientation 11

Session 2   You Are a Sunday School Leader 29

Session 3   Building a Healthy Sunday School 45

Session 4   You Are Called to Ministry 61

Session 5   Discovering Jesus' Leadership Qualities 77

Session 6   Developing Your Leadership Qualities 93

Session 7   Sharpening Your Leadership Skills 107

Session 8   The FACTS of Multiplication 125

Session 9   Multiplying Your Team 139

Session 10 Multiplying New Sunday School Units 155

Session 11 The Process of Multiplication 171

Session 12 Practicing FAITH 185

Session 13 Growing as a Ministry Leader 193

Session 14 Benefits of Leadership 209

Session 15 Where Do We Go from Here? 223

Session 16 Final Review 237

Supplemental Home Study Assignments 250

Overhead-Cel Masters 271

Using Your CD-ROM 344

The Writers

MARK H. ANDERSON is the senior pastor of Colonial Heights Baptist Church in Jackson, Mississippi. He previously served as the senior pastor of Lynwood Baptist Church in Cape Girardeau, Missouri, which is one of the 28 FAITH Originator Churches. Under his leadership Lynwood began a new mission church, Fruitland Community Church, by using FAITH Teams from the sponsoring church. Anderson teaches FAITH Basic at Colonial Heights in addition to leading a FAITH Team each semester.

Colonial Heights has seen its FAITH ministry grow by fully integrating the FAITH Sunday School Evangelism Strategy®. Colonial Heights had the privilege of hosting the first FAITH Clinic in Brazil with Igreja Batista Memorial in Rio de Janeiro in 2002. Since 1998 Colonial Heights has hosted several FAITH Clinics that have trained numerous pastors and churches.

Anderson is a graduate of Baylor University and Southwestern Baptist Theological Seminary. He and his wife, Karen, have four children: Ashley, Alyssa, Will, and Andrea.

GREG MILLER is the pastor of married adults at Colonial Heights Baptist Church in Jackson, Mississippi. He previously served as an editor at LifeWay Christian Resources of the Southern Baptist Convention in Nashville, Tennessee. He has also served churches in Tennessee and Kentucky. Miller teaches FAITH Discipleship studies at Colonial Heights and also serves as a FAITH Team Leader. He is married to Nancy, and they have three children: Kristy, Allison, and Joshua. Miller is a graduate of Georgia State University and The Southern Baptist Theological Seminary.

Expression of Commitment

FAITH Discipleship: Growing as a FAITH Leader

I commit myself to **FAITH** Sunday School evangelism training in my church. I recognize **FAITH** training as a way to help my church, to grow as a Great Commission Christian, and to obey God's command to be an active witness.

Signed _____

Address _____

City _____ State _____ ZIP _____

Phone number (home) _____ (business) _____

E-mail _____ Fax _____

I will faithfully attend and participate in this 16-week semester of FAITH training as: ❑ a Team Leader ❑ an Assistant Team Leader ❑ a Team Learner

My Team members _____

My Sunday School department/class _____

Dates of my *Growing as a FAITH Leader* training _____

Introduction

Congratulations for completing previous semesters of FAITH Sunday School evangelism training and for making a commitment to further growth as an on-mission Christian through FAITH Discipleship. This stop on your FAITH Discipleship journey is *Growing as a FAITH Leader*.

Leadership is important in any organization. It is even more important in churches because they deal with issues of eternal significance. Even so, many churches fail to understand the necessity of leadership, and they fail to cultivate leaders who are essential to their ministries. Leaders are essential to the church, Sunday School ministry, and FAITH strategy. Despite what some people may claim, leaders are not born; rather, they are developed. The material in *Growing as a FAITH Leader* was written to help you develop in your leadership, whether you are a Team Leader or an Assistant Team Leader. By the end of this semester, you should be able to indicate ways you have grown as a leader in each of the following areas.

1. *You will understand biblical leadership and evaluate yourself against those principles.* As believers, we turn to the Bible to discover leadership insights and principles. Our standard and model for leadership is Jesus Christ. This course will also reveal qualities and skills of other leaders in Scripture whose examples you will want to follow. Through both in-session and at-home activities you will consider ways you need to develop as a Christian leader.

2. *You will understand Sunday School as a strategy and become more effective in carrying it out.* As a FAITH Team Leader, you know that FAITH is a Sunday School strategy. An intentional partnership exists between Sunday School and FAITH, not only for evangelism but also for discipleship and ministry. During the next 16 weeks you will learn more about this connection and your important role in strengthening it in your Sunday School class and in your church.

3. *You will learn how to multiply yourself in your Team, in your Sunday School class, and in other disciples.* A FAITH leader is more concerned about multiplication than addition. This course will show that when you equip others to make disciples, who will in turn equip still others to make disciples, you will unleash a force that will have untold impact for evangelism and discipleship throughout the world.

4. *You will develop your skills as a FAITH Team Leader.* Because you lead different Learners each semester, you must learn to adapt your leadership style based on their needs. In this course you will learn how to encourage and motivate each of your Team members. Likewise, because every visit is different, you must learn to adjust to a variety of witnessing situations. Your Learners look to you for guidance in these situations, so you must continue to mature as a role model they can follow. This course will equip you with practical skills that will strengthen your Team leadership.

Your calling as a FAITH leader is a unique call to make disciples. Rely on God's power and guidance to equip you for spiritual leadership as you study and apply the concepts in this study.

Beside each session title, write the date of that training session in your church. The summary following each session title allows you to overview or review the content as needed.

Session 1: *Growing as a FAITH Leader*: An Orientation Date: _____
   Participants overview goals and content for this semester
   and examine general principles of Christian leadership.

Session 2: You Are a Sunday School Leader Date: _____
   Participants examine Sunday School as a strategy, learn
   the purposes of the church, and identify the role of FAITH
   in strengthening their Sunday School class and their church.

Session 3: Building a Healthy Sunday School Date: _____
   Participants explore practical ways to build a healthy Sunday School.

Session 4: You Are Called to Ministry Date: _____
   Participants understand the mandate and purpose of God's call to ministry.

Session 5: Discovering Jesus' Leadership Qualities Date: _____
   Participants explore Jesus' leadership qualities and learn ways
   to apply them to their leadership responsibilities.

Session 6: Developing Your Leadership Qualities Date: _____
   Participants learn how to develop biblical qualities of leadership.

Session 7: Sharpening Your Leadership Skills Date: _____
   Participants examine practical skills for effective Team leadership.

Session 8: The FACTS of Multiplication Date: _____
   Participants examine the biblical principle of multiplication
   and understand its meaning for their ministries as FAITH leaders.

Session 9: Multiplying Your Team Date: _____
   Participants study ways to multiply the ministry of their FAITH Teams.

Session 10: Multiplying New Sunday School Units Date: _____
   Participants learn ways to multiply Sunday School units in their church.

Session 11: The Process of Multiplication Date: _____
   Participants learn a biblical process for multiplication.

Session 12: Practicing FAITH Date: _____
   Participants spend time practicing in Teams.

Session 13: Growing as a Ministry Leader Date: _____
   Participants study ways to minister to their Sunday School
   class members, new members, and community.

Session 14: Benefits of Leadership Date: _____
   Participants examine the personal, church, and kingdom benefits
   of leadership.

Session 15: Where Do We Go from Here? Date: _____
   Participants consider the next steps they can take to influence
   others through FAITH.

Session 16: Final Review Date: _____
   Participants assess their growth as FAITH leaders this semester.

FAITH Visit Outline

Preparation

INTRODUCTION
INTERESTS
INVOLVEMENT

Church Experience/Background
- Ask about the person's church background.
- Listen for clues about the person's spiritual involvement.

Sunday School Testimony
- Tell general benefits of Sunday School.
- Tell a current personal experience.

Evangelistic Testimony
- Tell a little of your preconversion experience.
- Say: "I had a life-changing experience."
- Tell recent benefits of your conversion.

INQUIRY

Key Question: In your personal opinion, what do you understand it takes for a person to go to heaven?
Possible Answers: Faith, works, unclear, no opinion
Transition Statement: I'd like to share with you how the Bible answers this question, if it is all right. There is a word that can be used to answer this question: FAITH (spell out on fingers).

Presentation

F is for FORGIVENESS

We cannot have eternal life and heaven without God's forgiveness.

"In Him [meaning Jesus] we have redemption through His blood, the forgiveness of sins"
—Ephesians 1:7a, NKJV.

A is for AVAILABLE

Forgiveness is available. It is—

AVAILABLE FOR ALL

"For God so loved the world that He gave His only begotten Son, that whoever believes in Him should not perish but have everlasting life" —John 3:16, NKJV.

BUT NOT AUTOMATIC

"Not everyone who says to Me, 'Lord, Lord,' shall enter the kingdom of heaven" —Matthew 7:21a, NKJV.

I is for IMPOSSIBLE

It is impossible for God to allow sin into heaven.

GOD IS—
- LOVE

  John 3:16, NKJV
- JUST

  "For judgment is without mercy" —James 2:13a, NKJV.

MAN IS SINFUL
"For all have sinned and fall short of the glory of God"—Romans 3:23, NKJV.
Question: But how can a sinful person enter heaven, where God allows no sin?

T is for TURN
Question: If you were driving down the road and someone asked you to turn, what would he or she be asking you to do? (change direction)
Turn means *repent*.
TURN from something—sin and self
"But unless you repent you will all likewise perish"—Luke 13:3b, NKJV.
TURN to Someone; trust Christ only
(The Bible tells us that) *"Christ died for our sins according to the Scriptures, and that He was buried, and that He rose again the third day according to the Scriptures"—1 Corinthians 15:3b-4, NKJV.*
"If you confess with your mouth the Lord Jesus and believe in your heart that God has raised Him from the dead, you will be saved"—Romans 10:9, NKJV.

H is for HEAVEN
Heaven is eternal life.
HERE
"I have come that they may have life, and that they may have it more abundantly"—John 10:10b, NKJV.
HEREAFTER
"And if I go and prepare a place for you, I will come again and receive you to Myself; that where I am, there you may be also"—John 14:3, NKJV.
HOW
How can a person have God's forgiveness, heaven and eternal life, and Jesus as personal Savior and Lord?
Explain based on leaflet picture, FAITH (Forsaking All, I Trust Him), Romans 10:9.

Invitation

INQUIRE
Understanding what we have shared, would you like to receive this forgiveness by trusting in Christ as your personal Savior and Lord?

INVITE
- Pray to accept Christ.
- Pray for commitment/recommitment.
- Invite to join Sunday School.

INSURE
- Use *A Step of Faith* to insure decision.
- Personal Acceptance
- Sunday School Enrollment
- Public Confession

FAITH Participation Card

Name _____ Semester dates _____

Address _____ Phone _____

Sunday School class/department _____ Teacher _____

Other Team members _____

Check one: ❑ FAITH Team Leader ❑ FAITH Assistant Team Leader ❑ FAITH Team Learner

1 2 3 4 5 6 7 8 9 10 11 12 13 14 15 16   Totals

Class Participation
Place a check to indicate completion for the appropriate session.

Present	
Home study done	
Outline recited	

Visitation
Indicate a number for the following areas.

Number of tries	
Number of visits	
Number of people talked with	

Type of Visit (Assignments)

Evangelistic	
Ministry	
Baptism	
Follow-up	
Opinion Poll	

Gospel Presented

Profession	
Assurance	
No decision	
For practice	

Gospel Not Presented

Already Christian	
No admission	

Sunday School Enrollment

Attempted	
Enrolled	

Baptism Explained

Committed	
No decision	

Life Witness

Profession	
Assurance	
No decision	

SESSION 1

Growing as a FAITH Leader: An Orientation

In this session you will—

HEAR IT by learning the purpose of this course and by being introduced to general principles of Christian leadership;

SAY IT by practicing the *Presentation* portion of the FAITH Visit Outline;

STUDY IT by overviewing Home Study Assignments.

IN ADVANCE
- Preview the content of all sessions.
- Read the teaching suggestions and content for session 1. Pay special attention to the description of this course (see pp. 13–16) and to the teachings on Christian leadership (see pp. 16–21). Examine and be prepared to overview the format of Home Study Assignments (see the first week's assignments, pp. 26–28).
- Decide whether to use the session 1 computer presentation (on the CD-ROM inside the back cover of this Facilitator Guide) or overhead cels 1–8 (see pp. 271–78). To make overhead cels for this training course, duplicate the masters provided on pages 271–343 of this guide.
- Make copies of the Celebration Time Report shown on pages 22–23, using the file provided on the CD-ROM (inside the back cover of this Facilitator Guide).
- Prepare the room for teaching.
- Pray for participants.
- Distribute Journals as participants arrive. When you are ready to begin the orientation, direct participants to open their Journals to page 12.

TEACHING TIME

HEAR IT

Step 1 (5 mins.)

Welcome participants to *Growing as a FAITH Leader.* Ask volunteers to share ways they have experienced God at work in their lives through previous semesters of FAITH. Lead in prayer, thanking God for the ways He has changed lives and asking Him to continue His work to develop leaders and change lives for eternity.

Step 2 (5 mins.)

Direct participants to turn to page 12 in their Journals and to fill in the blanks as you share the goals of FAITH Discipleship courses. Use the computer presentation or overhead cel 1.

> Goals
> of FAITH
> Discipleship

Your Journey in FAITH Continues

Congratulations for completing previous semesters of FAITH Sunday School evangelism training and for making a commitment to additional growth as an on-mission Christian through FAITH Discipleship. In *A Journey in FAITH* you learned to use the FAITH Visit Outline to present the gospel to lost persons and to use your Sunday School testimony in witnessing visits. You also learned the importance of making Sunday School ministry visits. You gained valuable experience in making witnessing visits, as well as in sharing FAITH in everyday situations.

In *Building Bridges Through FAITH* you learned the importance of following up with new Christians to lead them to their next steps of growth and commitment. You learned and practiced additional skills for connecting people with Christ, the church, and Sunday School. You saw how these vital connections occur in daily life, in intentional visits, in ministry actions, and in other ways.

The next phase of your journey is FAITH Discipleship.

Goals of FAITH Discipleship

FAITH Discipleship begins with the Great Commission: " 'Go, therefore, and make disciples of all nations, baptizing them in the name of the Father and of the Son and of the Holy Spirit, teaching them to observe everything I have commanded you. And remember, I am with you always, to the end of the age' " (Matt. 28:19-20). In the Greek language the only imperative (command) is the phrase "make disciples"; yet the other verbs carry the equivalent force of commands. We cannot make disciples without going to them, and baptism and teaching are essential parts of the discipleship process.

In FAITH Basic and Advanced you learned about going to the lost and leading them to understand the importance of baptism and church membership. In FAITH Discipleship courses you learn more about being a Christ-follower (a disciple) and leading others to follow Christ. *Discipleship* can be defined as "a personal, lifelong, obedient relationship with Jesus Christ in which He transforms your character into Christlikeness; changes your values into Kingdom values; and involves you in His mission in the home, the church, and the world."[1] Just as evangelism and discipleship are like two sides of a coin, FAITH Discipleship complements FAITH evangelism training by helping you grow as a disciple and disciple Team Learners, who will continue the process.

Here are some ways FAITH Discipleship helps you become a more effective on-mission Christian.

- By teaching you important **biblical** **truths** you need to know and show as a growing disciple
- By equipping you to respond to difficult **questions** you may encounter in witnessing
- By helping you develop as a **life** **witness** for Christ, taking advantage of daily opportunities to practice what you've learned in witnessing situations
- By helping you develop as a **Team** **Leader** or as an **Assistant** Team Leader
- By suggesting ways you can **disciple** Team Learners
- By helping you lead your Sunday School class to become a **reaching**, **teaching**, **ministering**, and **multiplying** group

This phase of your FAITH Discipleship journey is *Growing as a FAITH Leader*.

Purposes of Growing as a FAITH Leader

> **LEADERS ON LEADERSHIP**
> *"To aspire to leadership in God's kingdom requires us to be willing to pay a price higher than others are willing to pay." —Oswald Sanders[2]*

Consider a team without a coach or a captain, an army without an officer or a sergeant, or a company without a president or a manager. It's not difficult to imagine the chaos that might result when leaders are missing from these strategic positions. It is more difficult to imagine that any of these groups could plan or accomplish anything, especially the purpose for which they were intended, without appropriate leaders. Leadership is the key that brings about the advance or decline of these groups.

Leadership is equally important in a church. In fact, it is more important because churches deal with issues of eternal significance. Author and researcher George Barna, writing about leadership in the church, states, "Nothing is more important than leadership."[3] Even so, many churches fail to understand the necessity of leadership, and they fail to cultivate leaders who are essential to their ministries. In addition, many churches narrowly define who fits into the leadership category, thinking only of persons who are approved by the church for certain positions.

Leaders are essential to the church, to Sunday School ministry, and to FAITH. Despite what some people may claim, leaders are not born; rather, they are developed. The material in *Growing as a FAITH Leader*

Step 3 (15 mins.)

Direct participants to turn to page 13 in their Journals and to fill in the blanks as you present the four "Purposes of *Growing as a FAITH Leader.*" Using the computer presentation or overhead cel 2, elaborate on the material that introduces how participants will—
- understand biblical leadership and evaluate themselves against those principles;
- understand Sunday School as a strategy and become more effective at carrying it out;
- learn how to multiply themselves in their Teams, in their Sunday School classes, and in other disciples;
- develop their skills as FAITH Team Leaders.

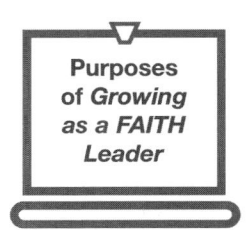

Purposes of *Growing as a FAITH Leader*

was written to help you develop in your leadership, whether you are a Team Leader or an Assistant Team Leader. By the end of this semester, you should be able to indicate ways you have grown as a leader in each of the following areas.

You will understand <u>biblical</u> <u>leadership</u> ***and evaluate yourself against those principles.***
If you go into a typical bookstore, you can find hundreds of books devoted to leadership. Written by CEOs, generals, athletes, and politicians, these books promise the latest insights and techniques. They offer countless examples of ways persons throughout our society have reached the top through their leadership practices, and they suggest that if you follow their principles, you can be the leader you were meant to be. Although these principles may seem valuable for a time, soon they are replaced by a bigger and better leader promoting a different technique. In addition, many of these contemporary leadership philosophies do not align with biblical principles. So where are we to turn?

As believers, we turn to the Bible, where we discover that our standard and model for leadership is Jesus Christ. How was Jesus a leader? Although we will look more in-depth at Jesus' leadership qualities in session 5, here are some examples.

- Jesus remained focused on His purpose regardless of His situation. His temptation (see Luke 4:1-13) is one example; another is the occasion when the people wanted to force Him to become their king (see John 6:14-15).
- Jesus challenged people to move from where they were to where they should have been, as seen in His encounter with the rich young man (see Mark 10:17-23).
- Jesus guided people to see with their hearts before they saw with their eyes. An example of this is His teaching on heaven in Matthew 13:44-46.
- Jesus mentored others so that they could fulfill their potential. Teaching the disciples to pray (see Luke 11:1-13) is an example.
- Jesus led by example, as when He washed His disciples' feet (see John 13:1-17).
- Jesus was balanced in His responses to people. For example, He sternly rebuked Peter (see Matt. 16:23) and later gently restored him (see John 21:15-17).
- Jesus prioritized His life and work. We see this quality in the priority He gave to prayer and time alone with God (see Mark 1:35).
- Jesus recognized that people are more important than procedures. Observe the way He dealt with the woman caught in adultery (see John 8:1-11).
- Jesus stayed at the task until He completed His mission. On the cross He proclaimed, " 'It is finished' " (John 19:30).

This course will also reveal qualities and skills of other leaders in Scripture whose examples you will want to follow. Through both in-session and at-home activities you will consider ways you need to develop as a Christian leader. Although you may get discouraged thinking about how far you are from the leadership standard set by Jesus, His words in Luke 6:40 should encourage you to continue on your journey of discipleship: " 'A disciple is not above his teacher, but everyone who is fully trained will be like his teacher.' "

You will understand __Sunday__ __School__ *as a* __strategy__ *and become more effective at carrying it out.*
If you asked different people to define the purpose of Sunday School, you might get a variety of responses.
- "It's for Bible study."
- "It's where people get together with friends."
- "It's a time to learn about and pray for others' needs."

Although these responses are valid, they are only part of the purpose of Sunday School. While many people think of Sunday School only as a 60-minute program on Sunday morning, it is actually a 24-7 strategy for helping churches fulfill the Great Commission. In session 2 you will begin learning more about the purpose and strategy of Sunday School.

You may be tempted to ask, Why are we concerned about Sunday School when this is the FAITH ministry? As a FAITH Team Leader, you are aware of the importance of leadership to the FAITH ministry. Ultimately, however, a FAITH leader doesn't function only in the FAITH arena. This is because FAITH is more than a stand-alone ministry.

FAITH is more correctly referred to as the *FAITH Sunday School Evangelism Strategy*®. This title points to the intentional partnership between Sunday School and FAITH, not only for evangelism but also for discipleship and ministry. During the next 15 sessions you will learn more about this connection and your important role in strengthening it in your Sunday School class and in your church.

You will learn how to __multiply__ *yourself in your Team, in your Sunday School class, and in other disciples.*
When you put money into a retirement account, you are not as interested in how much you put into the account as in how much the money will grow over the years. Your concern is more for multiplication than addition. In the same way, the greater concern in the FAITH Sunday School Evangelism Strategy® must be for multiplication. Though we rejoice when one person comes into a saving relationship with Jesus Christ, we weep when we consider how many more people in our world are moving toward an eternity in hell because they do not know Christ.

The situation can seem discouraging because we have such a limited number of faith-sharing disciples in the world. The answer lies in the principle of multiplication. This course will show that as FAITH leaders equip others to make disciples, who will in turn equip still others to make disciples, we will unleash a force that will have untold impact for evangelism, discipleship, and ministry throughout the world.

You will develop your skills as a FAITH __Team__ __Leader__. Regardless of how many semesters you have participated in FAITH and have led FAITH Teams, you can always enhance your leadership skills. Because you lead different Learners each semester, you must learn to adapt your leadership styles based on their needs. In this course you will learn how to encourage and motivate each of your Team members. Likewise, because every visit is different, you must learn to adjust to a variety of witnessing situations. Your Learners look to you for guidance in these situations, so you must continue to mature as a role model they can follow. This course will equip you with practical skills that will strengthen your Team leadership.

Why Do Churches Need Leaders?

The church is only one generation from extinction. If all believers decided not to reproduce themselves in someone else's life, the church and Christianity would die. This has happened in other cultures in previous eras and is happening in some parts of the world today.

Tragically, the United States is one of the places it is happening. Even though a number of churches are growing, the majority of Southern Baptist churches are losing ground. From 1996 to 2001, 69 percent of Southern Baptist churches were __plateaued__ or __declining__ in average Sunday School attendance.[4] Because Sunday School attendance usually indicates what is happening in our churches, we are confronted with a problem. Likewise, when we look at baptisms in Southern Baptist churches, the average has stayed around 384,000 for the past 50 years.[5] This echoes the problem: although we have more members and more resources than perhaps any other time in history, we are not seeing significant increases each year in the number of people who come to know Christ. While our country's population is rapidly increasing, __kingdom__ __growth__ is not keeping pace.

The problem can be traced to a void in __biblical__ __leadership__. The world has provided the wrong models of leadership. These have found their way into the church, where they have proved to be ineffective at best or harmful at worst. Our churches need to return to genuine biblical leadership, which has stood the test of time and is successful for any church, regardless of size, location, or a variety of other characteristics.

Step 4 (5 mins.)

Ask participants to turn to page 16 in their Journals and to fill in the blanks as you summarize "Why Do Churches Need Leaders?" Using the computer presentation or overhead cel 3, remind participants that kingdom growth has declined in many churches and that other churches are dying because leaders are not reproducing themselves in others' lives.

> Why Do Churches Need Leaders?

This model must be the same for the pastor, the staff, and the laity. Many churches are in conflict because the staff has a different perspective on leadership than do the members of the congregation. The Scriptures provide a model that is the same for everyone, and through this study you will understand and incorporate this model into your life.

What Is a Leader? *slide*

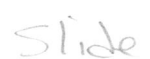

A leader is someone who reproduces himself in the lives of others. Paul outlined the process of reproduction in 2 Timothy 2:2, a verse that is an essential part of the FAITH strategy.

Receive *(learn): "what you have heard from me."*
A leader is always ready to learn, especially God's truth. We can never be satisfied in our Christian walk, thinking we have arrived. God wants us to experience Him daily. An intentional, daily pursuit of what God wants to teach us through personal discipleship is essential for a leader.

The FAITH strategy depends on Learners who are willing to receive training from others who have gone ahead of them. Likewise, the strategy can continue only if FAITH leaders recognize the need to keep learning.

Repeat *(teach): "commit to faithful men."*
What we learn or receive from God is not for us alone; we are to share that truth with others. This verse makes clear that we are to give away what we have received. The principle of stewardship does not apply just to financial resources but to spiritual resources, as well.

This principle is a crucial element in the FAITH strategy. FAITH gives you an opportunity to go and share with others the forgiveness and eternal life you have received through Jesus Christ. It also provides you an opportunity to teach others to do the same.

Reproduce *(train): "who will be able to teach others also."*
This is where the process often breaks down. We learn truth and teach it, but we fail to train others to the point that they can train others to share. Reproduction is an essential part of leadership, especially in FAITH. If the process stops with your Learners, the FAITH strategy ends and the Great Commission will not be accomplished.

Leadership authority John Maxwell writes about a conference he attended where Peter Drucker, the well-known management authority, emphasized, "There is no success without a successor."[6] Ultimately, a leader is not a leader until he has reproduced himself in someone else. This means a leader can turn things over to someone else who will carry

---

Step 5 (10 mins.)

Instruct participants to select partners and discuss: Who was the best leader you've ever known? What made that person so effective? Allow pairs five minutes to share responses. Then read 2 Timothy 2:2. Direct participants to turn to page 17 in their Journals and to fill in the blanks as you present the points in "What Is a Leader?" Use the computer presentation or overhead cel 4. Emphasize that it is not enough just to receive and repeat; we must also reproduce ourselves in others' lives.

What Is a Leader?

Session 1: Growing as a FAITH Leader: An Orientation / 17

on the mission. This is true biblical leadership and a vital component of your leadership responsibilities in FAITH.

Who Are Leaders?

Henry and Richard Blackaby have noted that "spiritual leadership is not restricted to pastors and missionaries. It is the responsibility of all Christians whom God wants to use to make a difference in their world."[7] This means you are a leader, as are all believers. Even though God has given some believers the spiritual gift of leadership, __all__ __Christians__ are called to be spiritual leaders.

This realization may make you feel inadequate, unworthy, and ill equipped. These feelings, however, come not from God but from Satan. Your enemy is trying to convince you that you are not a leader and can never be a leader. Even so, when you look at the 12 men Jesus chose as His disciples, you should be encouraged. They were ordinary people. Though they all failed Jesus at some point in their lives, all except Judas eventually developed into the leaders Christ called them to be.

The disciples were given the same challenge we are given today: to make disciples. They embraced the challenge, and though they often struggled with it, they endured and became successful leaders. The fact that we have a relationship with Christ points to their effectiveness in reproducing themselves in others' lives. You may also struggle with the challenge, but God's command is clear, and His plan is still the same: God wants you to join His work of __making__ __disciples__, who in turn will go and make disciples. You can be a successful leader with God's power enabling you and with ongoing training.

If we are going to build on-mission Christians and Great Commission churches, what will make the difference? These outcomes will happen only when all believers are convinced that they are called to be leaders.

Where Are You to Lead?

The context of leadership is important. Through *Growing as a FAITH Leader* you will learn to apply biblical leadership principles in five areas.

Your relationship with __God__
God wants you to grow as a Christian, and in a sense you have a role in leading yourself to mature in your faith. Your personal walk of discipleship is both your most important qualification and your greatest resource for spiritual leadership. Each week during this course you will have

---

Step 6 (5 mins.)

Ask participants to turn to page 18 in their Journals and to fill in the blanks as you present the material in "Who Are Leaders?" Use the computer presentation or overhead cel 5. Note that though some believers have the gift of leadership, every believer has the responsibility to be a spiritual leader.

> Who Are Leaders?

Step 7 (10 mins.)

Instruct participants to fill in the blanks as you present the points in "Where Are You to Lead?" Use the computer presentation or overhead cel 6.

> Where Are You to Lead?

---

18 / Growing as a FAITH Leader Facilitator Guide

opportunities to evaluate your personal life and determine what you will do to grow into the disciple and biblical leader God wants you to be.

Your relationship with your ___FAITH___ ___Team___
One of your primary roles as a FAITH leader is to reproduce yourself in the lives of your Team members. Your goal is to train your Learners to the point that they can lead Teams next semester. Your goal is not to teach an outline but to develop soul-winners, who will in turn develop others. This task begins before the first session and continues after the final session.

Your relationship with your ___Sunday___ ___School___ ___class___
In many churches the Sunday School is not growing due to a lack of leadership. As a FAITH leader, you must catch the vision of reproducing new Sunday School units, as well as new leaders. This is an essential part of the FAITH Sunday School Evangelism Strategy®, and you are a key leader in that strategy. Through this study you will discover ways to lead your class to join God in His mission of making disciples.

Your relationship with the ___lost___
As a disciple, you have a leadership responsibility with those who don't know Christ: taking the initiative to reach out to them with the gospel message. People without Christ are headed for an eternity in hell, and this is one primary reason for the FAITH strategy—to reach out to the lost and minister to them while seeking to lead them to salvation.

Your relationship with your ___family___ *and* ___church___
As a believer, you are a part of the body of Christ, and you are essential to helping your church fulfill God's purposes for it. The Book of Acts identifies these purposes as evangelism, discipleship, fellowship, ministry, and worship. You must not only actively work to fulfill these purposes but also lead others to do the same.

When Are You to Lead?

The structure of the Greek text in 2 Timothy 2:2 indicates that reproducing leaders is a ___command___. We must do it, and we must do it now. Because leadership is a lifestyle, the fact is that you are leading today, whether or not you realize it. The question you must ask yourself is, *How am I leading today?* You might be a soul-winner, and you might even teach others who are soul-winners, but are you teaching others to teach still others to be soul-winners? True biblical leadership is ___reproducing___ ___reproducers___.

Slide
Direct participants to discuss with a partner this question: In which of the five areas do you struggle most to fulfill your leadership responsibilities?

Step 6 (5 mins.)

Instruct participants to turn to page 19 in their Journals and to fill in the blanks as you present the points in "When Are You to Lead?" Using the computer presentation or overhead cel 7, remind participants of the immediate need for leaders to fulfill their responsibilities.

When Are You to Lead?

Step 7 (10 mins.)

Ask participants to turn to page 20 in their Journals and to fill in the blanks as you present the material in "How Do You Grow as a Leader?" Use the computer presentation or overhead cel 8. Explain the format of Home Study Assignments, referring to this week's assignments on pages 26–28 as an example. Encourage participants to use their Home Study Assignments to grow as FAITH leaders.

> How Do You Grow as a Leader?

Emphasize the roles of accountability partners throughout this semester. Remind participants that this person functions in addition to the two prayer partners whom participants will enlist from their Sunday School classes or departments. Allow time for participants to choose an accountability partner (perhaps the partner with whom they have already shared responses in this session) and to record the partner's name in the blank on page 21.

You must assume this responsibility now. Delaying obedience is _____**disobedience**_____. The hour is urgent, and there is no better time than the present to assume your God-ordained position of leadership. Jesus said, " 'We must do the works of Him who sent Me while it is day. Night is coming when no one can work' " (John 9:4). Sharing the same concern, Paul emphasized, "Pay careful attention, then, to how you walk—not as unwise people but as wise—making the most of the time, because the days are evil. So don't be foolish, but understand what the Lord's will is" (Eph. 5:15-17).

How Do You Grow as a Leader?

Although you will experience growth in your leadership during this course as you participate in weekly group sessions, your growth will continue after the classroom time. Your Home Study Assignments will provide material to be read and exercises to be completed during the week between group sessions. The purpose of these five daily segments is to allow you to respond to and apply what you learned in the previous session and begin preparing for the next session. Home Study Assignments will include Scripture readings, reflective questions, evaluative tools, and application projects to help you grow as a leader.

Your Home Study Assignments will help you focus on developing as a leader in five areas.
- Your relationship with __**God**__
- Your relationship with your __**FAITH**__ __**Team**__
- Your relationship with your __**Sunday**__ __**School**__ __**class**__
- Your relationship with the __**lost**__
- Your relationship with your __**family**__ and __**church**__

In addition to the 16 weeks of Home Study Assignments you will complete during this semester, 4 weeks of assignments are included at the back of this book, beginning on page 250. These assignments will help you continue to grow as a FAITH leader between semesters.

Another element is provided to help you grow as a leader. You will choose a participant in this study as an accountability partner who will help you continue to grow as a leader. This partner will be in addition to the prayer partners you enlist from your Sunday School class or department. Proverbs 27:17 states,

> As iron sharpens iron,
> so one man sharpens another.

To help you stay sharp as a tool in God's hand, your accountability partner will be available throughout the semester to—

20 / Growing as a FAITH Leader Facilitator Guide

- discuss questions you may have about the material in each session and in the Home Study Assignments;
- ask about opportunities you have had to witness and minister during the week;
- pray with you about your growth as a FAITH Sunday School leader, about your mentoring relationships with members of your FAITH Team, and about ways God will use you in witnessing situations;
- encourage you to continue developing, witnessing, and reproducing as a leader.

My accountability partner for this semester is _____.

The FAITH Process

Weekly Schedule

Growing as a FAITH Leader follows the format of FAITH Basic and Advanced courses. The FAITH schedule should not exceed three hours.

1. Team Time (15 minutes)
    - CHECK IT—Leading Team Time
    Leaders meet with Learners and check their memory work, homework, and Journal.
2. Teaching Time (45 minutes)
    - KNOW IT—review of the previous week's material
    - HEAR IT—presentation of the current week's material
    - SAY IT—practice of the FAITH Visit Outline (selected sessions)
    - STUDY IT—preview of Home Study Assignments
    FAITH Discipleship meets while Learners are in FAITH Basic.
3. Visitation Time (90 to 110 minutes, depending on your church's schedule)
    - DO IT
    Teams pray in cars before leaving the church.
4. Celebration Time (30 minutes)
    - SHARE IT
    Celebration Time will increase as the number of Teams increases. However, a time may come when your ministry will grow large enough to have FAITH training on more than one night.

Prayer and Practice

When your FAITH ministry grows to more than five Teams, you will generally begin dividing into groups. A group should generally have no more than five Teams. Each group should have a Group Leader, who helps Team Leaders in his or her group stay on target and serves as their accountability partner.

Break (10 mins.)

Step 8 (10 mins.)

Review the FAITH training schedule, using the computer presentation. Because a videotape is not included in this course, point out that SEE IT will not be a part of this course as it has been in some other FAITH Discipleship courses.

Using the computer presentation, review the dates this course will begin and end, as well as when Team Time, Teaching Time, Visitation Time, and Celebration Time will begin each week.

Explain how Prayer and Practice will be done in your church, as well as how this information will be communicated.

Beginning no earlier than session 5, one group should be assigned a night to remain at church to pray for those who are visiting and to practice the FAITH gospel presentation. If a church has five or fewer Teams, enlist a Team (instead of a group) to remain at church. Waiting until session 5 gives Learners an opportunity to have heard and memorized the visitation outline. Otherwise, they have nothing to practice. The Group Leader guides the prayer time and supervises the practice time.

Celebration Time

During the first few weeks of Celebration Time, each Team Leader should model how to give a report. You may not believe that following the guidelines for giving a report is important when you have only a few Teams. However, your FAITH ministry will grow. What you do at the beginning is what will be followed later. Model your reports as though 50 Team Leaders were standing in line behind you. A sample of a model report is shown below.

Distribute copies of the Celebration Time Report and recommend that Teams use them. Copies may be made from the file provided on the CD-ROM at the back of this guide.

CELEBRATION TIME REPORT

My name is (first name only) _____

My Team members are _____ and _____

We contacted (first names only) _____
_____
_____

Answer to the Key Question (check one):   ❑ Faith   ❑ Works
Gospel presented?   ❑ Yes   ❑ No
Results: ❑ Profession   ❑ Assurance   ❑ No decision
If not presented, why?   ❑ Already Christian   ❑ Ministry visit
❑ Other (please explain): _____
_____
_____

Our Team went through *A Step of Faith*   ❑ and showed picture
❑ and prayed   ❑ and enrolled in Bible study   ❑ to completion.
How many enrolled? _____
Follow-up appointment made? ❑ Yes   If so, when? _____   ❑ No
Other significant information: _____
_____

(See back of card on next page.)

1. Use only first names of those who are on your Team and only first names of those you visited to protect their privacy.
2. Report only on contacts made; please do not report on persons who were not at home. If reporting on Opinion Polls, report the total number attempted and the number completed, but explain only one significant visit.
3. Keep the report positive in tone; report only what will benefit the entire group as a learning experience. Do not give names of churches or denominations.
4. Reports must be limited to one minute; lengthy reports cause sessions to run late and hurt the ministry. Use the time before and after (not during) Celebration Time to share details.

Team reports should include—

Information About whom you visited, questions asked, and responses made.
Inspiration That which edifies and inspires the group, such as professions, assurance decisions, and so on.
Intercession Individuals for whom you wish to request prayer.

Reports during Celebration Time should be—
1. *Brief*. Reports should be no more than one minute per Team.
2. *Precise*. Reports should not give unnecessary details.
3. *Accurate*. Reports are not designed to embellish but to celebrate what actually happened on the visit.
4. *Sensitive*. By not using last names and giving details that may have been shared in confidence, these reports protect persons being reached.
5. *Affirming*. The reports encourage others who may not have enjoyed a good visit and motivates those who are learning how to share.

FAITH Resources

Participation Card
A sample FAITH Participation Card appears on page 10. This card is used each week as a name placard and to record numbers and types of visits attempted and made by the Team. Complete your card each week so that you will be able to help your Team members complete theirs. If you have not completed the top portion, please do so now.

Be familiar with all of the categories on the card and explain the card to your Learners. Help them complete their cards after each Celebration Time.

Highlight procedures for giving reports during Celebration Time.

SAY IT

Step 9 (10 mins.)

Ask accountability partners to practice the *Presentation* portion of the FAITH Visit Outline with each other.

HEAR IT

Step 10 (10 mins.)

Overview the resources needed this semester. The following are available.

1. *Journal.* Each participant needs a copy. Order item 0-6330-9006-9.
2. *Facilitator Guide.* This guide contains the same sessions trainees have in their Journals, plus teaching suggestions in the margins. Additional copies may be ordered (item 0-6330-9332-7). Note some differences between your Facilitator Guide and those in other FAITH Discipleship courses. In one resource it offers the following teaching aids.
   - *Overhead-cel masters.* This set of 73 masters, provided at the back of the Facilitator Guide (pp. 271–343), can be used to produce cels that support session content. Permission is granted for you to duplicate the masters.
   - *CD-ROM.* You may prefer an Adobe Acrobat® presentation to overhead cels. The CD-ROM provided inside the back cover of this guide is Macintosh®/Windows® compatible. The readme file provides directions for adding customized PowerPoint® slides to each session's computer presentation. The CD-ROM also provides FAITH forms in Microsoft Word® and Adobe Acrobat® formats, as well as a FAITH catalog and an order form. Permission is granted for you to duplicate the forms.
3. *Prayer-Partner Commitment Cards.* Distribute these cards to participants in session 2 for their use in enlisting prayer partners (pkg. of 15, item 0-6330-1876-7). Order enough cards for all participants and their Team Learners.

The information on the card should correspond to the Report Board and Celebration Time Report. Remember that it is the Team Leader's responsibility to teach the members the process and to listen as they eventually give the report during Celebration Time.

Visitation Notebook

It is essential that every Team have a visitation notebook. Each notebook should include the following:
- Plastic pouch to hold tracts, pens, Opinion Polls, and so forth
- Pocket in front to hold visitation assignment forms
- Pocket in back to contain Sunday School material, including the appropriate class/department roll, and information about the church

FAITH Visit Outline

There is no new memory work in *Growing as a FAITH Leader*; you will continue to practice and share the FAITH Visit Outline.

Growing as a FAITH Leader Journal

As was true in FAITH Basic and Advanced, the Journal will be your main resource. After you have filled in the blanks during each session's Teaching Time, it can be helpful between sessions to reread the previous session to get the big picture. Besides the content studied during Teaching Time, the following sections are included in your Journal.

- *Leading Team Time.* The Leading Team Time suggestions each week will help you as a Team Leader debrief, practice, and review with your Team. Suggestions are based on Learners' *A Journey in FAITH Journal* Team Time agenda for each week.
- *Leaders on Leadership.* These quotations by Christian leaders provide insights into leadership and inspiration for growing as a leader.
- *Home Study Assignments.* Each week between group sessions Home Study Assignments provide daily devotional segments to help you apply the principles you are learning about leadership to critical areas of your life and witness.
—*FAITH Tip.* Selected sessions include optional readings that apply prayer to a witness's life of evangelism and Sunday School ministry.
—*FAITH at Work.* Selected sessions include testimonies about the difference FAITH has made in participants' lives.

Sunday School Ministry

Your Sunday School class or department is a primary resource. Sunday School is the unique dynamic of FAITH. Your class/department can be a place where names become people, needs become visible, and assimilation becomes more than a term. This link is created by attending the weekly Sunday School leadership meeting (and the Group Leader meeting, if appropriate).

Your Walk with God

Three components of your walk with God will provide essential spiritual direction as you participate in this course.

- *Your willingness to join God's work.* Evangelism is God's activity, and you must be willing to be on His agenda and timetable in this endeavor. Ask that His Holy Spirit guide what you say and do; empower you for divine confidence, strength, and wisdom; and prepare each lost person's heart for the seeds you will sow. During the next 15 sessions, expect God to work in your life, in your Sunday School/church, in the lives of the people you will meet, and in your Team.
- *Bible study.* You will be exposed to a lot of biblical content during this course. Your Facilitator will not have time to cover in-depth each passage in your Journal. Spend time between sessions reading and reviewing the passages so that you will be better prepared to give the "reason for the hope that is in you" (1 Pet. 3:15). Never underestimate the power of God's living and active Word to speak with an authority of its own (see 2 Tim. 3:15-17; Heb. 4:12).
- *Prayer.* Prayer is your most important and most powerful resource for FAITH training. The Lord has promised to hear us when we call on Him (see Matt. 18:19-20; 21:22; Luke 11:9-13). Call on Him throughout *Growing as a FAITH Leader*.

In addition to personal prayer, you are asked to enlist two faithful prayer partners in your Sunday School class to uphold you in prayer during this semester. Your Sunday School class as a whole should also pray for your involvement in FAITH. Your class's prayer coordinator can do four things: (1) make members aware of your prayer needs; (2) lead the class to pray for divine appointments for your FAITH Team, for evangelism and ministry opportunities to be evident, for people to be saved, and for believers to grow as on-mission Christians; (3) give brief reports from FAITH Team visits; and (4) report prayer concerns and results to Sunday School leaders.

---

[1] Avery T. Willis, Jr., *MasterLife 1: The Disciple's Cross* (Nashville: LifeWay Press, 1996), 5.
[2] J. Oswald Sanders, *Spiritual Leadership* (Chicago: Moody Press, 1994), 115.
[3] George Barna, *Leaders on Leadership* (Ventura, CA: Regal Books, 1997), 18.
[4] Annual Church Profile of Southern Baptist Churches for the five-year period 1997–2001.
[5] *Strategic Planning Indicators* (North American Mission Board), no. 2 (summer 2000).
[6] John C. Maxwell, *Developing the Leaders Around You* (Nashville: Thomas Nelson, Inc., 1995), 11.
[7] Henry and Richard Blackaby, *Spiritual Leadership* (Nashville: Broadman & Holman Publishers, 2001), 14.

STUDY IT

Step 11 (5 mins.)

Overview the Home Study Assignments for session 1.

Remind participants that home visits will begin in session 2. Close this session by asking accountability partners to pray with each other, asking God to guide them in growing as soul-winners, leaders, and disciples during this semester.

Home Study Assignments

Day 1: Your Relationship with God

How would you define *biblical leadership*? <u>focused on Jesus and His</u> <u>mission and able to lead that by example</u>

Read below the qualities of Jesus' leadership. Place a star beside the quality that reflects your strongest trait as a leader and an X beside your weakest.
___ Remained focused on His purpose regardless of His situation
___ Challenged people to move from where they were to where they should be
___ Guided people to see with their hearts before they saw with their eyes
___ Mentored others so that they could fulfill their potential
_X_ Led by example
___ Was balanced in His responses to people
___ Prioritized His life and work
_X_ Recognized that people are more important than procedures
_X_ Stayed at the task until He completed His mission

Write a goal for growing in your relationship with God this semester.

<u>Prioritize my life and work.</u>

Day 2: Your Relationship with Your FAITH Team

Memorize 2 Timothy 2:2. How does your FAITH Team carry out this command?

_____

Write your definition of *spiritual multiplication*. <u>equipping others to</u> <u>equip others to share the gospel</u>

How will you communicate the importance of multiplication to your Team?

<u>through encouragement — motivation</u>

Write a goal for growing as a Team Leader this semester.

<u>To be an encouragement to my team.</u>

Day 3: Your Relationship with Your Sunday School Class

Circle a number on the scale to indicate how well your Sunday School class understands the FAITH strategy.

Low   1   2   3   4   5   6   ⑦   8   9   10   High

What are you doing to lead others to understand the strategy of FAITH and Sunday School working together?

Monthly leadership meetings. — FAITH events

Write a goal for growing as a Sunday School leader this semester.

To be an example and resource to the Sunday School teachers.

Spend time praying for your class, asking God to use you to help others catch the vision for fulfilling the Great Commission through Sunday School.

Day 4: Your Relationship with the Lost

Write the name of at least one lost person you are praying for this semester.

_____

Read the following Scriptures and record what they say about your relationship with lost persons.

Matthew 9:36-38 _____

_____

Luke 15:1-7 _____

_____

Write a goal for growing in your relationships with lost persons this semester.

_____

_____

Day 5: Your Relationship with Your Family and Church

When you think of biblical leadership principles, what person in your church stands out as a model of those principles? Why?

_____

_____

_____

What is your church doing to develop leaders who follow biblical leadership principles?

_____

_____

How has your fellowship with God and His Word influenced your leadership in your family?

_____

_____

in your church? _____

_____

_____

Write a goal for growing as a leader in your family and church this semester.

_____

_____

SESSION 2
You Are a Sunday School Leader

In this session you will—

CHECK IT by engaging in Team Time activities;

KNOW IT by reviewing content from session 1;

HEAR IT by understanding Sunday School as a strategy, by learning the purposes of the church, and by identifying the role of FAITH in strengthening your Sunday School class and your church;

STUDY IT by overviewing Home Study Assignments;

DO IT by leading your Team in making visits;

SHARE IT by celebrating.

IN ADVANCE
- Overview content.
- Preview teaching suggestions. Prepare key points. Decide whether to use the session 2 computer presentation or overhead cels 9–15 (see pp. 279–85).
- Obtain Prayer-Partner Commitment Cards (item 0-6330-1876-7) for all participants and their Team Learners.
- Make copies of "Questions for Evaluating Whether Your Bible-Study Group Is an Open Group" for all participants, using the file on the CD-ROM at the back of this guide.
- Prepare the room for teaching.
- Pray for participants and for Teams as they prepare for their first home visits.
- As Teaching Time begins, direct participants to open their Journals to page 32.

TEAM TIME

CHECK IT (15 MINS.)

If the computer presentation is used, display the agenda for Team Time. Add other points to the agenda as needed.

CHECK IT agenda:
- ✔ FAITH Visit Outline
- ✔ Sunday School Testimony
- ✔ Other Home Study Assignments
- ✔ Session 1 Debriefing
- ✔ Help for Strengthening a Visit

Leading Team Time

All Team members participate in Team Time. They are primarily responsible for reciting the assigned portion of the FAITH Visit Outline and for discussing other Home Study Assignments.

As you direct this important time of CHECK IT activities with your Team, keep in mind that Learners look to you as a role model, motivator, mentor, and friend. Team Time activities can continue in the car as the Team travels to and from visits.

Lead CHECK IT Activities

Team Leaders must be model disciplers so strive to set a good example. Arrive early to review visit assignments and to check your Team members' homework. You want to give Learners adequate time to recite memory work and to otherwise encourage them. Because this is the first week for Team Time activities, provide any additional explanation that is needed. Make good use of the 15 minutes that begin each session.

✔ *FAITH Visit Outline*
- ❏ Team members should be ready to recite all aspects of **Preparation** up to INQUIRY and the key words in **Presentation** (FORGIVENESS, AVAILABLE, IMPOSSIBLE, TURN, HEAVEN) and *Invitation* (INQUIRE, INVITE, INSURE).
- ❏ Indicate your approval by signing or initialing Journals. Encourage Learners throughout this review process.

✔ *Sunday School Testimony*
- ❏ The Team Leader is responsible for checking the testimonies of his or her Learners. Help evaluate each testimony to make sure it includes one or two of the following aspects: friendship/support received, assistance received during a crisis, personal benefits of Bible study through the class, or ways they have grown as a Christian through experiences in or through the Sunday School class. Discuss how benefits can and do change, reflecting different experiences.
- ❏ If the written testimony is acceptable, make sure each Team member understands the importance of learning to share it naturally, in his or her own words. Ask for permission to print the testimony in any church materials that publicize FAITH and/or that encourage persons to share their testimonies.

✔ *Other Home Study Assignments*
- ❏ Check to be certain that the Learners are reading Scriptures and recording their thoughts in their Journals between sessions. As a general rule, when they discontinue writing in their Journals, they

30 / Growing as a FAITH Leader Facilitator Guide

are about two weeks away from dropping out of FAITH. Show them Home Study Assignments. It will motivate them to see your work.

✔ Session 1 Debriefing
❑ Make sure major concepts from session 1 are understood, since this session provides an orientation to the course.

✔ Help for Strengthening a Visit
❑ This is the first session in which Teams will make home visits. Encourage members and try to ease any concerns. Explain that the Team Leader will take the lead in the INTRODUCTION portion of the visit(s) following this session.
❑ Identify a Team member(s) who would be prepared to share a Sunday School testimony at the Team Leader's prompting during a visit. Be sensitive to persons who are ready to share.
❑ Once prayer partners are enlisted, they might be asked to pray by name (first name only) for the persons contacted that week.

Notes

Actions I Need to Take with Team Members This Week

Transition to classrooms for instruction on the content of the session. (5 mins.)

TEACHING TIME

KNOW IT

Step 1 (5 mins.)

Ask participants to turn to "A Quick Review" on page 32 in their Journals and to complete the activities. Review answers, using the computer presentation or overhead cel 9:
1. a, c, d, f, g
2. The church is only one generation away from extinction, and a tremendous void of biblical leaders exists in many churches.

Be careful not to exceed the five-minute time limit.

A Quick Review

A Quick Review

1. Last week you learned the purposes and goals of this study. Check the following items that represent legitimate purposes of this course.

    - ☑ a. To help you become a better FAITH leader as you learn more about biblical leadership
    - ☑ b. To help you become a successful leader in every area of your life
    - ☑ c. To help you evaluate yourself as a FAITH leader, based on the unchanging standard of Scripture
    - ☑ d. To help you understand the strategy of Sunday School and its connection to FAITH
    - ☐ e. To give you fellowship ideas that will help you draw closer to those in your Sunday School class
    - ☑ f. To help you accept your responsibility as a FAITH leader to influence your Sunday School ministry
    - ☑ g. To help you become more effective in multiplying yourself as a FAITH leader
    - ☐ h. To help you gain a position of responsibility in your church's Sunday School ministry

2. In your own words, explain why your church needs more leaders.

    We are always one step away from being ineffective – due to poor leadership. We need to multiply ourselves.

LEADERS ON LEADERSHIP

"Sunday School is the most effective organization ever developed to meet the church's needs for Bible study because Sunday School has all five church growth functions operating at the same time. Sunday School helps believers reach others for Christ and prevents the church from becoming ingrown and exclusive." —James T. Draper, Jr.[1]

Sharpen the Focus of Sunday School

When you pick up a pair of binoculars and attempt to look through them, what's usually the first thing you have to do? You almost always have to focus them before you can clearly see something in the distance. Without the capability to focus, the binoculars would be of limited value.

In the same way, it is important to be properly focused as we think about growing as a FAITH leader. That means understanding the nature and purpose of Sunday School, on which the FAITH strategy is built. This definition may help you understand the full implications of Sunday School: "Sunday School is the foundational strategy in a local church for leading people to faith in the Lord Jesus Christ and for building on-mission Christians through open Bible study groups that engage people in evangelism, discipleship, fellowship, ministry, and worship."[2]

Sunday School is a ____strategy____.
The fact that Sunday School is a strategy means that it's more than just a 45-minute program each week; rather, it's a 24-7 ministry that operates primarily outside the classroom.

Sunday School leads people to know ____Jesus____.
Look at the first two action words in the definition: *leading and building*. Sunday School intentionally helps people come to know Jesus Christ as Savior and Lord and then guides them to be on mission with Him. This is the essence of the Great Commission (see Matt. 28:18-20) and must be the driving force of our Sunday Schools.

Sunday School utilizes ____open____ Bible-study groups.
An open Bible-study group is open to anyone at any time and does not require people to have prior information before participating in the class. An open group intentionally seeks to involve new people, both believers and non-Christians, and intentionally positions itself for change and multiplication. The focus is on Bible study that transforms lives.

Sunday School helps accomplish the work of the ____church____.
Notice the last action word: *engage*. Sunday School doesn't just seek to tell people what they need to know. It also intentionally seeks to involve people in accomplishing the purposes of the church: evangelism, discipleship, fellowship, ministry, and worship. Again, this is where the 24-7 aspect comes in: Sunday School functions 24 hours a day, 7 days a week.

Having the purposes of Sunday School in focus will help us understand the important role FAITH plays in the Sunday School ministry.

HEAR IT

Step 2 (10 mins.)

Instruct participants to pair with their accountability partners and discuss: What do most members of my Sunday School class think is the purpose of Sunday School? Allow partners to share for no more than five minutes. Then ask participants to turn to page 33 in their Journals and to fill in the blanks as you present the material in "Sharpen the Focus of Sunday School," using the computer presentation or overhead cel 10.

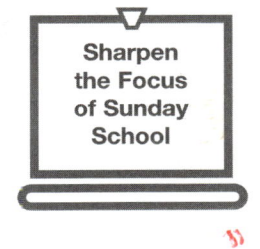

Sharpen the Focus of Sunday School

"It is about the people..."

Strengthen the FAITH Connection to Your Sunday School

Step 3 (5 mins.)

Ask participants turn to page 34 in their Journals and to fill in the blanks as you present the material in "Strengthen the FAITH Connection to Your Sunday School." Use the computer presentation or overhead cel 11. Emphasize ways FAITH is a part of the Sunday School strategy and ways FAITH keeps Sunday School focused on evangelism.

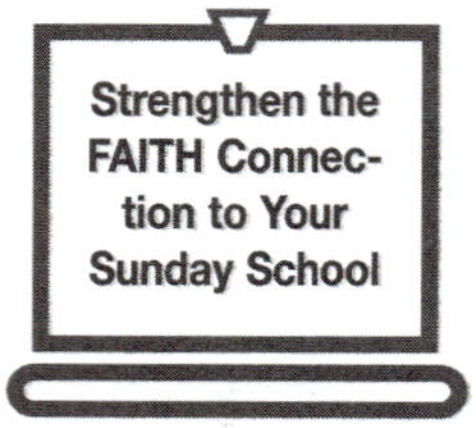

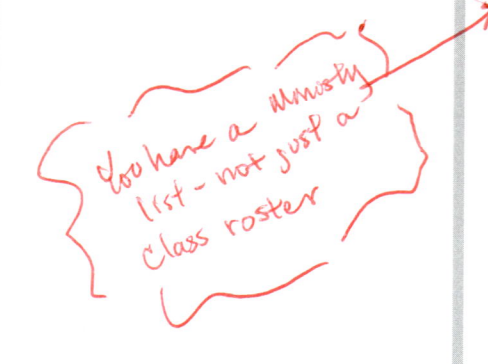

> Strengthen the FAITH Connection to Your Sunday School

Many churches that have a passion for evangelism often maintain a two-track system. One track is an outreach or visitation ministry, and the second track is a Sunday School ministry. Because one purpose of Sunday School is evangelism, which includes outreach, having a two-track system becomes a problem. These two ministries often find themselves competing for leaders, prospects, and a time to visit. FAITH solves this problem by uniting evangelism, ministry, and Sunday School.

FAITH links _____evangelism_____ ***to Sunday School.***
In too many churches Sunday School is viewed as a place where people hear a good Bible lesson and help take care of one another. It often becomes a close-knit group of folks who sincerely love one another but miss the entire purpose of Sunday School.

We must always remember that the birthright of Sunday School is evangelism. Consider these statements.
- "Through the years Sunday Schools that have been positively evangelistic kept on growing. Sunday Schools grow fastest when the fires of evangelism burn the hottest."[3]—J. N. Barnette
- "Evangelism is not a plus added to the regular program; it is the main work of the Sunday School and must be interwoven in all the activities of all the departments."[4]—Arthur Flake
- "The Sunday School is the prime evangelistic agency. When evangelism declines in Sunday School, evangelism sets its face toward the open door of departure from the church."[5]—P. E. Burroughs

Each statement asserts that the primary outlet of evangelism is through Sunday School ministry.

FAITH links _____ministry_____ ***to Sunday School.***
Some Sunday School leaders who are not involved in FAITH may ask, "If we focus our attention on evangelism, what about those already in our class?" As a FAITH leader, you know that FAITH is designed to encourage ministry visits as well as prospect visits. You know that each FAITH Team, ideally composed of three members from the same Sunday School class, is visiting prospects for its class. As a leader, you also model for Learners how to make a ministry visit, whether to encourage an absentee or to minister in times of death, illness, and so on. The beauty of the FAITH strategy is watching ministry and evangelism come together. In fact, many FAITH churches strive to strengthen this relationship by making assignments that reflect a ratio of 40 percent ministry visits and 60 percent evangelistic visits throughout the semester.

[handwritten note: You have a ministry list—not just a class roster]

Strengthen the FAITH Connection to Your Church

Sunday School and FAITH are also vitally linked to the mission of your church. Implementing the FAITH Sunday School Evangelism Strategy® helps your church stay focused on its purposes. Acts 2:42-47 records five purposes the first church carried out. Rather than describing the work of the church, this passage shows us the church at work. These purposes are the model for the ministries in which our churches are to engage. Sunday School and FAITH have important roles in each of these ministries.

A church exists for _____**evangelism**_____.
Evangelism is sharing the message of Christ with people who are on their way to a Christless eternity. It is a critical function of the church. Without it a church will not grow or prosper and will not fulfill God's will. "How can a minister, believer, or church say they believe that salvation can be received only through Jesus Christ in an act of supernatural grace and not share that news with others? To say we believe something as incredible as God's love and then be reluctant to share this good news with others with enthusiasm and joy is beyond belief."[6]

When we lead people to Christ through evangelism, we escort them into God's family. The early church recognized the priority of evangelism, and it willingly and frequently witnessed about Christ—His atoning death for the sins of humanity, the forgiveness of sins that He offers, the free gift of eternal life to those who believe, and the abundant life that comes from believing in Him. Then, as now, "Evangelism is the good news spoken by believers and lived out in their lives."[7]

Evangelism is a crucial part of both the FAITH ministry and the ongoing Bible-study ministry. As a FAITH leader, keep in mind that FAITH is not just about visiting people and inviting them to your church. Rather, it is about sharing the message of Jesus Christ with people who need Him. This happens on Sunday mornings and throughout the week.

A church exists for _____**discipleship**_____.
Another function that is as important as evangelism is discipleship, which Gene Mims has noted "is much talked about but probably is practiced the least of all church functions."[8]

Discipleship is a lifelong process in which we continue to grow in our knowledge of and love for the Lord while we become more like Him and live His will in our daily lives. In the discipleship process we are not only engaged as learners but also lead other believers to love, trust, and obey Jesus Christ and then to teach other believers to do the same.

Step 4 (10 mins.)

Ask participants to turn to page 35 in their Journals and to fill in the blanks as you present the material in "Strengthen the FAITH Connection to Your Church." Use the computer presentation or overhead cel 12.

> State that prayer is one way fellowship develops in the body of Christ. Remind participants of the need to enlist two persons to be their prayer partners throughout this study. These should be persons who are not participating in FAITH and are not partners for someone else. Distribute Prayer-Partner Commitment Cards and ask participants to enlist their prayer partners and to return their cards when they arrive for session 3. Give participants enough cards to distribute to their Team Learners also.

As you participate in *Growing as a FAITH Leader* and other FAITH Discipleship courses, as well as in your Sunday School class, you are following Christ's example and growing as a disciple and a discipler.

A church exists for _____fellowship_____.

Fellowship is another crucial function for the family of God. Through fellowship believers come to know one another and live as disciples in a community of faith. Fellowship is sharing lives together—not only in good times but also in difficult ones. In fact, fellowship may be best understood as shared suffering. However, fellowship is not automatic. It develops only when God's Spirit has His way within individual Christians and within the church as He cultivates the unity He desires.

"The fellowship of the church provides an atmosphere in which believers can mature and be nourished. Without this fellowship and our accountability to the Lord and other believers, we might be tempted to live our lives away from Him and apart from other believers."[9]

Biblical fellowship develops as you and the other persons on your FAITH Team meet together, pray together, and visit together during the semester. You come to know one another on a deeper level and develop the concern for and accountability to one another that God desires for those who are a part of His family. In the same way, your Sunday School class should be experiencing a different dynamic because the FAITH ministry is strengthening relationships.

A church exists for _____ministry_____.

Ministry is another essential function of the church that was practiced by the early believers. "Ministry is the discovery and use of spiritual gifts and abilities to meet the needs of others in Jesus' name."[10] We practice it in the church as we support one another during difficult times. This is what John commanded when he wrote, "We must not love in word or speech, but in deed and truth" (1 John 3:18).

While we understand the importance of caring for those within the church, ministry also includes meeting needs of people who are not in the church. Often we use the term *missions* to designate the ministry we provide to the unchurched, especially those who are a part of a different culture. As we minister, we seek to lead people to know and follow Jesus Christ as Savior and Lord.

As your FAITH Team makes ministry visits to persons connected to your Sunday School class, you express love in action to class members who are having difficulty. You may be able to reclaim inactive members who want to be part of a fellowship that cares about them.

A church exists for _____worship_____.

Worship may be the most misunderstood function of the church. We understand the corporate dimension of worship—gathering with other believers to praise God, listen to His Word, and respond to His leading. But worship also has a personal dimension: coming into the presence of the living God, listening to Him speak through His Word, opening our lives to be transformed by Him, and responding to Him according to His will. James emphasized these dimensions of worship when he wrote, "Draw near to God, and He will draw near to you" (Jas. 4:8).

Our personal worship has a great impact on our corporate worship. "True worship should lead worshipers to a deeper appreciation for God, a better understanding of His ways, and to a deeper commitment to Him. Encountering God in worship transforms us more and more into His likeness."[11]

As you participate in FAITH, you should experience deeper worship of God as you seek to fulfill His purposes in order to bring Him glory.

Recognize the Importance of Small Groups

Because the previous actions are commanded in God's Word and were modeled in the first church, they are goals for every church. The following five reasons indicate ways small groups provide an effective structure for carrying out a church's ministries.

Small groups offer _____**connection**_____ _____**points**_____.
As FAITH Teams participate in visitation, they have opportunities to reach new people for Christ and enroll them in Sunday School classes. One natural result of the FAITH strategy is that Sunday School classes grow, thus creating the need for additional classes to be started. As more and more classes are made available, a variety of connection points are established for new people to get involved in the church.

Small groups offer _____**accountability**_____ *for evangelism.*
The saying "Everybody's business is nobody's business" is especially true of evangelism. Because FAITH is an integral part of the Sunday School strategy, FAITH participants can keep Sunday School members focused on the importance of sharing the gospel with non-Christians. FAITH also provides a structure for training Sunday School members, step-by-step, to share their faith and to train others to do the same.

Small groups provide _____**effective**_____ _____**ministry**_____.
It is difficult to care for people you don't know. If you don't know someone personally, you likely are unaware of the person's need because most people don't freely share their needs in large groups (such as a worship

Step 5 (5 mins.)

Ask participants to turn to page 37 in their Journals and to fill in the blanks as you present the material in "Recognize the Importance of Small Groups." Use the computer presentation or overhead cel 13.

> Recognize the Importance of Small Groups

service) or with strangers. FAITH works as a partner with Sunday School to provide ministry to people in need in the context of a small group. Because relationships develop, the natural results are regular contact between individuals and concern for those in need.

Small groups enhance _____spiritual_____ _____maturity_____.
Almost any type of Bible study can potentially help persons grow as disciples. However, the most effective Bible study allows persons to ask questions, utilizes different teaching approaches to meet a variety of learning needs, and provides practical ideas for putting into practice what members learn. Ideally, this happens in Sunday School classes. In addition, participants in FAITH have the opportunity to grow in their faith as they learn to witness and minister in obedience to Christ.

Small groups provide an avenue for _____service_____.
Ephesians 4:11-12 emphasizes that God gave the church certain leaders "for the training of the saints in the work of ministry, to build up the body of Christ." God intended for all of His people to be ministers, not just a select few. He provided pastors and other leaders to train believers in how to fulfill the ministry to which God called and gifted them. This model is seen in the FAITH strategy: pastors train believers, who then train others in an ongoing process.[12]

Cultivate Open Bible-Study Groups

To determine whether the small-group process is working in your church, it is important to answer this fundamental question: Are your Sunday School classes open to new people? Before you answer, consider these features of an open group. An ___open___ Bible-study group—
- is an evangelistic group that seeks to include new people, especially unbelievers, at any time;
- doesn't require that someone have prior content knowledge or preparation in order to participate;
- regularly sees people coming and going—new people coming into the class and others leaving the class to serve somewhere else.

In contrast, a ___closed___ group focuses more on spiritual maturity than on evangelism. A closed group—
- requires people to prepare for the class, and the content of the class progressively builds from session to session, making it difficult or impossible for a new person to join after a study has begun;
- usually exists for a limited time, such as for the length of a particular study, then disbands.

Step 6 (5 mins.)

Ask participants to turn to page 38 in their Journals and to fill in the blanks as you present the material in "Cultivate Open Bible-Study Groups." Use the computer presentation or overhead cels 14–15.

Cultivate Open Bible-Study Groups

It has been estimated that more than half of Adult Sunday School classes in Southern Baptist churches are __**closed**__ __**groups**__. This may be the primary reason more than two-thirds of our churches are plateaued or declining. Although new people, including unbelievers, may come to a worship service, they will have little, if any, genuine connection with other believers if they are not involved in a small group. And if the small groups are not open to them or are not functioning as they should, then these people cannot get into a group! Thus, individuals will not grow, and the church will be weakened.

As a FAITH leader, you must determine whether your Sunday School class is a properly functioning open group. Read the following list and check the boxes that describe your class. An open Bible-study group—

- means that both believers and unbelievers are invited to participate and that the class has an intentional evangelistic purpose;
- is open at any time for new unbelievers or believers to enter;
- studies God's Word with an intentional focus on teaching that guides people toward conversion and assimilation;
- is intentionally formed around transforming learners' lives through the study of God's Word;
- constantly sends out leaders to serve in other areas of the church;
- is organized so that relationships for ongoing ministry are built and maintained with believers and unbelievers;
- has been conditioned by its leader to the idea of starting new units;
- is willing to do whatever it takes to reach one more person.[12]

What are you doing to make sure other class members understand the distinction between open and closed groups? What are you doing to make sure your class becomes or remains an open group? If you don't assume the responsibility in this area, no one else may know enough or care enough to do something about it.

If your church is going to grow, it is critical that you understand the FAITH Sunday School Evangelism Strategy®. It is just as critical that you understand your role as a leader in implementing this strategy and its role in the ministries of your Sunday School and church. Your leadership can make a tremendous difference in your Team, your class, your church, and the kingdom.

In the next session you will discover how to effectively implement FAITH and how to incorporate kingdom principles into your class and your church.

To learn more about the way open groups support Sunday School as a strategy, see *Essentials for Excellence: Connecting Sunday School to Life* (LifeWay Press, 2003).

If time permits, give participants a moment to complete the checklist. If not, ask them to complete it before session 3.

Duplicate and distribute copies of "Questions for Evaluating Whether Your Bible-Study Group Is an Open Group" from the CD-ROM at the back of this guide. Encourage participants to use this tool to evaluate their Sunday School classes.

STUDY IT

Step 7 (5 mins.)

Overview the Home Study Assignments for session 2.

Transition to assemble with FAITH Teams to prepare for home visits. (5 mins.)

[Handwritten note: This is not the only reason we should do FAITH - It is not about growing your church, but the Kingdom. (by product - growth)]

DO IT (110 MINS.)

Visitation Time

DO IT

1. The Team Leader guides preparation for all visits. Remind Team members to stay alert to prospect and ministry needs.
2. Alert Team members in advance if they need to be ready to give Sunday School or evangelistic testimonies.
3. Team members have been introduced to the Key Question. Discuss responses to the question and emphasize the importance of the **Preparation** phase of the visit.
4. Keep in mind the visitation tips Learners have been asked to review (p. 35, A Journey in FAITH Journal). Highlight any you feel are especially helpful or needed.
5. Most of all, encourage Team members as they make their first home visits. Be prepared to take the lead in all visits. Model a visit and debrief what happened so that Team members can learn.

Celebration Time

SHARE IT (30 MINS.)

SHARE IT

1. Explain the purpose and importance of Celebration Time and encourage members to stay for this time each week.
2. Encourage Team members to listen carefully as reports are shared, especially about decisions made in visits; the information can be helpful in follow-up.
3. Take the lead in sharing reports.
4. Complete the necessary forms: Evaluation Cards, Participation Cards, and church visitation forms updated with the results of visits.

---

[1] James T. Draper, Jr., *Bridges to the Future: A Challenge to Southern Baptists* (Nashville: Convention Press, 1994), 52.
[2] Alan Raughton and Louis B. Hanks, *Essentials for Excellence: Connecting Sunday School to Life* (LifeWay Press, 2003), 24.
[3] J. N. Barnette, in Bill L. Taylor, *The Power to Change Lives* (Nashville: Convention Press, 1998), 67. Out of print.
[4] Arthur Flake, *The True Functions of the Sunday School* (Nashville: Convention Press, 1955), 81. Out of print.
[5] P. E. Burroughs, in Bobby H. Welch, *Evangelism Through the Sunday School: A Journey of FAITH* (Nashville: LifeWay Press, 1997), 11.
[6] Gene Mims, *Kingdom Principles for Church Growth, Revised and Expanded* (Nashville, LifeWay Press, 2001), 34–35.
[7] Ibid., 35.
[8] Ibid., 39.
[9] Ibid., 51.
[10] Bill L. Taylor and Louis B. Hanks, *Sunday School for a New Century* (Nashville: LifeWay Press, 1999), 17. Out of print.
[11] Mims, *Kingdom Principles*, 57.
[12] Adapted from Dale Galloway, *The Small-Group Book: The Practical Guide for Nurturing Christians and Building Churches* (Grand Rapids: Fleming H. Revell, 1995), 10.
[13] Adapted from John McClendon, *Beyond the Walls: Multiply Your Ministry* (Nashville: LifeWay Press, 2002), 6. Out of print.

Home Study Assignments

Day 1: Your Relationship with God

Learning about leadership is important, but your greatest resource for developing as a leader is a close relationship with God. Read Luke 6:39-43. What does this Scripture say about the importance of continuing to learn from God?

"a disciple is not above his teacher, but everyone who is perfectly trained will be like his teacher."

How are you depending on God to equip and empower you to be the leader He created you to be? Check all that apply and add your own ideas.
- [x] Having a daily quiet time that includes Bible study and prayer
- [x] Staying in contact with God throughout the day
- [x] Going first to God for direction when you face choices or problems
- [ ] Studying biblical leadership resources in a group or on your own
- [ ] Taking notes on your pastor's sermons
- [x] Seeking guidance from more mature believers
- [x] Participating in discipleship and ministry opportunities

Day 2: Your Relationship with Your FAITH Team

Look up the word *strategy* in a dictionary. Then define it in your own words.

a determined planned set of actions for attaining a specific goal

How can understanding Sunday School as a strategy enhance your leadership in Sunday School?

We have to move out beyond ourselves — we have the plan — now lets obtain the goal

on your FAITH Team? *We must work together to be accomplished*

Spend time praying for your Team members.

Day 3: Your Relationship with Your Sunday School Class

Listed below are the reasons a church should have small groups. Check the one that addresses the greatest need in your Sunday School class.
- ☑ Offer connection points
- ❏ Enhance spiritual maturity
- ❏ Offer accountability for evangelism
- ❏ Provide an avenue for service
- ❏ Provide effective ministry

Circle the number representing the degree to which you think most members of your Sunday School class understand the role of the FAITH strategy in your Sunday School and church. Low 1 2 3 4 5 6 ⑦ 8 9 10 High
What can you do to help others better understand the strategy?

weekly/monthly meetings (S.S)

Read James 1:22-25. How does this Scripture passage relate to the members of your class and the need to carry out the Sunday School strategy?

We need to be doers, and not just hearers

Day 4: Your Relationship with the Lost

Read and meditate on Romans 10:11-15. What is God saying to you through this Scripture?

_____

Suppose that a lost person visited your Sunday School class. Circle a percentage representing your level of confidence that the person would learn how to become a Christian over a short period of time.

5%   10%   25%   35%   50%   65%   ⓻⓹%   100%

How would the lost person experience the FAITH Sunday School Evangelism Strategy® in action?

"evangelism fly's on the wings of ministry"

What steps can you take to ensure the FAITH strategy is implemented in your Sunday School class so that a lost person can learn how to become a Christian?

_____

_____

Day 5: Your Relationship with Your Family and Your Church

Match the purposes of the church with their definitions.

D 1. Evangelism
C 2. Discipleship
A 3. Fellowship
E 4. Ministry
B 5. Worship

a. Developing relationships as you live within the community of faith
b. Coming into God's presence; opening your life to be transformed by Him
c. Growing in the knowledge of and love for Christ; becoming more like Him
d. Sharing the message of Christ with those who don't know Him
e. Using spiritual gifts and abilities to meet others' needs in Jesus' name

On a scale of 1 to 10, with 10 being the highest, how would you rate your church on fulfilling each purpose of the church?

Evangelism	1 2 3 4 5 6 7 8 **9** 10
Discipleship	1 2 3 4 5 6 **7** 8 9 10
Fellowship	1 2 3 4 5 **6** 7 8 9 10
Ministry	1 2 3 4 5 6 **7** 8 9 10
Worship	1 2 3 4 5 6 7 **8** 9 10

What percentage of the members of your church do you estimate are aware of the purposes of the church?

5%   10%   25%   35%   **50%**   65%   75%   100%

Answers to matching exercise on this page: 1. d, 2. c, 3. a, 4. e, 5. b

FAITH AT WORK

Although I accepted Christ when I was 12, unfortunately I was 35 before I realized the importance of sharing my faith. I always used the excuse that I was living my faith daily, so I didn't need to tell anyone. What a devastating lie from Satan!

When my husband and I joined our church, we heard about the FAITH ministry, but both of us responded that we would not participate because going and telling others were not necessary. Besides, we weren't called to that ministry. But God saw otherwise and began to convict us. We finally agreed to participate in a semester of FAITH training. Little did we know that our lives would never be the same!

After we had completed the semester, God led us to start a new Sunday School class for single parents. If not for FAITH, we would never have been equipped to begin teaching in this new ministry area.

It's exciting to think about the work God has done in our class through the FAITH ministry. One class member had grown up in a local church, but when our FAITH Team visited her home, she admitted that she had never personally accepted Christ. She prayed to receive Christ as her Savior and Lord during that FAITH visit. She was baptized and became an active member of the Single-Parent Sunday School Class and the church.

On another night we visited a single-parent home, but the man we were going to see was not home. However, another single parent was house-sitting for him with her son, and after we shared the FAITH outline, her son prayed to receive Christ. Now the boy's mother and the man we were originally going to see are prospects for our class. One of our FAITH Teams has also had the opportunity to minister to a single parent whose former wife was murdered.

I am sad when I think that I wasted all those years in rebellion, thinking I didn't have to share my faith verbally, but I am thankful that God is now allowing my husband and me to participate in His glorious work with single parents through the FAITH Sunday School Evangelism Strategy®. Seeing Him at work in people's lives in tangible ways is a joy and a blessing. For us, each FAITH visit is a divine adventure!

> Beth Cuvelier
> Colonial Heights Baptist Church
> Jackson, Mississippi

SESSION 3
Building a Healthy Sunday School

In this session you will—

CHECK IT by engaging in Team Time activities;

KNOW IT by reviewing content from session 2;

HEAR IT by discovering practical ways to build a healthy Sunday School;

STUDY IT by overviewing Home Study Assignments;

DO IT by leading your Team in making visits;

SHARE IT by celebrating.

IN ADVANCE
- Overview content.
- Preview teaching suggestions. Prepare key points. Decide whether to use the session 3 computer presentation or overhead cels 16–19 (see pp. 286–89). (Because "A Quick Review" calls for subjective responses in this session, no corresponding overhead-cel master is provided for reviewing these answers.)
- Use the file provided on the CD-ROM (inside the back cover of this Facilitator Guide) to make copies of the Leadership-Meeting Planning Sheet for all participants.
- Prepare the room for teaching.
- Pray for participants and for Teams as they prepare to visit.
- As Teaching Time begins, direct participants to open their Journals to page 48.

TEAM TIME

CHECK IT (15 MINS.)

If the computer presentation is used, display the agenda for Team Time. Add other points to the agenda as needed.

CHECK IT agenda:
- ✔ FAITH Visit Outline
- ✔ Other Home Study Assignments
- ✔ Session 2 Debriefing
- ✔ Help for Strengthening a Visit

Leading Team Time

All Team members participate in Team Time. They are primarily responsible for reciting the assigned portion of the FAITH Visit Outline and for discussing other Home Study Assignments.

As you direct this important time of CHECK IT activities with your Team, keep in mind that Learners look to you as a role model, motivator, mentor, and friend. Team Time activities can continue in the car as the Team travels to and from visits.

Lead CHECK IT Activities

✔ *FAITH Visit Outline*
- ❑ Be prepared to check off each Learner's memorization of all of **Preparation** (through Transition Statement) and the key words in **Presentation** and **Invitation**.
- ❑ Indicate your approval by signing or initialing each Learner's Journal. Encourage Learners as you do and indicate any notes you have jotted down that might be helpful.

✔ *Other Home Study Assignments*
- ❑ Give as much time as needed to helping Learners understand different responses people might make to the Key Question and ways to answer those responses in love. Indicate that such answers will become clearer throughout FAITH training/visits.
- ❑ Discuss how FAITH Tips and/or other readings can provide specific help or answer some questions from sessions.
- ❑ Indicate specific content areas that may appear again on the session 16 written review.

✔ *Session 2 Debriefing*
- ❑ Answer any questions that remain from session 2. Emphasize the importance of a good beginning in building trust that can ultimately result in the gospel's being shared. Highlight ways the Sunday School testimony helps build bridges to people.
- ❑ Review Learners' written Sunday School testimonies.
- ❑ Indicate specific content areas that may appear again on the session 16 written review.

✔ *Help for Strengthening a Visit*
- ❑ Answer any questions that emerged from home visits following session 2.
- ❑ Review ways to begin a visit.

46 / Growing as a FAITH Leader Facilitator Guide

- ❑ Identify actions Team members took during last week's visits that were particularly effective and others that might need to be changed.
- ❑ Suggest ways Team members can improve sharing their Sunday School testimonies.
- ❑ Call attention to the evangelistic testimony you shared during last week's visit(s). Mention that Team Learners will be introduced during this session to ways to share their testimonies during a visit.

Notes

Actions I Need to Take with Team Members This Week

Transition to classrooms for instruction on the content of the session. (5 mins.)

TEACHING TIME

KNOW IT

Step 1 (5 mins.)

Direct participants to turn to "A Quick Review" on page 48 in their Journals and to complete the activities. Review answers, using the computer presentation. (Because "A Quick Review" calls for subjective responses in this session, no corresponding overhead-cel master is provided for reviewing these answers.)

1. As a strategy, Sunday School operates 24 hours a day, 7 days a week, primarily outside the classroom, to help the church fulfill its purposes. This contrasts to Sunday School as a program, an hour-long event each week in which people "come in, fill up, and go out."
2. FAITH helps reach people for Christ, minister to their needs, connect them to a class, and disciple them so that they can repeat the process.
3. *Evangelism:* FAITH shares the gospel with others. *Discipleship:* FAITH helps people grow in their relationship with Christ so that they can help others do the same. *Fellowship:* FAITH allows a Team of three class members to draw closer together as they meet, pray, and visit together. *Ministry:* FAITH Teams show love to class members in need. *Worship:* FAITH leads people to a greater dependence on God, thus to a greater love for Him and a greater desire to glorify Him.

A Quick Review

In session 2 you learned the concept of Sunday School as a strategy, examined the purposes of the church, and discovered the importance of small groups to the ministries of your Sunday School and church. Review by answering the following questions in your own words.

1. How does the idea of Sunday School as a strategy differ from the idea of Sunday School as a program?

   It is an on going thing - that should have no end - everybody needs evangelism/ministry

2. How does FAITH help carry out the Sunday School strategy?

   By using evangelism - ministry

3. How does the FAITH strategy support the five purposes of the church?

   Evangelism: *Sharing the gospel message*
   Discipleship: *lifelong process of growing/knowing Christ*
   Fellowship: *Sharing our lives together*
   Ministry: *using spiritual gifts to help others*
   Worship: *Coming into the presence of the Lord*

> **LEADERS ON LEADERSHIP**
> "Many Sunday School programs have failed to produce growth results because they lack vision for the total work and consequently lose balance." —Ken Hemphill[1]

Develop a Healthy Sunday School Class

While it's important to understand the strategy of Sunday School and the purpose of the church, it's just as important to actively participate in the Sunday School strategy and help fulfill its purposes. Healthy Sunday School classes intentionally seek to carry out the strategy you studied in session 2.

As a FAITH leader, you may already understand Sunday School as a strategy, and you may be helping to fulfill its purposes. Yet in certain areas your Sunday School class may need additional help to do all it was designed to do. As a leader, you can be the catalyst to bring about change where it is needed. To know where a change is needed and yet ignore the change will cause problems. The Bible states that not doing something good we know we should do is a sin (see Jas. 4:17).

Where should you start if changes are needed?

Make the area of need a matter of __prayer__.
God wants your class and your church to be effective and to live up to His standards. In Revelation 2—3 He sent messages to seven churches through the apostle John to remind them of His standards and call them to obey Him. Because He also has a message for your class, He may use you as His messenger, so listen closely to what He says.

Discuss the need with __FAITH__ __Teams__.
Your FAITH Team and other individuals on FAITH Teams from your class may not have leadership responsibilities in your class, but they are perhaps the best candidates for helping to initiate change where it's needed. Those who will step out in faith and obedience to participate in FAITH will be more likely to follow in faith and obedience to make the Sunday School class more effective.

Consult with __class__ __leaders__.
Someone once said, "As the staff goes, so goes the church." In the same way, we can say, "As the Sunday School class leadership goes, so goes the class." This means that leaders must understand and do what is best if the class is going to follow. And for leaders to know and be motivated to do what is best, they must regularly meet together.

[Handwritten note: "If there is an absence of genuine leadership - people will look for the next best thing"]

HEAR IT

Step 2 (10 mins.)

Ask participants to turn to page 49 in their Journals and to fill in the blanks as you present the material in "Develop a Healthy Sunday School Class." Use the computer presentation or overhead cel 16. Remind participants that even though they may be involved in helping to fulfill the Sunday School strategy and the purposes of the church, their Sunday School classes may still need to make changes in order to do all they were designed to do.

Ask accountability partners to share one area in which change is needed in their Sunday School classes to help them accomplish their purposes. Emphasize the three things participants can do when changes are needed: pray, discuss the need with your FAITH Team, and discuss the need with class leaders.

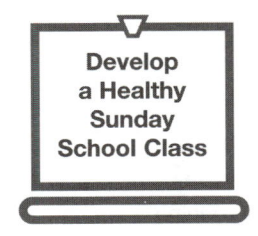

Develop a Healthy Sunday School Class

Step 3 (10 mins.)

Ask each participant to consider, on a scale of 1–10, with 10 being the highest, the priority their class places on leadership-team meetings, then to write that number in the margin on page 50 in the Journal. Instruct participants to fill in the blanks in their Journals as you present the material in "Give Priority to the Sunday School Leadership Meeting," using the computer presentation or overhead cel 17. Emphasize that it is important for any team to meet and evaluate its work, encourage one another, make corrections, and plan. Briefly share the functions of a Sunday School leadership meeting: building a team spirit, developing deeper relationships, and sharing names of persons who need a FAITH visit or results of FAITH visits.

Duplicate copies of the Leadership-Meeting Planning Sheet from the CD-ROM and distribute them. Point out that additional copies can be made and used to help guide leadership meetings. Remind participants that God may have raised them up as FAITH leaders to be catalysts for change in strengthening the work of their Sunday School classes.

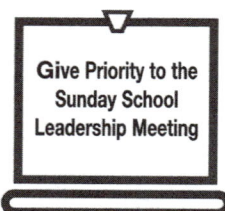

Give Priority to the Sunday School Leadership Meeting

Give Priority to the Sunday School Leadership Meeting

What level of importance does your class place on Sunday School leadership meetings? Hopefully, you give them high priority, because they are a critical part of the Sunday School strategy. What are the benefits of a leadership team meeting?

The leadership meeting equips ___leaders___.
In the world of sports, a team won't function effectively without practice, which is a time to evaluate weaknesses, work on skills, make plans, and so forth. In the same way, a Sunday School class won't fulfill its purposes unless the leadership team regularly meets for evaluation, encouragement, correction, and planning. The leadership meeting is a setting in which some leaders begin to understand the objectives of Sunday School and all leaders plan ways to carry out the strategy.

The leadership meeting strengthens ___teamwork___.
A sense of team develops when leaders recognize that they are working together to accomplish the church's mission. This sense of team grows as leaders build relationships with one another, share their lives with one another, and support one another with prayer.

The leadership meeting promotes ___communication___.
In leadership meetings, communication is strengthened among leadership team members who are working in different areas to accomplish the same goal. Team members can share concerns, joys, challenges, and opportunities they have discovered that others need to know about in order to better minister to members and prospects. As a part of the sharing time, FAITH Team assignments and follow-up reports can be shared with other leaders who are not participating in FAITH. Such communication can enhance planning and evaluation for the class.

A weekly leadership team meeting is ideal because the Sunday School class also meets weekly. A weekly meeting is especially valuable during the FAITH semester because it allows leaders who are not involved in FAITH to stay connected to the heart of Sunday School—evangelism and ministry. As FAITH Team members share updates about their visits and discuss visits that are needed (such as ministry visits), the class as a whole will be more effective in fulfilling the Sunday School strategy week after week.

Some class leadership teams find it difficult, however, to meet each week. Does this mean they can forget about meeting together? No! In such cases the leadership team may be able to get together every other

50 / *Growing as a FAITH Leader Facilitator Guide*

week or at least monthly. Given the technology available today, leaders may be able to get together through Instant Messenger, e-mail, or a conference call. Still, a monthly, face-to-face meeting should be a minimum requirement for every class leadership team.

What can you do if you are not the designated leader in a class? Even if another person convenes and moderates the meeting, you as a FAITH leader can introduce elements of the Sunday School strategy that need attention in your class. As you remind other leadership-team members of the biblical basis for these actions, you can help build the case for making these actions a part of your class. While the task of convincing others about these actions may seem daunting in some cases, a part of leadership includes speaking the truth for the good of the group, then allowing God to bring conviction about changes that are needed.

Assimilate New Members

Imagine that you are a member of a Sunday School class that doesn't want new members. Your class would be interested in the following list.

TOP 10 WAYS TO KEEP NEW PEOPLE AWAY FROM YOUR CLASS

10. Install locks on the classroom door and give keys only to members.
9. Meet in a different location each week. Tell only the current members each new location.
8. Hot-wire empty chairs so that any visitor who sits in one receives a mild electric shock.
7. Put a No Vacancy sign on the door.
6. Announce that your class is conducted in pig Latin.
5. If new people attend, ignore them during class.
4. Invite new people to a fellowship, but provide the wrong information about the place and time.
3. If new people show up, ask, "Do you know the password?" and refuse entry to those who don't.
2. Require new people to pay a service fee of $100 to attend.
1. Advertise a need for new members whose spiritual gift is martyrdom.

Although the items in this list range from humorous to ludicrous, the philosophy they represent is prevalent in too many classes. While few classes would admit to being closed to new people, many are functioning as unhealthy or dysfunctional open groups.

Step 4 (5 mins.)

Ask participants to turn to page 51 in their Journals and to read along as you read aloud the Top-10 List. Ask participants to indicate whether their Sunday School class is an unhealthy or dysfunctional open group. Mention that although the Top-10 list may seem humorous, the mind-set of disinterest in others is prevalent in many classes.

Ask participants to fill in the blanks as you present the material in "Assimilate New Members." Use the computer presentation or overhead cel 18. Emphasize that because FAITH participants reach people for Christ, for Sunday School enrollment, and for church membership, they are vital to helping assimilate people into the church.

Assimilate New Members

What is the antidote to such a condition? Continuing to stay focused on and involved in the FAITH Sunday School Evangelism Strategy® will keep a class open to new members. When your class is involved in FAITH, new people will come to Christ, enroll in the class, and attend the class. However, that's not the end of the process. Your class must still work to assimilate new members—to plug them in to the life and work of the class. Unless assimilation becomes a team effort and a priority of the class, however, members will soon turn inward. At that point you might as well hang a Closed sign on the door.

Assimilating new people begins even before a new member joins the class. Here are some suggestions to help people get connected and stay connected to your class and church.

Station a **class** **greeter** *at the door.*
By making sure your class has at least one greeter at the door, preferably someone with the gift of hospitality, you will convey a good first impression as a class that cares about people. This greeter could be a member of a FAITH Team who may have already met the person through a home visit. Greeters must be careful not get so caught up in conversations with members that they ignore guests or give them just a token welcome.

Wear **name** **tags** .
Name tags are helpful for both newcomers and long-time members. Name tags create a more open feeling in the class and make it easier for new people to remember the names of existing members. Use the same type of name tags for everyone so that no one appears to be an outsider.

Enlist **good** **neighbors** .
Enlist members to sit with new people and to introduce them to others. FAITH Team members may have already visited the newcomers or will likely visit them during the coming week. Talking with new people, good neighbors may discover interests newcomers have in common with someone else in the class and can encourage new friendships to develop.

Assign prospects and new members to **care** **groups** .
This practice ensures that newcomers will be regularly contacted and ministered to when (not if) they have a need or experience a crisis. Care groups must be small, must be focused on ministry to members, and must be led by someone who will maintain connections with members to ensure that no one is ignored or forgotten.

Utilize **fellowship** .
By planning fellowship events every month or so and inviting every guest and class member (including class members serving in other age groups), you provide opportunities for people to share their lives and

get to know one another better. In addition, service projects, supper clubs, and small prayer groups can be used to connect new people to your class. As you keep these groups dynamic—moving people in and out after several months—you help develop relationships on a broader scale and keep cliques from forming that would damage the class.

Take the __lead__.
As a FAITH leader, take the initiative to ensure that the people you visit, witness to, and minister to get connected to your class and feel that they belong. To do otherwise would be like bringing a new baby home from the hospital and ignoring her, expecting her to make it on her own. Even after someone joins your class, you may want to make a ministry visit to the person to make sure connections are being made. How can you know when people have been assimilated?

- They have a regular pattern of involvement—not only attending the class but also investing themselves in the church's life and work.
- They have made genuine friends who keep up with and encourage one another not just on Sunday morning but throughout the week, as well (see Heb. 3:13). It has been suggested that a person needs seven friends in a church to stay involved.
- They help others get and stay connected to the church in the same way other persons did for them.

Maintain Connections

As class members grow in their faith, they will begin to hear God's call, recognize how He has equipped them, and begin to serve where He leads them. Often this will be in another area of Sunday School, whether working with a class in another age group or helping to start a new adult class. Many times those who leave are FAITH-trained individuals who step out on faith and obey God's call to serve in another area.

How many members have left your class to serve in other areas? What has happened to them after they left the class? It is essential for your class to maintain a connection with anyone who leaves to serve elsewhere in the church. Use ideas like these to do so.

Assign them to __care__ __groups__.
Care groups enable your class to stay in contact with in-service members and to continue ministering to their needs.

Include them in __fellowship__ *activities*.
When class fellowships and activities are planned, in-service members should be invited and introduced to new members of the class.

Step 5 (5 mins.)

Ask participants to turn to page 53 in their Journals and to fill in the blanks as you highlight the material in "Maintain Connections." Use the computer presentation or overhead cel 19. Ask participants to answer the questions that begin the second paragraph. Remind them of the necessity that their class stay in contact with and minister to those who have left their class to serve in other areas.

Maintain Connections

Establish a service __hall__ *of* __fame__.
Set up a service hall of fame that is displayed in the classroom. Include the photos of those who are serving elsewhere, along with labels that identify their places of service.

As members see that their class continues to support those who leave to serve elsewhere, it will be much easier for them to follow God's leadership if He guides them to serve in a similar way. Conversely, members may be hesitant or unwilling to serve in other areas if the class has an out-of-sight, out-of-mind philosophy.

Understand the Difference Between Growth and Health

What's your most important concern about your body—your growth or your health? Most likely it's your health, which can be affected by your growth! In the past few decades Sunday Schools and churches have emphasized growth. Although most growth principles are valid, the greater emphasis should be on health. Just as a human body can grow too large and become unhealthy, so can a Sunday School or a church. When a class places its focus on health, however, it is positioned for growth that will be beneficial rather than detrimental.

The FAITH Sunday School Evangelism Strategy® is designed to build a healthy church—one that is balanced in accomplishing the purposes of the church. As a FAITH leader, you are interested not only in seeing people make professions of faith but also in connecting them with the body of Christ, where they can be discipled, receive and provide ministry, develop relationships with other believers, and worship the Lord.[2]

By following the principles in this session, your class and your church can be healthy. You can be the key to nurturing health in your class because, as a leader, you know what should be done, and you have the motivation to do it. The power to do it comes through the Holy Spirit, who is able to accomplish "above and beyond all that we ask or think" (Eph. 3:20).

To learn more about building a healthy Sunday School, see the following resources.
- *Essentials for Excellence: Connecting Sunday School to Life* (LifeWay Press, 2003)
- *Ten Best Practices to Make Your Sunday School Work* (LifeWay Press, 2001)

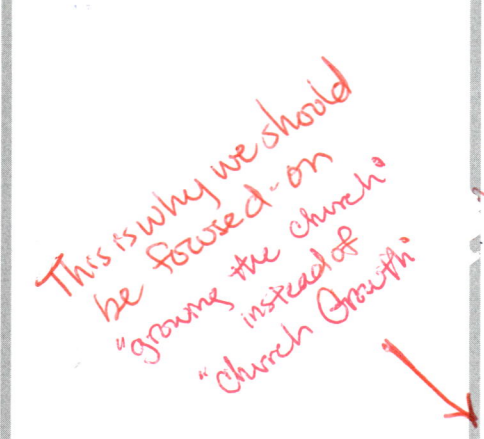

Sidebar

> *This is why we should be focused on "growing the church" instead of "church Growth"*

Step 6 (5 mins.)

Present the material in "Understand the Difference Between Growth and Health," using the computer presentation.

Ask participants to return the Prayer-Partner Commitment Cards they used to enlist prayer partners during the past week. Encourage those who have not enlisted partners to do so as soon as possible so that they will have prayer support during this semester.

STUDY IT

Step 7 (5 mins.)

Overview the Home Study Assignments for session 3.

Transition to assemble with FAITH Teams to prepare for home visits. (5 mins.)

Visitation Time

DO IT
1. Assign specific responsibilities to your Team Learners. Ask one to share a Sunday School or evangelistic testimony. Ask one to be the navigator to arrange the visitation schedule. Suggest that this person start with the prospect's home that is farthest away. Then work your way back toward the church. Assign another Team Learner to gather age-appropriate materials for your visit. This procedure will save time and will provide good training for Learners.
2. Pray before you go.
3. Review in the car. Share your evangelistic testimony and ask Learners to share what they would like to include in theirs.
4. Debrief each visit. Facilitate by asking specific questions.

Celebration Time

SHARE IT
1. Hear reports and testimonies.
2. Complete Evaluation Cards.
3. Complete Participation Cards.
4. Update visitation forms with the results of visits.

---
[1] Ken Hemphill, *Revitalizing the Sunday-Morning Dinosaur* (Nashville: Broadman & Holman Publishers, 1996), 21.
[2] Many of the ideas in this session were adapted from Topper Reid, *Beyond the Walls: Focus on Adults and Young Adults* (Nashville: LifeWay Press, 2000), 18. Out of print.

DO IT (110 MINS.)

SHARE IT (30 MINS.)

Home Study Assignments

Day 1: Your Relationship with God

Read Joshua 1:7-9. Match the verse or verses that relate to each item.

_____ 1. Strength   a. Verse 7
_____ 2. Courage   b. Verse 8
_____ 3. Obedience to God's Word   c. Verse 9
_____ 4. Meditation on God's Word
_____ 5. Confidence
_____ 6. Encouragement

In the previous list, circle the qualities and disciplines you need to develop to become a more successful leader.

What fears do you have as a leader? _____
_____

What will you do to stay focused on God as you fulfill the leadership role He has given you?

_____

Day 2: Your Relationship with Your FAITH Team

How are you helping your Team Learners catch the vision of the FAITH Sunday School Evangelism Strategy®?

_____

Think about the Learners on your FAITH Team. How do you hope to be able to describe them as leaders two semesters from now?

_____

List three ways you are helping Learners become future FAITH Team Leaders.

1. _____
2. _____
3. _____

Day 3: Your Relationship with Your Sunday School Class

How many people are enrolled in your class? _____
How many attend on a typical Sunday? _____

Do you consider your Sunday School class to be a healthy class? Check three characteristics or practices you think make your class healthy.
❑ Ministry to members
❑ Evangelistic outreach
❑ Large numbers in attendance
❑ In-depth Bible teaching
❑ Many FAITH-trained members
❑ Close fellowship
❑ Members leaving the class to serve elsewhere
❑ Guests every week

One action of a healthy class is starting other classes. When is the last time your class helped start a new class? _____

How can you share the vision of starting a new class? _____
_____

Day 4: Your Relationship with the Lost

Write the name(s) of one or two lost persons you are regularly praying for.
_____

Check events your class could use to build relationships with the lost.
❑ Picnic or cookout
❑ Softball or volleyball league
❑ Habitat for Humanity or another service project
❑ Fishing or rafting trip
❑ Golf or tennis tournament
❑ Scrapbooking seminar
❑ Community prayer survey
❑ Other: _____

Whom will you invite this week to visit your class with you?

_____

Day 5: Your Relationship with Your Family and Your Church

How is your leadership in FAITH having an impact on your family?

_____

_____

_____

_____

Ask your pastor to allow a FAITH Sunday School testimony to be shared in a worship service. Pray about volunteering to share a testimony.

Make an appointment with your pastor. Ask how you can help him communicate and fulfill the vision God has given him for FAITH and Sunday School.

Answers to matching exercise on page 56: 1. a, 2. a, 3. a, 4. b, 5. c, 6. c

FAITH TIP

Using FAITH to Start and Strengthen Churches

In recent years an effort has flourished to plant more churches in the United States and around the world. The FAITH Sunday School Evangelism Strategy® is an excellent way to help start new churches. Think of the possibilities if your church commissioned FAITH Teams for two years to help start a new work.

Lynwood Baptist Church in Cape Girardeau, Missouri, is one of the 28 FAITH Originator Churches. In 1999 about 20 adults and their families from Lynwood, along with a church planter, established Fruitland Community Church in a new-growth area just north of Cape Girardeau. Almost all of these adults had participated in FAITH and realized the potential of starting a new church with FAITH Teams. That first semester four FAITH Teams began to visit. Within two years the church averaged more than 150 in attendance and is still growing today.

The FAITH Team Leaders at Fruitland Community Church saw their role as more than leading Learners. They were people of great vision who understood how God could use the FAITH strategy to start a church. He can also use you, a FAITH leader, to help start a new church.

God can also use you to help another struggling church in your area. You may become a partner with the church to help it begin the FAITH strategy. Pastor Joe Little of Lula Baptist Church, a small, rural church just outside the Jackson, Mississippi, metro area, approached Colonial Heights Baptist Church in Jackson about sending some FAITH leaders to help train his members in FAITH. Little had attended a clinic at Colonial Heights but was not able to have any of his members attend. Four leaders from Colonial Heights committed to help for one semester. God began to do amazing things as those FAITH Teams saw people won to Christ, new believers baptized, and people enrolled in Sunday School. As a result, Lula Baptist Church renewed its vision and focus for reaching people in the community.

In both of these examples God blessed not only the churches that were helped but also the mother churches and the leaders who heard and obeyed God's voice. Combining your role as a leader in the FAITH ministry with a kingdom view of God's work opens many opportunities for God to use you for His purpose and glory.

FAITH AT WORK

We recently discovered a void in our church of young couples who had been married for less than five years and did not have children. This discovery led three couples to begin a new Sunday School class to target these couples. We recognized that young couples were not attending church for different reasons. Some had dropped out after high school and had never gotten back into the habit, while others had moved to a new city and had not joined a church. We knew that because most young couples are consumed with work and are highly recreational, they make little time for God and church.

Given these facts, we spent the first month praying about and planning how to make a difference in the lives of young couples. We divided class responsibilities and leadership roles, then launched our class with a very simple mission—to reach unchurched young couples. We knew that if we could connect with them socially, we might be able to connect with them spiritually, so we started hosting monthly supper clubs to which each leader couple would bring an unchurched couple. In almost every case on the following Sunday at least one of the visitor couples attended our class.

One couple who came to a supper club was Chris and Shaunta. Shortly afterward Chris's reserve unit was deployed to the Middle East, and Shaunta was forced to move to a smaller apartment. Our class quickly acted by renting a truck, moving her, and helping her get settled. Shaunta's care-group leader ministers to her, and our class's two FAITH Teams also make regular ministry visits to her. Shaunta recently joined our Sunday School class, and we believe it was because she felt loved and accepted. This past Sunday she even brought someone else with her to church. We continue to pray, encourage, and support her and her husband during this difficult time.

Grounding our young couples in their faith and in their marriages is important to us. Using the Explore the Bible curriculum, we focus the Scripture passage and lesson theme on their specific needs. We also have marriage-builder moments that directly apply the Scripture passage to their marriages.

The first few months as a new class were difficult, mainly because we started during the summer, when many couples were on vacation and our FAITH ministry was between semesters. Yet we used that time to connect as a class leadership team and to focus on our purpose as a class. When fall came, however, we began to see God's blessings as we identified and targeted more couples. Each month we continue to discover prospects. We are committed to minister to them in the midst of their struggles; to help them connect with the Lord, our class, and our church; and to guide them in developing strong marriages through obedience to the truths of God's Word.

Jim Randall
Colonial Heights Baptist Church
Jackson, Mississippi

SESSION 4
You Are Called to Ministry

In this session you will—

CHECK IT by engaging in Team Time activities;

KNOW IT by reviewing content from session 3;

HEAR IT by understanding the mandate and purpose of God's call to ministry;

STUDY IT by overviewing Home Study Assignments;

DO IT by leading your Team in making visits;

SHARE IT by celebrating.

IN ADVANCE
- Overview content.
- Preview teaching suggestions. Prepare key points. Decide whether to use the session 4 computer presentation or overhead cels 20–26 (see pp. 290–96).
- Use the file provided on the CD-ROM (inside the back cover of this Facilitator Guide) to make copies of the Spiritual-Gifts Worksheet for all participants.
- Prepare the room for teaching.
- Pray for participants and for Teams as they prepare to visit.
- As Teaching Time begins, direct participants to open their Journals to page 64.

TEAM TIME

CHECK IT (15 MINS.)

If the computer presentation is used, display the agenda for Team Time. Add other points to the agenda as needed.

CHECK IT agenda:
- ✔ FAITH Visit Outline
- ✔ Evangelistic Testimony
- ✔ Sunday School Testimony
- ✔ Other Home Study Assignments/Session 3 Debriefing
- ✔ Help for Strengthening a Visit

Leading Team Time

All Team members participate in Team Time. They are primarily responsible for reciting the assigned portion of the FAITH Visit Outline and for discussing other Home Study Assignments.

As you direct this important time of CHECK IT activities with your Team, keep in mind that Learners look to you as a role model, motivator, mentor, and friend. Team Time activities can continue in the car as the Team travels to and from visits.

Lead CHECK IT Activities

✔ FAITH Visit Outline
- ❏ Listen as each Learner recites the appropriate portion of the FAITH Visit Outline (all of **Preparation,** adding the Key Question and Transition Statement, plus key words for **Presentation** and **Invitation**).
- ❏ Indicate your approval by signing each Learner's Journal.
- ❏ Involve an Assistant Team Leader in this part of Team Time, if you have this Team member.

✔ Evangelistic Testimony
- ❏ Review the first draft of written evangelistic testimonies, due this session. Use the criteria from the session 3 FAITH Tip in *A Journey in FAITH Journal.* Explain why you are making your suggestions. Indicate that most testimonies undergo revisions. Be sensitive in helping Team members develop their testimonies, keeping their stories intact. As a reminder, these are the criteria Learners have used to develop their testimonies:
  - Define a specific event before (pre-conversion) and after your conversion (benefits).
  - Do not answer the Key Question in your testimony.
  - Keep your testimony brief (three minutes or less).
  - Do not give too many unnecessary details; instead, concisely reflect your experience.
  - Conclude your testimony with the assurance that you are going to heaven.

✔ Sunday School Testimony
- ❏ If possible, provide time for Team members to practice their Sunday School testimonies. Review of the evangelistic testimony, however, should be your priority.

✔ **Other Home Study Assignments/Session 3 Debriefing**
❑ Answer other questions Learners may have from session 3 or as a result of their Home Study Assignments.

✔ **Helps for Strengthening a Visit**
❑ Identify ways Team members can improve sharing their evangelistic testimonies in a visit.
❑ Help your Team, especially Learners, know how to handle the following issues.
- Dialogue with someone who answers the Key Question with a faith answer by discussing his or her journey of faith in Christ.
- Briefly explain to a person who answers the Key Question with a works answer that many people feel that doing good things gets them into heaven. Discuss the various ways such a response might be verbalized.
- Look for opportunities to ask permission to share what the Bible says about how a person goes to heaven.
- Look for ways to get clarification or explanation if someone shares an unclear response to the Key Question.
- Prayerfully look for ways to talk with a person who indicates no opinion about the Key Question.

Notes
_____
_____
_____
_____

Actions I Need to Take with Team Members This Week
_____
_____
_____
_____

Transition to classrooms for instruction on the content of the session. (5 mins.)

TEACHING TIME

KNOW IT

Step 1 (5 mins.)

Direct participants to turn to "A Quick Review" on page 64 in their Journals and to complete the activities. Review answers, using the computer presentation or overhead cel 20:
1. Pray. Discuss the need with FAITH Teams. Consult with class leaders.
2. Station a class greeter at the door. Wear name tags. Enlist good neighbors. Assign prospects and new members to care groups. Utilize fellowship. Take the lead.
3. Growth focuses on getting larger; health focuses on staying balanced, naturally resulting in growth.
4. FAITH is a part of the Sunday School strategy, which is designed to build a healthy church that is balanced in accomplishing five purposes: evangelism, discipleship, fellowship, ministry, and worship.

Be careful not to exceed the five-minute time limit.

A Quick Review

A Quick Review

In session 3 you learned more about the strategy of Sunday School and ways you as a FAITH leader can keep it focused on fulfilling the purposes of the church. Answer the following questions to recall ways you can enhance the ministry of your Sunday School.

1. What process can you follow as a FAITH leader to help bring about needed changes in your Sunday School class?

   _____

   _____

   _____

2. In your FAITH visits you lead people to Christ and enroll them in Bible study. What are some essential steps your class should take to assimilate these persons and other newcomers?

   _____

   _____

   _____

3. What is the difference between church growth and church health?

   _____

   _____

4. How does the FAITH strategy advance church health?

   _____

   _____

LEADERS ON LEADERSHIP
"When God calls people, he enables them to fulfill their callings even in the most unlikely circumstances." —John Ortberg[1]

---

64 / *Growing as a FAITH Leader Facilitator Guide*

Recognize Your Calling

What if someone asked you, "Have you been called into the ministry?" If you are like many Christians, your response might be "No, I'm just a _____," filling in the blank with your vocation. Such a response would indicate that you've accepted the myth that God's call to ministry comes only to those in vocational ministry, such as pastors and ministers of education.

Other myths associated with God's call to ministry are just as unfortunate:
- God won't call me to ministry because I'm a new Christian.
- God won't call me to ministry because I don't have the right gifts or abilities.
- I can minister only after I have been trained by a seminary.

All of these statements damage the cause of Christ. Unfortunately, many Christians believe them. Satan uses these myths to keep believers from recognizing and responding to God's call on their lives.

When we consider the call to ministry, we must begin with the church of the first century. Who were the early disciples of Christ, the early ministers of the gospel, and the early church leaders? They were all **laymen**, not paid professionals. They were ordinary people. Few of them had been trained in the religious schools of their day. They had a variety of gifts and abilities. Whether new or mature Christians, they were committed to Christ and allowed His Spirit to control their lives.

We should also look at our own day. Who is starting the vast majority of churches around the world today? Who is ministering to people in schools, in the workplace, and in the community? They are laypersons who have different gifts and abilities. Not all may know a lot of theology, but they have a **love** **relationship** with Jesus Christ that motivates them to **obedience**. Most will never see any compensation here on earth for their ministry, but one day all of them will receive a great reward in heaven and hear Jesus say, "Well done!"

Writing to the believers in Ephesus, Paul noted that God "gave some to be apostles, some prophets, some evangelists, some pastors and teachers, for the training of the saints in the work of ministry" (Eph. 4:11-12). Paul's words remind us that God calls all believers—"the saints"—to serve Him in ministry. God gave certain leaders, including pastors, to the church to train Christians to fulfill their callings.

Yes, you are called by God into the ministry. A specific part of your calling is as a leader in the FAITH Sunday School Evangelism Strategy®. But there's more to your ministry than just being involved in FAITH. This session will help you clarify the full implications of God's calling on your life.

HEAR IT

Step 2 (5 mins.)

Instruct accountability partners to discuss with each other: Whom do you know who has been called into the ministry? After a minute or so, direct participants to turn to page 65 in their Journals and to fill in the blanks as you present the ideas in "Recognize Your Calling." Use the computer presentation or overhead cel 21.

State that God calls all Christians to ministry. Point out that God has used laypersons in ministry through the centuries. Remind participants of Paul's emphasis in Ephesians 4: 11-12—that God gave certain leaders, such as pastors, to the church to train Christians to fulfill their calls to ministry. Emphasize that God's primary ministry for us is to be His witnesses (see Acts 1:8).

Recognize Your Calling

Step 3 (5 mins.)

Ask participants to turn to page 66 in their Journals and to fill in the blanks as you summarize "Understand the Command of God's Call," using the computer presentation or overhead cel 22.

> Understand the Command of God's Call

Step 4 (10 mins.)

Direct participants to fill in the blanks in their Journals as you present the material in "Identify the Characteristics of God's Call." Use the computer presentation or overhead cel 23. Summarize the ways God called Moses, David, and Peter. Point out the characteristics of God's call that we also experience.

> Identify the Characteristics of God's Call

Understand the Command of God's Call

To what primary ministry have you been called? Acts 1:8 states, " 'You will receive power when the Holy Spirit has come upon you, and you will be My witnesses in Jerusalem, in all Judea and Samaria, and to the ends of the earth.' " All believers are called by God to be His witnesses. We were empowered by the Holy Spirit on the day of our salvation to live our faith with boldness and perseverance. God has called us not only to **salvation** but also to **service**. And that service centers on proclaiming the **gospel** of **Christ** so that all people might bring **glory** to **God**.

The Learners on your FAITH Team have been working on their evangelistic testimonies during the past week. They know how and when God saved them, and they are learning to tell others about God's salvation. Although they may have begun highly motivated to participate in FAITH training, some of them are already listening to Satan's words of doubt and discouragement, and they are questioning whether God has called them to be involved in FAITH. Continue to remind them that God has called them to ministry and that their primary function as ministers—whatever their occupation—is to be Christ's witnesses.

Identify the Characteristics of God's Call

Are you still having difficulty accepting that God has called you to ministry? Let's look at some examples of God's call in Scripture.

In Exodus 3—4 God spoke to Moses through a burning bush. Having been a shepherd for many years, Moses felt inadequate to fulfill the task to which God was calling him. He expressed several concerns about leading God's people out of Egypt. Eventually, however, Moses understood that God was calling him to fulfill God's purposes.

In 1 Samuel 16 David was called to be the king of Israel. God had rejected Saul as king and had instructed Samuel to go to Jesse's house and anoint the new king. Though reluctant, Samuel obeyed God. "When they arrived, Samuel saw Eliab and thought, 'Surely the Lord's anointed stands here before the Lord.' But the Lord said to Samuel, 'Do not consider his appearance or his height, for I have rejected him. The Lord does not look at the things man looks at. Man looks at the outward appearance, but the Lord looks at the heart' " (1 Sam. 16:6-7). All of

66 / Growing as a FAITH Leader Facilitator Guide

Jesse's sons appeared before Samuel except David, who was tending the sheep. Samuel called for him and announced that David was to be the anointed king. David understood that God was calling him to fulfill God's purposes.

Peter was a fisherman. Even so, God chose Him to be a disciple of Jesus Christ. Mark 1:16-18 states, "As He was passing along by the Sea of Galilee, He saw Simon and Andrew, Simon's brother. They were casting a net into the sea, since they were fishermen. 'Follow Me,' Jesus told them, 'and I will make you fishers of men!' Immediately they left their nets and followed Him." Peter had many lessons to learn about God's call, but eventually, he too understood that God was calling him to fulfill God's purposes.

From these biblical examples we can identify several common characteristics of God's call.

A time of ____preparation____ is needed.

Before your first semester of FAITH training, you may never have shared the gospel with anyone else, perhaps because you didn't know what to say. Your FAITH training provided you with an outline you could follow to share God's message. You spent many weeks learning and practicing to be an effective witness.

Whenever God calls His people to ministry, He also prepares them for His assignment, often even before they are aware of the call.

____God____ initiates the call.

Imagine that you've heard that a friend will give a special dinner party. Do you call the friend and ask whether you can attend? No, you wait and hope for an invitation.

Likewise, we don't go to God and tell Him something we want to do. Instead, we intentionally watch for and respond to His initiatives and directions. In many areas He has already taken the initiative in telling us His plan for us, for example, through His Word.

God's call is first to a ____relationship____.

Can you imagine a man asking a woman he has never met to marry him? Although arranged marriages are common in some cultures, in our society a marriage is usually preceded by a time in which the man and woman get to know each other. They develop a relationship.

Similarly, God wants you to join Him in ministry, but His primary desire is to have a relationship with you. Think about it. Does God really need our help to accomplish His will? He could have told all people about His free gift of salvation through supernatural means. Instead, He chose to allow people to experience Him through an intimate relationship, which then gives others the opportunity to experience the same relationship as believers share from the overflow in their lives.

God does __extraordinary__ *things through ordinary people.*
When you see a muscular athlete lifting a lot of weight in the Olympics, you might not be surprised. After all, you would almost expect a conditioned athlete to be able to pick up so much weight. However, if you saw a 98-pound weakling lift the same amount of weight, you would be shocked and might think, *There's no way he really did that!*

God's work through human beings is like that. <u>He uses unlikely people to accomplish unbelievable things so that people will see what only He could do and will praise Him as a result.</u>

God calls us to a life of __sacrifice__.
In baseball most batters want to get on base or get around the bases as quickly as possible. While they concentrate on a hit, they hope for a home run. If the coach calls for them to make a sacrifice—work toward a hit that will advance a runner even though they will make an out—the batter will likely be less excited because he knows he won't get the cheers that come from an important hit.

<u>In our society, making sacrifices is also an unpopular concept, because a sacrifice means giving up something that's important to us.</u> Even so, Jesus said, " 'If anyone wants to come with Me, <u>he must deny himself, take up his cross daily, and follow Me</u>' " (Luke 9:23). We must be willing to leave everything to follow God's call. Too many people, including Christians, think they couldn't live on less or do without certain things, and thus they refuse God's call, like the rich young man who questioned Jesus (see Matt. 19:16-22). Yet many others throughout the centuries have discovered the gain that comes from giving up what they have to follow God's call.

God's call and your specific role are __unique__ *to you.*
Think about people you know. Though you may have some things in common, probably a lot more things are different, such as looks, personality, abilities, background, and education.

<u>God loves variety. He created you as a unique person for a unique purpose.</u> Though others may be called to the same ministry as you, they will not carry it out the same way as you. Because you have a different spiritual gift, different experiences in life, a different personality, different abilities, and a different passion, your ministry will naturally be different from that of any other Christian. This is according to God's design.

God expects instant __obedience__.
Perhaps you've heard a parent tell a child to do something, then count to three while they wait for the child to obey. Often the parent waits between numbers or counts by fractions, hoping the child will do as he or she was told. This practice may condition a child to delay obedience, which is really disobedience.

68 / *Growing as a FAITH Leader Facilitator Guide*

Obedience is doing something right away, the right way, and with the right attitude. Once God calls, immediately respond with a resounding, "Yes, Lord" and then get to it! In Romans 10:9, which you have memorized in the FAITH outline, many Christians overlook the part of the verse affirming the lordship of Jesus Christ. To confess "the Lord Jesus" (NKJV) or that "Jesus is Lord" (HCSB) means that we must do what He tells us to do. To do otherwise means that we are calling the shots, which indicates that Jesus is not Lord—master, ruler, boss—of our lives.

Fulfilling your call from God brings glory to Him. In addition, your life will be blessed and fulfilled by bringing glory to His name. God has called everyone to serve Him and be His witness. Your role as a FAITH leader is not only to fulfill your own calling but also to help those you are training to understand and live God's call in their lives.

Discover the Purpose of God's Call

Sometimes we fail to understand the purpose of God's call on our lives. Have you ever known Christians who were convicted to be witnesses, made that their priority, but then burned out? What happened?

Read again the words of Jesus in Mark 1:17: " 'Follow Me,' Jesus told them, 'and I will make you fishers of men!' " Notice that Jesus wants us to **follow** first, then to be His **witnesses**. Many believers have done just the opposite, and that is why they burn out. They have lost the close walk with God that fuels all other disciplines of their faith. In His words to the church in Ephesus (see Rev. 2:1-6), the Lord noted the believers' deeds and endurance; yet they had turned away from their original love for Him.

To stay always at the task of witnessing without maintaining our relationship with the Lord is like constantly using a cell phone without frequently recharging it. Eventually, the phone will be useless because it's out of power and will remain that way until it is recharged or connected to another power source.

In the same way, we can't constantly **work** for God without **walking** with God. To follow Christ means that we remain close to Him and stay connected to Him. This was Jesus' emphasis in John 15, where He noted that believers (the branches) who stay connected to Him (the vine) will produce abundant fruit.

The purpose of God's call is that all people will come to **know** Him and **glorify** Him. As you focus on developing your relationship with Christ, the fellowship that results will naturally lead you to fish for people, and you will do it in His power, not your own.

Step 5 (5 mins.)

Ask participants to consider silently their answers to this question: Do you know someone who at one time was completely focused on witnessing for Christ but eventually seemed to burn out? Direct participants to "Discover the Purpose of God's Call" on page 69 in their Journals and to fill the blanks as you present the material. Use the computer presentation or overhead cel 24. State that daily fellowship with the Lord must be our main priority if we want to bear fruit for God's kingdom.

Discover the Purpose of God's Call

Step 6 (5 mins.)

Direct participants to turn to "Connect Your Calling" on page 70 in their Journals and to fill in the blanks as you present the material. Use the computer presentation or overhead cel 25. Emphasize that God calls us to work together as believers to lead people to glorify Him.

[Connect Your Calling]

Connect Your Calling

Though we may recognize God's call, we can still become confused about our roles in God's plan. Many Christians have the erroneous idea that everything hinges on them, and if they don't or can't do it all, then the kingdom will crumble. This attitude is a sign of spiritual immaturity.

It is <u>important for us to recognize that our calling connects us with every believer in God's family</u>. God never intended for us to live or minister in isolation. Instead, He planned for us to be a part of His body, the church. Paul emphasized that Christ placed us "in the body just as He wanted" (1 Cor. 12:18).

Believers in the church in Corinth had trouble understanding this truth. They not only misunderstood the purpose of spiritual gifts but were also divided over the leader they felt was better. Paul emphasized in 1 Corinthians 3:6-8, "I planted, Apollos watered, but God gave the growth. So then neither the one who plants nor the who waters is anything, but only God who gives the growth. Now the one who plants and the one who waters are equal, and each will receive his own reward according to his own labor."

Many people who start out in FAITH become discouraged because they do not see many professions of faith when they visit. They sit through the Celebration Time each week and hear others share about people who made professions of faith as a result of FAITH visits. Sometimes they become envious of others who have led people to Christ, even though their Teams have been just as faithful in witnessing but have not seen the same results. These FAITH participants may even wish they could be on Teams that seem more effective.

<u>If you have been active in a church for very long, you may have seen people align themselves with a certain leader. Often this group resisted any changes that might diminish the person's leadership, so factions developed in the church that harmed the church's ministry.</u>

<u>This was the problem in the church in Corinth and the reason for Paul's correction in 1 Corinthians 3:6-8. These verses set forth three important elements in a believer's calling.</u>

The __role__ we are given

In verse 6 <u>Paul wrote that he planted</u> the seed of the gospel. He may not have seen much in the way of immediate results as he had seen at other times and in other places. Paul recognized that his task was simply to share the gospel message in Corinth. Later, <u>Apollos came and watered</u> that seed, reaffirming and clarifying Paul's message. Both leaders played a different role, and both had important callings. However, Paul emphasized that it was <u>God who made the seed grow.</u>

70 / Growing as a FAITH Leader Facilitator Guide

Paul's words are a reminder that God is in control of the entire salvation process, especially those elements we experience in this life: regeneration—experiencing new life in Christ—and sanctification—maturing in Christ. God uses His people in this process, and everyone has a role to play, according to His will.

The __reason__ we are called

Paul also emphasized in verse 8 that those who planted and those who watered were equal. They both had one purpose: to prepare people for God's work. God wants to use His people as instruments to accomplish His will, not to divide the church. He wants to be glorified as He accomplishes what only He can do in the lives of people.

Some church members develop such a strong connection to a particular leader that they follow that person's leadership. If people focus on a leader instead of on Christ, the result can be division in the church.

As a FAITH leader, help your Learners understand the reason God has called them—to work with Him in bringing about transformation in the lives of people so that God will be glorified.

The __reward__ we will receive

Paul noted in verse 8 that those God uses to accomplish what He desires will be rewarded. The Bible is filled with verses about the rewards that await believers for acts of service. Because people have different gifts and abilities, their rewards will also be different.

We are not rewarded, however, just on the basis of what we've received. Paul noted that we are rewarded according to our labor. Those who labor more will be rewarded more. Paul did not imply that those who see more professions of faith than others will be rewarded more but that those who faithfully fulfill the role God gives them will be rewarded more.

Your responsibility is to join God in making disciples. This is what you are doing as a FAITH Team Leader. Faithfully share the gospel with as many people as you can while you can. Guide those who accept Christ to continue growing in Him and begin sharing Him with others. Don't worry about others' success or even your own so-called success. God will reward you according to your faithfulness.

Step 7 (5 mins.)

Direct participants to turn to page 72 in their Journals and to fill in the blanks as you summarize "Find Your Place in Ministry." Use the computer presentation or overhead cel 26. Emphasize that because God has made every believer unique, every Christian's ministry is unique. State that the acrostic S.E.R.V.E. can help us understand our makeup and discover the ministry God has for us.

Duplicate copies of the Spiritual-Gifts Worksheet from the CD-ROM, distribute them, and challenge participants to complete them this week.

Find Your Place in Ministry

STUDY IT

Step 8 (5 mins.)

Overview the Home Study Assignments for session 4.

Transition to assemble with FAITH Teams to prepare for home visits. (5 mins.)

Find Your Place in Ministry

Although you may be convinced that you are called to ministry, you may still be uncertain about exactly how or where God can use you. Finding your place in ministry is a process of __listening__ to God and __following__ His direction. Sometimes where you start is not where you end up. Philip followed God's call to minister by waiting on tables (see Acts 6:2-5), but later God used him as an evangelist (see Acts 8:4-8,26-40).

You have begun the process of discovering your place of ministry by obeying God's Word to be a witness for Him. As you look at different areas of your life, God may show you a better picture of how He has prepared you for ministry and what He wants to do with and through you.

S.E.R.V.E. is a profile from *Jesus on Leadership* that you can use to picture what God has done in your life up to this point.

THE S.E.R.V.E. PROFILE

S stands for __spiritual__ __gifts__.

E stands for __experiences__.

R stands for __relational__ __style__ (personality).

V stands for __vocational__ __skills__.

E stands for __enthusiasm__ (passion).

Thinking about these areas of your life can help you begin to discover the place God has for you in ministry.[2]

To learn more about your call to ministry, see the following resources.
- *Jesus on Leadership: Becoming a Servant Leader* (LifeWay Press, 1996)
- *Every Christian a Minister: Finding Joy and Fulfillment in Serving* (LifeWay Press, 2001)

Visitation Time

DO IT

1. Your visitation assignments will include evangelistic prospects, recent guests who visited the church and are already believers, and absentees from Sunday School. Approach evangelistic visits with the expectation that you will ask the Key Question. If the person gives a strong faith answer, your Team will have an opportunity for practice. If the prospect does not respond in faith, you as the Team Leader will have an opportunity to demonstrate how to present the gospel. Remember that you are there to fulfill God's divine purpose, whether in an evangelistic or a ministry role. Remember 2 Timothy 2:2.
2. Pray before you go.
3. Use the time in the car to review, allowing Learners to ask questions. Because they studied ministry visits in this session, ask them what ministry visits they think the Sunday School class needs. Remind them to listen to prayer requests and other discussions in Sunday School that might reveal ministry needs.
4. After each visit allow Learners to debrief it. Facilitate the debriefing by asking specific questions: What were their feelings about the visit? How could the visit have gone more smoothly? How does this visit compare with the previous week's visits?

Celebration Time

SHARE IT

It is important that everyone attend Celebration Time. Emphasize this as an important part of the FAITH process. This is an opportunity to rejoice for decisions that were made. Demonstrate for your Team Learners how to do the following.
1. Hear reports and testimonies.
2. Complete Evaluation Cards.
3. Complete Participation Cards.
4. Update visitation forms with the results of visits.

---

[1] John Ortberg, *If You Want to Walk on Water, You've Got to Get Out of the Boat* (Grand Rapids: Zondervan Publishing House, 2001), 72.
[2] Joe Sherrer, *Adult Class Leader Administration Kit* (Nashville: LifeWay Press, 1999), item 21.

DO IT (110 MINS.)

SHARE IT (30 MINS.)

Home Study Assignments

Day 1: Your Relationship with God

Memorize John 15:5. What one thing could you do that would be most beneficial in helping you remain or abide in Christ each day?

_____

_____

Commit this action to God. In addition, contact your accountability partner today and ask that person to help keep you accountable for your commitment to grow in this area.

Spend time in prayer asking God to clarify His calling to you, either as a lay minister, a bivocational minister, or a vocational minister.

Day 2: Your Relationship with Your FAITH Team

Place an X and an O on the scale to indicate how well you think the other two members of your FAITH Team understand God's call to ministry.

Low   1   2   ③(X)   4   5   6   7   8   9   10   High

What can you share with your Team Learners from this session to help them understand their call to ministry?

That we have all been called - that there is always a place serve - Help them understand that need to make themselves available.

Pray that God will clarify His calling to your Team members and that they will embrace His vision for reaching the world.

Day 3: Your Relationship with Your Sunday School Class

Read Exodus 3—4. Think about persons in your class who are making excuses for not serving in ministry. Read the list below and check some of the excuses you've heard.
- ☑ I don't have time.
- ❏ I wouldn't know what to do.
- ❏ I'm just a new Christian.
- ☑ I've already served my time.
- ❏ I haven't heard a definite word from God.
- ❏ I need to learn more about the Bible.
- ❏ There's no place for me to serve.
- ❏ That's why we pay the pastor.
- ❏ Other: _____

List the names of persons in your class who are making excuses and begin praying for them. Ask God to show you how you can help them see their potential to be used by Him.

_____ _____ _____

_____ _____ _____

_____ _____ _____

Day 4: Your Relationship with the Lost

Read Mark 1:16-18. Write one way your following Christ has influenced your fishing for people.

_____

_____

If someone you are praying for comes to know Christ and begins sharing his or her faith with others based on your example, how likely would that person be to focus on following Christ before fishing for men?
❏ Not at all likely ☑ Somewhat likely ❏ Very likely

Ask God to reveal to you anything that is keeping you from following Him. Ask Him to make you a more effective fisher of people as you focus first on following Him.

Day 5: Your Relationship with Your Family and Your Church

List members of your family who have heard the gospel but have not accepted Christ. Ask God to show you how you can water the seed that has been planted in them.

_____ _____ _____

_____ _____ _____

_____ _____ _____

Look again at the elements of your S.E.R.V.E. profile that you should have completed on the Spiritual-Gifts Worksheet you received during session 4. Which area was most difficult for you to complete?

_____

How can an awareness of your unique makeup strengthen your ministry in your church?

You now know your weakness and strengthens so, you can utilize your gifts/talents.

Pray that God will raise up more leaders in your church who will understand and follow God's call.

SESSION 5
Discovering Jesus' Leadership Qualities

In this session you will—

CHECK IT by engaging in Team Time activities;

KNOW IT by reviewing content from session 4;

HEAR IT by exploring Jesus' leadership qualities and learning ways to apply them to your leadership responsibilities;

SAY IT by practicing the *Presentation* portion of the FAITH Visit Outline;

STUDY IT by overviewing Home Study Assignments;

DO IT by leading your Team in making visits;

SHARE IT by celebrating.

IN ADVANCE
- Overview content.
- Preview teaching suggestions. Prepare key points. Decide whether to use the session 5 computer presentation or overhead cels 27–29 (see pp. 297–99).
- Prepare the room for teaching.
- Pray for participants and for Teams as they prepare to visit.
- As Teaching Time begins, direct participants to open their Journals to page 80.

TEAM TIME

CHECK IT (15 MINS.)

If the computer presentation is used, display the agenda for Team Time. Add other points to the agenda as needed.

CHECK IT agenda:
- ✔ FAITH Visit Outline
- ✔ Evangelistic Testimony
- ✔ Key Question/Transition Statement
- ✔ Other Home Study Assignments
- ✔ Session 4 Debriefing
- ✔ Help for Strengthening a Visit

Leading Team Time

All Team members participate in Team Time. They are primarily responsible for reciting the assigned portion of the FAITH Visit Outline and for discussing other Home Study Assignments.

As you direct this important time of CHECK IT activities with your Team, keep in mind that Learners look to you as a role model, motivator, mentor, and friend. Team Time activities can continue in the car as the Team travels to and from visits.

Lead CHECK IT Activities

✔ FAITH Visit Outline
- ❑ Call on each Learner to recite the assigned portion of the FAITH Visit Outline (all of *Preparation*, plus key words in *Presentation* and *Invitation*).
- ❑ Indicate your approval by signing each Learner's Journal. Be prepared to answer any questions Learners may have. Make suggestions for improvement.

✔ Evangelistic Testimony
- ❑ Call for final written copies of Learners' evangelistic testimonies. Congratulate Team members for achieving another important milestone.
- ❑ Make sure any revisions include criteria discussed in sessions 3 and 4. Ask for permission to print these testimonies in church materials that publicize the FAITH strategy or that encourage persons to share their faith.
- ❑ Emphasize to Team members the importance of sharing their testimonies naturally, in their own words, in actual visits.

✔ Key Question/Transition Statement
- ❑ Practice the Key Question/Transition Statement, helping Learners comfortably use their hands to spell the word *FAITH*.

✔ Other Home Study Assignments
- ❑ Look over Learners' Home Study Assignments. Are Learners on track? Clarify or emphasize key points from FAITH Tips and/or *Evangelism Through the Sunday School: A Journey of FAITH* as needed.

✔ Session 4 Debriefing
- ❑ Review the importance of and approach for making Sunday School ministry visits. Help Team members understand how such visits reconnect many inactive members to church life. Highlight ministry

visitation assignments and indicate why certain comments are made during different types of ministry visits (to absentees, nonattenders, members with ministry needs). As inactive members return to Sunday School or church, remind Team members they had a part.
- ❏ Ask any questions you feel would solidify Learners' understanding of session 4, including questions that will appear on the final written review (ses. 16).

✔ Help for Strengthening a Visit
- ❏ Be prepared to discuss ways to strengthen a visit, based on what has been discovered in previous sessions.
- ❏ Be prepared to model an Opinion Poll visit during Visitation Time.
- ❏ Identify which Team member(s) will take the lead in sharing a Sunday School testimony. Ask another Team member to be prepared to share his or her evangelistic testimony. With sensitivity to Learners and person(s) being visited, be prepared to resume the visit after Team members have shared.

Notes

_____
_____
_____
_____
_____

Actions I Need to Take with Team Members This Week

_____
_____
_____
_____
_____

Transition to classrooms for instruction on the content of the session. (5 mins.)

TEACHING TIME

KNOW IT

Step 1 (5 mins.)

Direct participants to turn to "A Quick Review" on page 80 in their Journals and to complete the activities. Review answers, using the computer presentation or overhead cel 27:
1. God calls us first to walk with Him—to stay connected to Him as our source of life—and then to work for Him.
2. God calls every believer to ministry, and He works with us as we work together, like the parts of the body, to lead others to know and love Him.
3. Choices a, c, d, f, g, h, and i are correct.

Be careful not to exceed the five-minute time limit.

A Quick Review

A Quick Review

In session 4 you learned about God's call to ministry. Take a moment to respond to the following questions about God's call.

1. If the Learners on your FAITH Team were struggling with the primary purpose of God's call on their lives, what would you tell them?

   _____

   _____

   _____

   _____

2. As a FAITH Team Leader, how does your call to ministry connect you to the calls of other Christians?

   _____

   _____

   _____

   _____

3. Check the seven common characteristics of God's call.
   - a. A time of preparation is needed.
   - b. A sure sign of God's call is the gift of ecstatic utterances.
   - c. God initiates the call.
   - d. God's call is first to a relationship.
   - e. God's call is always to vocational service.
   - f. God does extraordinary things through ordinary people.
   - g. God calls us to a life of sacrifice.
   - h. God's call and your specific role are unique to you.
   - i. God expects instant obedience.
   - j. Once you are called, you will no longer have to do unpleasant tasks when you serve God and others.

LEADERS ON LEADERSHIP

"Leaders are active, not passive people. They initiate. They do. They risk." —Leith Anderson[1]

Identify Your Role Model

Answer the following questions.

Who has had a major impact on your life? _____

_____

In what ways did that person influence you? _____

_____

All of us have known individuals who have positively influenced us. Most of us have also known certain leaders who had a great impact on our lives because their example and leadership affected the choices we made and the direction we took in life. Their impact may have come through a book they wrote, a seminar they presented, or the life they lived. We tend to follow these leaders and emulate them, hoping that we can become more like them.

Unfortunately, many Christians and many churches have followed leaders who were influenced by secular models of leadership. The result has been ineffectiveness for the kingdom of God. If we truly want to have an impact in our churches and in the kingdom, we must follow biblical leadership principles.

Follow the Greatest Leader

Though we could focus on many biblical leaders, we will concentrate on the greatest leader the world has ever known, Jesus Christ. Notice seven characteristics of Jesus as our model of leadership.

Jesus remained ___focused___ on His purpose regardless of His situation.

Have you ever been doing something in one part of your house and realized you needed something that was at the other end of the house? Perhaps as you walked through a room, you saw something that needed to go in a room near where you were going, so you took it with you. After you got to that room and put the object in its place, you found a light bulb burned out and went to find a replacement. After replacing the bulb, you went back to the other end of the house and later remembered the thing you wanted to get from the other part of the house in the first place! Some people have a hard time staying focused, regardless of the task.

HEAR IT

Step 2 (5 mins.)

Briefly acknowledge the Spiritual-Gifts Worksheet you asked participants to complete between sessions. Encourage them to study *Jesus on Leadership* (LifeWay Press, 1996) or to attend spiritual-gifts classes being planned by your church.

Direct participants to the section "Identify Your Role Model" on page 81 in their Journals and ask them to write answers to the two questions. Emphasize the difference between persons who have influenced our lives for a brief period and leaders who have had a great impact by changing the course of our lives. Summarize the other ideas, stating that Jesus Christ is our primary model of leadership.

Step 3 (25 mins.)

Instruct participants to fill in the blanks while you present "Follow the Greatest Leader," using the computer presentation or overhead cels 28–29. Emphasize using each quality to strengthen leadership in Sunday School classes and on FAITH Teams.

> Follow the Greatest Leader

Session 5: Discovering Jesus' Leadership Qualities / 81

Just after Jesus was baptized, He faced the first test in His public ministry. Luke 4:1-13 records the temptation of Jesus. Verses 1-2 note that Jesus "was led by the Spirit in the wilderness, for 40 days to be tempted by the Devil." On three occasions in this encounter Satan tried to derail Jesus' ministry by tempting Him to focus on other needs and opportunities. Jesus, however, stayed focused on God's mission for Him, which was to open the door for salvation to all humanity through His death on the cross. By focusing on His purpose, He was able to resist Satan's attempts to get Him off track.

Another distraction came when Jesus' followers wanted to make Him king: "When the people saw the sign He had done, they said, 'This really is the Prophet who was to come into the world.' Therefore, when Jesus knew that they were about to come and take Him by force to make Him king, He withdrew again to the mountain by Himself" (John 6:14-15).

How did Jesus remain focused on His purpose while He was on earth?

- Jesus recognized that __God__ was with Him. Just as He was led by the Spirit into the wilderness, He was guided by the Spirit during the 40 days He was tempted. We can always be certain that God is with us. He has promised, "I will never leave you or forsake you" (Heb. 13:5). In the Great Commission Jesus said, " 'Remember, I am with you always, to the end of the age' " (Matt. 28:20).
- Jesus did not allow His __personal needs__ to get in the way of God's purpose. We can get sidetracked from God's purpose for our lives when we focus on ourselves and our needs. Jesus reminded us that our Heavenly Father knows what we need and will provide it. Our responsibility is to stay focused on Him and His righteousness (see Matt. 6:25-33).
- Jesus did not allow other __opportunities__ to distract Him. If Satan can't dissuade us from following God, he may present us with a number of good opportunities in an attempt to distract us from the primary task God has for us. If we are not maintaining intimate fellowship with God, we might settle for the good at the expense of the best.
- Jesus did not allow __popular opinion__ to sway Him. Jesus knew when to be with people and when to be alone with God. It's easy for our ego to get in the way when someone says, "We can't do it without you" or "You are the unanimous choice for this important position." Unless we place our ego under the Spirit's control, we may get preoccupied by flattering words and thus stray from God's purpose. It's also easy to focus on trying to please all people so that we remain popular with everyone. If we focus on pleasing people, we will get distracted from God's purpose.

As a FAITH Team Leader, remain focused on your mission regardless of your situation. Although you may have already learned how to keep distractions in perspective, your Team members may still struggle with

[Margin notes: "It is about the people!" and "Edging God Out"]

them. Help your Learners stay focused on God's purpose despite the situation. Some of them are already thinking about dropping out of the FAITH ministry. They may wonder whether God is really with them as they prepare and share testimonies and parts of the FAITH outline. Or they may have become more aware of personal needs that suddenly seem to cry out for their attention, whether related to job, children, spouse, or other priorities. New, important opportunities may be presented that seem to be once-in-a-lifetime experiences. Regardless of what they face, you can use Jesus' example, as well as situations in your life, to encourage your Team Learners to remain focused.

> *[margin note: you can't if you are not]*

Jesus ____**challenged**____ *people to move from where they were to where they should have been.*

On a radio call-in show dealing with personal finances, a caller identifying herself as recently married commented on her debt and her husband's debt, her savings and his savings. Then she asked a question about buying a house. The host interrupted to remind her of the pastor's words during the wedding ceremony that the two of them had become one flesh. The host emphasized that she should quit thinking about what was his or hers and instead think about theirs: their debt, their savings, and their house. This radio host challenged the caller to move from where she was in her thinking about marriage—two persons operating independently— to where she should have been—two functioning together.

One of the most tragic incidents in the Bible is Jesus' encounter with the rich young man in Mark 10:17-22. This man desperately wanted to know how he could experience eternal life. Claiming to have obeyed the Ten Commandments, he was a good man, but Jesus knew what it would take for him to understand complete surrender of his life to God. Jesus wanted him to move beyond his current understanding to a new level of faith. Jesus challenged him to sell all he had, give to the poor, and follow Him. Tragically, this was more than the man was willing to do, and as a result, "he went away grieving" (Mark 10:22).

> *[margin note: Read 10:17-22]*

Your goal as a FAITH leader is first to help people assess where they are and then to lead them to take the next step in their spiritual journeys. This is true not only for the Learners you mentor but also for people to whom you witness. God's desire is that people come to know Him as Savior and Lord and continue to grow in faith, which means taking one step after another regardless of where they are in their spiritual lives.

Jesus ____**mentored**____ *others so that they could fulfill their potential.*

Have you ever taught someone to drive? If so, you know that the teaching process takes time and attention. You might have required the learner to read manuals or books or to watch videos on driving. But you couldn't

> *[margin note: Why do we like the back seat when it comes to leadership? the view is better from up front!]*

have taught the person to drive until you got in the car, explained what to do, and sat in the passenger seat (perhaps with fear and trembling!) to give feedback. You continued guiding and teaching until eventually, the person was ready to take a driving test and get a driver's license.

Jesus mentored 12 men for three years by pouring His life into them. He walked with them. He ate with them. He spent time with them. Much of what the early disciples learned from Him was caught rather than taught. They learned perhaps the greatest lesson when they witnessed Christ's suffering and death on the cross. That one event caused them to learn incredible lessons about love, forgiveness, humility, mercy, and obedience. How did Christ teach these lessons?

- *Love.* As a sinless Man who died for the sins of all humanity, Jesus expressed the greatest love anyone could ever imagine.
- *Forgiveness.* Jesus spoke words of genuine forgiveness to those who had wronged Him; He didn't threaten or retaliate.
- *Humility.* Jesus had the power to call for the angels' help, but He would not do so. Instead, He suffered and died in accordance with His Father's will.
- *Mercy.* Jesus promised a thief who was being crucified beside Him that the man would be with Him in paradise that day—the very opposite of what the man deserved.
- *Obedience.* Jesus prayed for the cup of suffering and death to be removed if possible; yet He yielded Himself to His Father's plan.

Only once did the disciples ask Jesus to teach them something—how to pray. Luke 11:1-13 records the model Jesus gave them to follow, which we know as the Lord's Prayer. This simple but significant prayer taught them to pray. Jesus also modeled the practice of prayer in His own life on many occasions.

One of the most effective ways you will lead others is by mentoring them—spending quality time with them so that your words and actions influence them to adopt what you have. But a leader must also intentionally teach through the experiences of life. Just as a child learns to function by the intentional mentoring of loving parents who are farther down the road of physical life, a child of God learns by the mentoring of loving believers like you who are farther down the road of spiritual life.

Jesus led by ____example____.

Have you ever worked for someone who gave you detailed instructions for handling a certain issue but then didn't follow the same procedure when he or she had to deal with the same issue? What did you think of that person's leadership?

In contrast, Jesus led by example throughout His ministry. One very significant instance is recorded in John 13:1-17. The night before Jesus was crucified, He gathered His disciples in the upper room to celebrate the Passover. While everyone was reclining at the table, Jesus took a

84 / Growing as a FAITH Leader Facilitator Guide

basin of water and a towel and began washing His disciples' feet. Because this was normally a task relegated to the lowest servant in the house, the disciples were shocked. We can imagine tears streaming down their faces as they watched Jesus perform such a menial task. Afterward His demonstration of humility and servanthood Jesus said, " 'If I, your Lord and Teacher, have washed your feet, you also ought to wash one another's feet. For I have given you an example that you also should do just as I have done for you. I assure you: A slave is not greater than his master, and a messenger is not greater than the one who sent him. If you know these things, you are blessed if you do them' " (John 13:14-17).

No doubt the disciples would be willing to obey Jesus' command to wash one another's feet because He willingly did what He told them to do. This powerful example had a great impact on their lives. In the same way, you will have the greatest influence if you lead by example. When you encourage your FAITH Team Learners to do something, your words will have a greater impact if they see you doing what you have said.

Jesus was __**balanced**__ *in His responses to people.*
A school principal took pride in proclaiming, "I treat all of my students the same." And he did. He responded the same way to girls as well as boys, to slackers as well as honor students, to helpers as well as troublemakers. He was critical, harsh, and sarcastic to all, thinking that was the best way to influence those under his authority.

However, Jesus responded to people based on the situation and on their need. He knew when to be firm and when to be gentle. He knew when to rebuke and when to encourage. Jesus strongly rebuked Peter in Matthew 16:23 when Peter argued with Jesus about His death. Jesus said, " 'Get behind Me, Satan! You are an offense to me, because you're not thinking about God's concerns, but man's.' " But Jesus gently restored Peter in John 21:15-17 after Peter had denied three times knowing Christ. Peter had great potential and needed to know that God could still use him, and Jesus knew exactly what to say to encourage him.

One of the clearest pictures of Jesus' balanced treatment of others is seen in the account of the woman caught in adultery. The religious leaders were ready to stone the woman. In approaching Jesus, they were primarily interested in discrediting Him. He knew how to deal with them as well as her. He said to them, " 'The one without sin among you should be the first to throw a stone at her' " (John 8:7). By confronting their hypocrisy, Jesus stopped them in their tracks.

Jesus then dealt with the woman in a different manner. Jesus asked her, " 'Woman, where are they? Has no one condemned you?' 'No one, Lord' she answered. 'Neither do I condemn you,' said Jesus. 'Go, and from now on do not sin any more' " (John 8:10-11). Jesus forgave the woman of her sin without condoning it. He encouraged her in a loving way to experience the power and freedom of a changed life.

| Remind Team Leaders to be sensitive in their responses to others rather than adopting a one-size-fits-all approach to their Learners.

As a FAITH leader, be sensitive in your response to others. Rather than take a one-size-fits-all approach, treat each individual and circumstance as a unique concern. Your two Team Learners are different, so you must be balanced in your responses to them. One could be highly motivated to confront unbelievers, wanting to condemn them if they won't listen to the FAITH outline. The other Learner may be more hesitant, wanting to walk away from the door if no one answers quickly. Both need training and correction, but these need to be balanced according to Learners' personalities, Learners' needs, and the situation.

Jesus _____ prioritized _____ His life and work.

Do you carry a calendar or a Personal Digital Assistant with a to-do list? Even if you don't, you probably have an unwritten list of tasks that need to be done each day. How do you determine which task is most important and which to do first? Setting priorities is a must for all leaders but especially for those who are leading other believers. And in any list of priorities one item must take the most important position. For any believer, and especially for you as a Christian leader, your time alone with God must be the top priority of your life if you want to have an effective ministry. Too many Christian leaders have become ineffective because they allowed something else to take top priority in their lives. Many later tell the same story: "It all began when I found myself drifting from the Lord. I lost that intimate relationship with Christ."

Regardless of your level of influence, you are not immune to Satan's trap. He will easily tempt you to become so busy that you lose your focus and move away from your priority of a growing relationship with God.

Jesus made His time alone with God a priority: "Very early in the morning, while it was still dark, He got up, went out, and made His way to a deserted place. And He was praying there" (Mark 1:35). Notice the way Jesus maintained His priority:

1. Jesus started early. He wanted to place Himself in a position to hear God's voice at the start of the day. He knew that the first actions of the day often set the course for the rest of the day.
2. Jesus chose a quiet, secluded place where He would not be distracted. By finding an isolated place, He would minimize the distractions that might come as people began to stir.
3. Jesus prayed. He didn't start His day by reading books, thinking about the tasks of the day, meeting with the disciples, catching up on the news, or planning His day's work. He spent time alone with His Father to hear God's voice and to get God's perspective on what He should do and the way He should do it.

These are critical steps for leaders, especially FAITH leaders. Get alone with God in order to hear His voice and have His mind in all that you do. Your effectiveness as a leader in your Sunday School class and on your FAITH Team is not determined as much by the weight of your works as it is by the depth of your relationship with Christ. Remember Jesus' words as He prepared His disciples for His departure: " 'The one who remains in Me and I in him produces much fruit, because you can do nothing without Me' " (John 15:5).

Jesus __persevered__ *until His mission was completed.* One characteristic of great leaders is finishing the job they are given to do. They stay on course, enduring challenges and setbacks, until their task was complete. Jesus was this type of leader during the three years of His earthly ministry. Throughout His ministry He faced challenges: Satan attacked Him. His disciples misunderstood and later betrayed Him. The religious leaders questioned and mocked Him. Yet He continued with His mission until the end. On the cross Jesus proclaimed, " 'It is finished' " (John 19:30). He had accomplished the work God sent Him to do, which opened the door for people to receive forgiveness for sin and eternal life in heaven.

How sad it is to see leaders who were once in the thick of the battle become discouraged and even bitter about the work and retreat in their service to God. Often they've been at the mission for a long time and eventually decide to give up. On the other hand, what an encouragement to see believers who still have passion, vigor, and joy in their service to the Lord. They may have been at the task for a long time too; yet they refuse to quit until the mission is complete.

God has a mission for you that is uniquely designed for you. Only you can do it. Others are watching you, both in your Sunday School class and on your FAITH Team. Some will model their leadership after you. You must stay at the task! Jesus said, " 'No one who puts his hand to the plow and looks back is fit for the kingdom of God' " (Luke 9:62). When you're tempted to quit, anticipate that day in heaven when someone comes to you and says, "Thank you for staying with it and not giving up. I watched your example. You encouraged me. Because you finished well, you encouraged me to do the same."

You've read powerful, practical lessons of leadership that Jesus modeled. You may be asking yourself, *How can I possibly measure up to the standard that Jesus set?* Remember that Jesus is on your team. He didn't come to show you up but to grow you up. He wants you to be effective as a leader, and He's provided the help you need through His Word and His Spirit. Because the Holy Spirit lives in you, you can lead in a way that is effective and biblical without making compromises. That's the kind of leadership God will bless.

> To learn more about Jesus' leadership qualities, see *Jesus on Leadership: Becoming a Servant Leader* (LifeWay Press, 1996).

Remind participants that this study of Jesus' leadership qualities is not meant to discourage them but to challenge them. State that Jesus is for them and wants to help them lead as He did. Emphasize that God "is able to do above and beyond all that we ask or think—according to the power that works in you" (Eph. 3:20). Point out that the power we have is the Holy Spirit, who enables us to become like Jesus and thus be better leaders than we could imagine.

SAY IT

Step 4 (5 mins.)

Ask pairs to practice sharing the *Presentation* portion of the FAITH Visit Outline with each other.

STUDY IT

Step 5 (5 mins.)

Overview the Home Study Assignments for session 5.

Transition to assemble with FAITH Teams to prepare for home visits. (5 mins.)

DO IT (110 MINS.)

Visitation Time

DO IT

1. Pray for God to lead your Team to a divine appointment. If someone is not home, go next door and conduct the Opinion Poll. It just may be God's divine appointment.
2. Use the time in the car to review, allowing Learners to ask questions. This week they have heard the full gospel presentation. Begin preparing them to share the outline in a few weeks. How do they feel about that?
3. Choose one letter in the FAITH Visit Outline and ask Learners how that concept applied to them when they accepted Christ.
4. After each visit allow Learners to debrief it. Facilitate the debriefing by asking specific questions.

Celebration Time

SHARE IT (30 MINS.)

SHARE IT

1. Share a divine appointment.
2. Not every Opinion Poll results in a profession of faith, but celebrate all attempts made. Highlight decisions made, prospects discovered, and other outcomes that would encourage and motivate other Teams.
3. Rejoice with other reports.
4. Complete Evaluation Cards.
5. Complete Participation Cards.
6. Update visitation forms with the results of visits.

---

[1] Leith Anderson, *Dying for Change* (Minneapolis: Bethany House Publishers, 1990), 195.

Home Study Assignments

Day 1: Your Relationship with God

Read the following passages and match each with one of the important leadership characteristics examined in this session.

___ 1. Isaiah 61:1-3   a. Focused
___ 2. Psalm 90:12   b. Challenged
___ 3. 1 Corinthians 11:1   c. Prioritized
___ 4. Hebrews 10:36   d. Mentored
___ 5. Matthew 17:20   e. Balanced
___ 6. Proverbs 4:25   f. Persevered
___ 7. 2 Timothy 2:2   g. Led by example

Consider one characteristic in which you need improvement. Ask God to work in you so that you will better demonstrate that leadership characteristic.

Day 2: Your Relationship with Your FAITH Team

Read John 13:12-17. Then review the section "Follow the Greatest Leader," beginning on page 81. Think about the seven characteristics of leadership and record one way you are exercising each.

Guiding Learners to stay focused on their purpose: _____

_____

Challenging Learners to move from where they are to where they should be:

_____

Mentoring Learners so that they can fulfill their potential: _____

Leading Learners by example: _____

Giving balanced responses to Learners: _____

Prioritizing your FAITH Team's work: _____

Challenging Learners to persevere until their task is complete: _____

_____

Day 3: Your Relationship with Your Sunday School Class

What positive things could happen if every leader in your class followed Jesus' leadership characteristics?

_____

_____

_____

What adjustments would have to be made in order for this to happen?

_____

_____

_____

Spend time praying that the leaders in your class will understand and follow Jesus' example.

Day 4: Your Relationship with the Lost

Review what it meant for Jesus to be balanced in dealing with lost people (see pp. 85–86). Think of lost persons you know or have visited. How have you been balanced in your responses to them, based on their questions, understanding, and backgrounds?

_____

_____

Describe a time when you felt like giving up in your efforts to reach out to those who are lost. How were you encouraged to persevere?

_____

_____

Pray and ask God to burden your heart for the lost. Ask Him to remind you of a person who needs to see and hear about Christ's love. Ask God to help you finish strong in His kingdom work.

Day 5: Your Relationship with Your Family and Your Church

Read 2 Timothy 2:1-2. Check things you are doing to mentor family members.
- ❏ Pray together
- ❏ Study the Bible together
- ❏ Discuss things we've studied
- ❏ Teach them how to witness
- ❏ Worship together
- ❏ Memorize Scripture together
- ❏ Spend time with them so that they can see my life
- ❏ Serve others together
- ❏ Play together
- ❏ Other: _____
  _____
  _____

Ask God to take control of you so that your family and church see love, forgiveness, humility, mercy, and obedience in your life as an example to follow. What are some tangible ways you can show these characteristics to your family at home and at church?

_____
_____
_____
_____

Answers to matching exercise on page 89: 1. e, 2. c, 3. g, 4. f, 5. b, 6. a, 7. d

FAITH AT WORK

FAITH has made a dramatic impact on my life. I've seen God's awesome power working in the people to whom I present the FAITH outline, as well as in my own life. I have learned that many people are wanting and waiting for someone to come and tell them about Jesus. He puts you in places and circumstances where He can use you if you allow Him.

The first time our church promoted FAITH, I had a tugging at my heart, and my dad and brother-in-law came to mind. I knew that God wanted me to witness to them, and I wanted to be obedient. I also wondered whether my dad was saved, but I didn't know how to ask him until I participated in FAITH. It took me three semesters before I was bold enough to ask him the Key Question. Sadly, his response was "I don't know." I asked him if I could share with him the way the Bible answers that question. After going through the FAITH outline, I asked him whether he would like to accept God's forgiveness and Jesus as personal Savior and Lord. He said, "No, not yet." I realize that he did not reject me; he rejected God. Now I know how to pray for him. At least I was there to plant the seed.

I work part-time doing ultrasound at a rehabilitation hospital. One of my patients was a paraplegic. When she came in, she looked very sad. At one point in our conversation she mentioned that her mother and her sister were estranged. I discussed forgiveness with her. Then I asked her the Key Question and went through the FAITH outline. She accepted Christ, and we prayed a commitment prayer. When I opened my eyes and looked at her face, it was as though light were shining around her face and head. It was one of the most beautiful sights I've ever seen. I know that God was present in that room and that I was exactly where God needed me, because my job and my desire as a Christian were to plant a seed or be used as a vessel for someone to come to Christ.

I've had the opportunity to lead more than 20 of my patients to the Lord. Before I started FAITH, I had led no one to Him. The patients I see today are no different from those I've seen for years. The difference is the way I see them—through eyes God has opened to His will.

I am a director in our three-year-old Sunday School Division. Because of FAITH I now see the importance of following up when a child has not been coming to Sunday School, so the family is assigned to a FAITH Team for a visit. Years ago I would never have seen myself asking others whether they would like to accept Christ, but now I can't see myself doing anything else.

Tamara Bullard
Colonial Heights Baptist Church
Jackson, Mississippi

SESSION 6
Developing Your Leadership Qualities

In this session you will—

CHECK IT by engaging in Team Time activities;

KNOW IT by reviewing content from session 5;

HEAR IT by learning how to develop biblical qualities of leadership;

STUDY IT by overviewing Home Study Assignments;

DO IT by leading your Team in making visits;

SHARE IT by celebrating.

IN ADVANCE
- Overview content.
- Preview teaching suggestions. Prepare key points. Decide whether to use the session 6 computer presentation or overhead cels 30–32 (see pp. 300–302). (Because "Quick Review" calls for subjective responses in this session, no corresponding overhead-cel master is provided for reviewing these answers.)
- Prepare the room for teaching.
- Pray for participants and for Teams as they prepare to visit.
- As Teaching Time begins, direct participants to open their Journals to page 96.

TEAM TIME

CHECK IT (15 MINS.)

If the computer presentation is used, display the agenda for Team Time. Add other points to the agenda as needed.

CHECK IT agenda:
- ✔ FAITH Visit Outline
- ✔ Other Home Study Assignments
- ✔ Session 5 Debriefing
- ✔ Help for Strengthening a Visit

Leading Team Time

All Team members participate in Team Time. They are primarily responsible for reciting the assigned portion of the FAITH Visit Outline and for discussing other Home Study Assignments.

As you direct this important time of CHECK IT activities with your Team, keep in mind that Learners look to you as a role model, motivator, mentor, and friend. Team Time activities can continue in the car as the Team travels to and from visits.

Lead CHECK IT Activities

✔ *FAITH Visit Outline*
- ❑ Listen while each Learner recites all of **Preparation**, **Presentation** through the Forgiveness statement and verse (Eph. 1:7a), as well as other key words in **Presentation** and **Invitation**.
- ❑ Indicate your approval by signing or initialing Journals. Encourage Learners.

✔ *Other Home Study Assignments*
- ❑ Check to see whether Learners shared their evangelistic testimonies with two different believers. Briefly discuss how these two believers responded to the testimonies.
- ❑ Discuss benefits Learners are discovering from assigned reading material in *Evangelism Through the Sunday School* and in the FAITH Tip "Nurturing a New Christian" in *A Journey in FAITH Journal*.
- ❑ Make sure Learners are writing in Your Journey in Faith (their journaling section).

✔ *Session 5 Debriefing*
- ❑ Learners have heard the entire gospel presentation by viewing the videotape, hearing the presentation during visits, and overviewing it in session 5. Ask Learners to share how comfortable they are becoming with understanding the significance of sharing the complete gospel presentation.
- ❑ Remind Learners that although the gospel presentation is built on the letters in FAITH, *A Step of Faith* is used to help lead a person to make a commitment to Christ and enroll in Sunday School. Indicate that each of the following six sessions will focus on a letter of the gospel presentation and on how to use the leaflet in leading a person to make a decision to follow Christ.

✔ *Help for Strengthening a Visit*
- ❑ Encourage Learners to be constantly in prayer for one another and for persons being visited. Emphasize the importance of looking for opportunities to build bridges that allow us to share the gospel while, at the same time, being sensitive to the needs of the person being visited. Call attention to the fact that many times a Team might inadvertently close a door to receptivity to the gospel because they come across as pushy.
- ❑ Remind Team members of the importance of being available to the Holy Spirit and of relying on Him to prepare someone for the gospel. We are to be prepared to share and to know how to compassionately lead someone to make the commitments that will change his or her life forever.

Notes

_____

_____

_____

_____

_____

Actions I Need to Take with Team Members This Week

_____

_____

_____

_____

_____

Transition to classrooms for instruction on the content of the session. (5 mins.)

TEACHING TIME

KNOW IT

Step 1 (5 mins.)

Direct participants to turn to "A Quick Review" on page 96 in their Journals and to follow the instructions to complete the activities. Then briefly discuss responses. (Because "A Quick Review" calls for subjective responses in this session, no corresponding overhead-cel master is provided for reviewing these answers.) Be careful not to exceed the five-minute time limit.

A Quick Review

In session 5 you studied Jesus' leadership qualities and learned how to follow His example to be a biblical leader. Reflect on what you learned as you complete the following activities.

1. Look at Jesus' leadership characteristics and evaluate how well you measure up to His standards. Circle the appropriate number for each statement (1 = poor; 5 = perfect).

I remain focused on my purpose regardless of my situation.	1 2 3 4 5
I challenge people to move from where they are to where they should be.	1 2 3 4 5
I mentor others so that they can fulfill their potential.	1 2 3 4 5
I lead by example.	1 2 3 4 5
I am balanced in my responses to people.	1 2 3 4 5
I prioritize my life and work.	1 2 3 4 5
I persevere until my mission is completed.	1 2 3 4 5

2. In what ways are your experiences and training as a FAITH leader helping you become more like Jesus?

   "How am I leading today?"

   Self evaluation – what do I need to work on and take notice of the things that need to change (God revealed things)

LEADERS ON LEADERSHIP

"Leadership growth is a process in which God invests Himself through Jesus and His Spirit in the lives of leaders He is raising up. This involves not only forming them in terms of their skills, abilities, and gifts, but also transforming them in terms of their persons and character."
—Leighton Ford[1]

Learning to Lead

What if you don't lead the way Jesus did? What if you're not as effective as He was? Many Christians who are in leadership positions experience frustration when they compare themselves to the Lord. Despite their best efforts, they often seem ineffective as leaders or, at least in their minds, unsuitable for leadership because they don't consistently measure up to Jesus' standards. As a FAITH leader, you may struggle with real or perceived ineffectiveness in your leadership.

All leadership is a process of learning. Though some people may seem to be natural leaders, they still had to develop their leadership qualities to improve their leadership performance. This is especially true for spiritual leaders. Even those with the spiritual gift of leadership (see Rom. 12:8) must develop their leadership qualities to fulfill the calling God has given them.

You can take certain actions that will help develop your leadership qualities. These steps are not one-time events but ongoing actions that must be carried out every day as part of your spiritual walk. As you read the following actions, consider what steps you need to take and will take to become a better leader.

Look Below

Don't _____**compartmentalize**_____.

Have you ever purchased a preowned car that had a new paint job, but soon rust came to the surface and body filler cracked to reveal that a lot of bodywork had been done on the car? You were shocked to discover that the car's appearance and its real condition were two different things, and you promised yourself that you wouldn't be deceived that way again.

Like cars, people can seem to be something they are not. Even Christians are not immune. What about you? When others look at you, what do they see? Do they see you acting differently in different places? Or are you consistent, regardless of where you are?

Many people think they can compartmentalize their lives. They see no problem in having a life at work, another at home, and still another on the golf course or ball field. If one day you saw them in one area and another day in a different area, you might wonder about the difference. These people rationalize that what they do in their private lives doesn't affect their performance at work, or they might insist that their family life and their work life are not connected.

You operate in different areas of life. However, you cannot view these different areas as computer files that can be opened and closed on demand

---

HEAR IT

Step 2 (5 mins.)

Ask participants to turn to "Learning to Lead" on page 97 in their Journals. Summarize the content, using the computer presentation. Encourage leaders not to get discouraged if their leadership is not what they want it to be but instead to continue learning as they develop their leadership qualities.

Step 3 (10 mins.)

Direct participants to fill in the blanks as you present the key points in "Look Below." Use the computer presentation or overhead cel 30.

Look Below

without having any effect on the other files. The areas of your life are interconnected. What happens in one area will have at least some influence on all the others. Ultimately, everything you do has an effect on your spiritual life, which in turn affects the kingdom of God. Conversely, the quality of your spiritual life affects every other area of your life.

Cultivate   *integrity*   .

One of your most important concerns as a FAITH leader is that your public life—what is seen from the outside—agrees with your private life—what is below the surface. This quality is known as integrity, which can be defined as *the quality or state of being complete or undivided.*[2] Closely related to this idea is the word *honesty*. These words suggest that all the areas of your life match so that you do not live a lie. The world sees the real you, regardless of where you are or what you are doing.

God's Word teaches that this real you is determined not by your external features but by your heart, which influences both your words and your actions. When Samuel examined Jesse's sons to select the king, the Lord instructed him, " 'Man looks at the outward appearance, but the Lord looks at the heart' " (1 Sam. 16:7). Paul wrote, "We speak, not to please men, but rather God, who examines our hearts" (1 Thess. 2:4). Because God looks at and judges your heart, spend time with Him each day, asking Him to search your heart and reveal to you any "offensive way" (Ps. 139:24) within you that would prevent you from being a person of integrity.

The Bible says, "The man of integrity walks securely" (Prov. 10:9). This is because he doesn't have to worry whether someone will find out that he's not really who he appears to be—he has nothing to hide. As you lead your FAITH Team, your Learners should discover that you are really who you appear to be—the same person on a FAITH visit as you are at a Sunday School fellowship or even at a local store. At some point they may discover that you have failed in some area or that you don't always have it all together. Even so, you can be honest about your failures and your desire not to fail in the same area again.

Although integrity alone will not guarantee that you will be an effective leader, a lack of integrity will guarantee that you will be ineffective in your leadership, even if it seems that everything is going well. Oswald Sanders writes that "a prominent businessman once replied to a question: 'If I had to name the one most important quality of a top manager, I would say, personal integrity.' "[3] If a person in the corporate world acknowledges the importance of integrity in a leader, shouldn't we also acknowledge its importance in spiritual leadership? Integrity is a quality you must cultivate daily to grow as a FAITH leader. To cultivate it, ask God to help you look below the surface of your life to identify anything that is contrary to what you profess in public.

Live Low

Resist ___pride___.

Have you ever known someone who was a novice at a sport but after a little success suddenly seemed to know it all? The person may have refused further instruction and even started telling others how they could improve! This happens not only in sports but also in other areas of life.

Such an attitude, known as pride, causes problems in the church as well, especially for leaders. Pride blinds people to their faults and causes them to give priority to themselves rather than to God. Even in the FAITH ministry, witnesses can become proud after leading several persons to Christ. If we begin to think, *Look what I've done*, we begin to rely more on self than on God. The Bible warns us that pride can cause us to forget God:

> "When I fed them, they were satisfied;
>   when they were satisfied, they became proud;
> then they forgot me" (Hos. 13:6; also see Deut. 8:14;
>   2 Chron. 32:25; Ps. 101:5).

Perhaps the most devastating word appears in both the Old and New Testaments: "God resists the proud" (Jas. 4:6; 1 Pet. 5:5; also see Prov. 3:34). The Greek word for *resists* pictures an army lined up against an opponent, ready for battle.[4] Because the army lined up against the proud person is God Almighty, all Christians must avoid the trap of pride.

Practice ___humility___.

The opposite of pride is humility, an essential quality for anyone who aspires to be an effective spiritual leader. Scripture tells us that God "gives grace to the humble" (Prov. 3:34; Jas. 4:6; 1 Pet. 5:5). God desires humility in His people:

> "This is the one I esteem:
>   he who is humble and contrite in spirit" (Isa. 66:2).

As we saw in session 5, Jesus Himself is our model for humility, and He taught His followers to be humble: " 'Whoever exalts himself will be humbled, and whoever humbles himself will be exalted' " (Matt. 23:12). However, because many believers have equated humility with weakness, they have not intentionally strived to cultivate this quality. Other Christians have been concerned about practicing humility because of what it might cost them. They may relate to the words of Gene Wilkes, a pastor who was speaking about servant leadership as taught by Jesus in Matthew 23:12. Wilkes explains, "When I quoted Jesus, I said, 'He who exalts

---

Step 4 (10 mins.)

Direct participants to turn to page 99 in their Journals and to fill in the blanks as you summarize "Live Low." Use the computer presentation or overhead cel 31.

Live Low

himself will be humbled, and he who humbles himself will be exhausted.' We all laughed, but then we agreed that this was how most of us felt about humbling ourselves! We feared that if we humbled ourselves, we would exhaust ourselves trying to do everything people asked us to do! We feared becoming doormats for others to walk on."[5]

These ways of thinking about humility, however, are faulty. Jesus wasn't weak in any way; yet He described Himself as "humble in heart" (Matt. 11:29). In the same verse Jesus said, " 'Take My yoke upon you and learn from Me … and you will find rest for your souls.' " Jesus' words show us the essence of humility—learning. To be humble means that we are teachable, that we recognize that we don't know it all. Jesus had a teachable spirit, as is evident in His words from John 8:28: " 'I do nothing on My own. But just as the Father taught Me, I say these things.' "

Learn from ____**Jesus**____.

Matthew 11:29 also teaches that learning from Jesus will bring rest for us. Jesus wasn't a doormat. He didn't do everything people asked Him to do. Instead, He did only what He saw His Father doing: " 'The Son is not able to do anything on His own, but only what He sees the Father doing. For whatever the Father does, these things the Son also does in the same way' " (John 5:19). As we practice humility by learning from Jesus, we won't be fatigued; instead, we will be fulfilled and strengthened because we are doing what He has told us to do (see Phil. 4:13).

As a FAITH leader, you can't sit back and think you've arrived. Continue to have a teachable spirit, recognizing that no matter how good a leader you are or how effective you are at witnessing, you still have more to learn. Then continue to stay connected on a daily basis to the One who invites you to follow His way and learn from Him. As you do these things, you will be a more effective and productive leader.

Let Go

Give God ____**control**____.

Have you ever been accused of being a backseat driver? Regardless of where you were sitting, you may have made a remark about the driver's speed, accelerating, shifting, braking, following, or turning. If you didn't say something, maybe you were thinking it.

Many Christians are backseat drivers in their spiritual lives. They ask God to take control of their lives, but they often interrupt and tell Him what they believe is the best way to do things. Others follow the "God is my copilot" philosophy—God is beside them to take over if things get rough or if they don't know what they're doing, but normally they're in the driver's seat and have control of their lives.

Step 5 (10 mins.)

Ask participants to turn to page 100 in their Journals and to fill in the blanks as you summarize "Let Go." Use the computer presentation or overhead cel 32. Encourage participants by emphasizing that leadership development is a process of growth.

[Let Go laptop graphic]

God wants to have control of your life to accomplish His will through you. The greatest thing you can do is to let go of the steering wheel, move into another seat, and allow God to drive!

Be filled with the ___Spirit___.

A Spirit-controlled life is especially important for leaders in the church. One quality of those chosen for leadership responsibilities in the first church was being "full of the Spirit" (Acts 6:3). Being full of God's Spirit meant they were emptied of self, they focused on God's will, and they willingly followed Him. In so doing, they grew as leaders. Stephen, one of the seven, was first given the responsibility to oversee the distribution of food among the widows. Eventually, he "was performing great wonders and signs among the people" (Acts 6:8), which was quite different from waiting on tables! Philip, also one of the seven, later led many to Christ in Samaria (see Acts 8:4-8), in addition to performing "signs and great miracles" (Acts 8:13). God eventually used Philip to bring salvation to an Ethiopian official, who may have taken the gospel into Africa.

Being Spirit-controlled is possible but not easy. Because the Bible commands us to be "filled with the Spirit" (Eph. 5:18), we know that God wants it to happen and that He will enable it. To be filled with the Spirit, means we must be emptied of self—our desires, plans, and ways of thinking. When we allow the Spirit to have control of us, He will produce incredible fruit in our lives, which will be both more and better than we can imagine: "love, joy, peace, patience, kindness, goodness, faith, gentleness, self-control" (Gal. 5:22-23). We cannot exhibit this fruit at will; it must come from the Lord. The fruit that the Holy Spirit has produced in our lives shows that He has filled us.

Be willing to ___grow___.

When you plant a young fruit tree, do you expect to find fruit on it the next day? No! The tree must have time to develop in order to produce fruit. During that time pruning, fertilizing, and spraying can encourage the tree to be productive. As the tree grows, you must continue to nurture it in order for it to continue to produce good, abundant fruit.

The same is true for leaders. All of God's leaders in the Bible—Moses, Deborah, Peter, Timothy, and many others—were human, so they all had to grow as leaders. For example, Exodus 18 relates that Moses learned from his father-in-law not to try to do everything himself but to delegate and share the load. John 21 records that Peter learned from Jesus not to be concerned about the tasks given to his peers but to focus on the mission he had been given.

Though Paul was an incredible leader in the early church, he was not the believer he wanted to be. Despite his successes Paul knew that he needed to keep growing: "Not that I have already reached the goal or am already fully mature, but I make every effort to take hold of it because

> *Life is a wild ride let God have the front seat and have a blast!*

STUDY IT

Step 6 (5 mins.)

Overview the Home Study Assignments for session 6.

Transition to assemble with FAITH Teams to prepare for home visits. (5 mins.)

DO IT (110 MINS.)

SHARE IT (30 MINS.)

I also have been taken hold of by Christ Jesus. Brothers, I do not consider myself to have taken hold of it. But one thing I do: forgetting what is behind and reaching forward to what is ahead, I pursue as my goal the prize promised by God's heavenly call in Christ Jesus" (Phil. 3:12-14).

Paul's words should challenge you in your spiritual life, as well as in your leadership role. As you continue to show integrity, live humbly, and give control of your life to the Holy Spirit, you will grow as a leader. As a result, you will strengthen your church's FAITH ministry, and you will help build the kingdom of God.

> To learn more about biblical leadership qualities, see *Kingdom Leadership: A Call to Christ-Centered Leadership* (Convention Press, 1996).

Visitation Time

DO IT

1. Learners have completed the letter *F.* Ask whether any of them are ready to lead the visit through **Preparation** and the Key Question. If so, instruct them: "After the Key Question is asked and the person responds with a works, unsure, or unclear answer, you can say, 'Would you mind if [name of Team Leader] shares with you how the Bible answers that question?' "
2. Use the time in the car to review, allowing Learners to ask questions.
3. After each visit allow Learners to debrief it. Facilitate the debriefing by asking specific questions.

Celebration Time

SHARE IT

1. Ask a Team member to take the lead in sharing reports.
2. Hear reports and testimonies.
3. Complete Evaluation Cards.
4. Complete Participation Cards.
5. Update visitation forms with the results of visits.

---

[1]George Barna, ed., *Leaders on Leadership* (Ventura, CA: Regal Books, 1997), 145.
[2]*Webster's Ninth New Collegiate Dictionary* (Springfield, MA: Merriam-Webster Inc., 1988), 628.
[3]Oswald Sanders, *Spiritual Leadership* (Chicago: Moody Press, 1994), 62.
[4]Marvin R. Vincent, *Word Studies in the New Testament* (Peabody, MA: Hendrickson Publishers, n.d.), 668.
[5]C. Gene Wilkes, *Jesus on Leadership* (Wheaton, IL: Tyndale House Publishers, 1998), 36.

Home Study Assignments

Day 1: Your Relationship with God

Read Acts 6:1-7. Being filled with the Spirit was essential for the first deacons, and it remains essential for all spiritual leaders today. Use a concordance to find other examples of believers who were filled with the Spirit. Record what happened as a result of their being filled. You might want to start with Luke 1:41.

_____

_____

What difference would it make in your church if all FAITH leaders allowed the Holy Spirit to have control of their lives?

_____

_____

Pray that God will empty you of yourself and will fill you with His Holy Spirit so that your leadership will bring glory to Him.

Day 2: Your Relationship with Your FAITH Team

Read 1 Timothy 4:11-16. Paul identified areas in which the young leader needed to develop. Consider the progress of the members of your FAITH Team. Mark below how well you are leading your Learners to grow in each area listed.
1 = doing a great job; 5 = need much improvement.

Taking more and more ownership of the visit		1 2 3 4 5
Completely memorizing each week's material		1 2 3 4 5
Completing their homework in *A Journey in FAITH*		1 2 3 4 5
Presenting the FAITH outline in a natural way		1 2 3 4 5
Realizing the importance of praying with prayer partners		1 2 3 4 5
Persevering in FAITH through the entire semester		1 2 3 4 5
Being an ambassador for the FAITH strategy in their Sunday School classes		1 2 3 4 5

Spend time praying for the members of your FAITH Team. Pray about their struggles, their successes, and their growth. Consider calling them today to encourage them in their journey of FAITH.

Day 3: Your Relationship with Your Sunday School Class

What is one element of leadership that has stood out to you this week as vital for a spiritual leader?

_____

How can you share what you learned this week with other leaders in your class?

_____

_____

Make a list of class members who have been absent lately or who have never attended. Plan a ministry visit to them in the coming week to check on them and to learn whether they have ministry needs. If you have too many members for a FAITH visit this week, plan a ministry visit for another time (besides your regular FAITH Visitation Time) and consider involving other Sunday School members who are not on a FAITH Team. This will give them an opportunity to minister and to see FAITH in action.

Day 4: Your Relationship with the Lost

Consider the importance of the leadership qualities you learned this week for your witness. Describe the way each action below can help you build relationships with lost persons.

Don't compartmentalize: *explain that anything we do will effect everything*

Cultivate integrity: *be the same personally / public*

Resist pride: *live humbly*

Practice humility: *do things for God's recognition*

Learn from Jesus: *study more - live what I learned*

Give God control: *Give God the driver seat in everything*

Be filled with the Spirit: _____

Be willing to grow: *personal study*

Day 5: Your Relationship with Your Family and Your Church

Read Galatians 5:22-25. Check one or more qualities below that you believe your life demonstrates. Then check whether family members and church members would agree that you are demonstrating that fruit.

	My Assessment	My Family's Assessment	My Church's Assessment
Love	☑	☑	☑
Joy	☐	☑	☑
Peace	☐	☐	☑
Patience	☐	☐	☑
Kindness	☐	☐	☑
Goodness	☑	☑	☑
Faith	☑	☑	☑
Gentleness	☐	☐	☑
Self-control	☑	☑	☑

Spend time praying for your family and your church, as well as for your spiritual-leadership development in both of these areas.

FAITH TIP

Practicing the Jethro Principle

After the Exodus, Moses was responsible for leading the children of Israel to the Promised Land. One of his responsibilities was to make decisions about disputes. The only problem was that there were millions of people! Moses sat from morning till evening settling arguments (see Ex. 18:13-16). Read Exodus 18:17-18. What was Jethro's observation of the way Moses was leading the people?

Leaders wear out their followers and themselves when they try to lead alone. Many church leaders burn out because they think they are the only ones who can do the task. But servant leaders know they are most effective when they trust others to work with them. Good leaders train and empower capable people to help them carry out their responsibilities. Read Exodus 18:19-23. What was Jethro's suggestion to Moses to meet the people's needs and carry out his responsibility as a leader?

Moses listened to his father-in-law. He taught the people and appointed judges over the nation. Moses delegated responsibility and authority to meet the needs of the people. The Jethro Principle of delegating ministry still works in churches today.

Check the box that best describes your feelings as a leader.
❏ I am tired and drained.
❏ I feel that I am the only one who can do what I have been asked to do.
❏ Enlisting and training others will take too much time, and my work will never get done.
❏ I am happy to delegate some of my responsibilities to others so that they can share in my joy of leadership.
❏ I have been given much responsibility and little authority.
❏ I have been trained as a leader and feel good about what I am asked to do.
❏ My church has enough trained leaders to meet our church's needs.

What needs exist in your church and community that require good leadership? List them below.

1. _____   4. _____
2. _____   5. _____
3. _____   6. _____

Circle the number beside the needs for which you are responsible. List members you can ask and train to help you meet these needs.

1. _____   4. _____
2. _____   5. _____
3. _____   6. _____

Ask God to show you how He wants you to lead—and to show you others who can lead with you.

Adapted from C. Gene Wilkes, *Jesus on Leadership: Becoming a Servant Leader* (Nashville: LifeWay Press, 1996), 24–26.

SESSION 7
Sharpening Your Leadership Skills

In this session you will—

CHECK IT by engaging in Team Time activities;

KNOW IT by reviewing content from session 6;

HEAR IT by examining practical skills for effective Team leadership;

STUDY IT by overviewing Home Study Assignments;

DO IT by leading your Team in making visits;

SHARE IT by celebrating.

IN ADVANCE
- Overview content.
- Preview teaching suggestions. Prepare key points. Decide whether to use the session 7 computer presentation or overhead cels 33–39 (see pp. 303–9).
- Prepare the room for teaching.
- Pray for participants and for Teams as they prepare to visit.
- As Teaching Time begins, direct participants to open their Journals to page 110.

TEAM TIME

CHECK IT (15 MINS.)

If the computer presentation is used, display the agenda for Team Time. Add other points to the agenda as needed.

CHECK IT agenda:
- ✔ FAITH Visit Outline
- ✔ Other Home Study Assignments
- ✔ Session 6 Debriefing
- ✔ Help for Strengthening a Visit

Leading Team Time

All Team members participate in Team Time. They are primarily responsible for reciting the assigned portion of the FAITH Visit Outline and for discussing other Home Study Assignments.

As you direct this important time of CHECK IT activities with your Team, keep in mind that Learners look to you as a role model, motivator, mentor, and friend. Team Time activities can continue in the car as the Team travels to and from visits.

Lead CHECK IT Activities

✔ *FAITH Visit Outline*
- ❑ Listen while each Learner recites all of **Preparation;** all of F and A, FORGIVENESS and AVAILABLE; the key words for I, T, and H in **Presentation;** and the key outline words in **Invitation.**
- ❑ Indicate your approval by signing or initialing Journals. Encourage Learners.
- ❑ Give Learners an opportunity to practice reciting the portion of the FAITH Visit Outline they have learned to this point.

✔ *Other Home Study Assignments*
- ❑ Check to see whether Learners listed two or three persons who might have a particular interest in knowing that God's forgiveness is available for them. Discuss how your FAITH Team can impact their lives with the gospel and with ministry. Also discuss the assigned reading material. Encourage Learners to continue writing in Your Journey in Faith (their journaling section).

✔ *Session 6 Debriefing*
- ❑ Learners are beginning to learn the gospel presentation. God's forgiveness becomes the foundation on which the rest of the gospel is shared. It is vital to understand that God's forgiveness is based on the free gift of grace that God gives because of Jesus' sacrificial death. As part of the gospel presentation, each letter is accompanied by at least one verse.

✔ *Help for Strengthening a Visit*
- ❑ Many people will not be aware of the free gift of forgiveness that God offers. Some are living with guilt and remorse because of sin in their lives. Others are insensitive to the fact that they are sinners who reject God's love and rebel against Him. The message of forgiveness may be an unfamiliar one to them. Emphasize the importance of showing compassion and understanding with each

person being visited. It helps to remember that your Team is not going to be judgmental but to share that real hope exists because God provides forgiveness through faith in Jesus.
- ❏ Have Learners had opportunities to practice parts of the gospel presentation in home visits? When they visit a Sunday School class member or fellow Christian, sometimes practice is a good option.
- ❏ Have Learners seen someone come to know Christ in a home visit?

Notes

_____

_____

_____

_____

_____

_____

_____

_____

Actions I Need to Take with Team Members This Week

_____

_____

_____

_____

_____

_____

_____

_____

Transition to classrooms for instruction on the content of the session. (5 mins.)

TEACHING TIME
KNOW IT

Step 1 (5 mins.)

Direct participants to turn to "A Quick Review" on page 110 in their Journals and to follow the instructions to complete the activities. Use the computer presentation or overhead cel 33 to review the answers:
1. a. compartmentalize, b. integrity, c. pride, d. humility, e. Jesus, f. control, g. Spirit, h. grow
2. Subjective response

Be careful not to exceed the five-minute time limit.

A Quick Review

A Quick Review

In session 6 you learned how to develop biblical leadership qualities. Review by completing the following activities.

1. Fill in the blanks to identify the actions you can take to acquire biblical qualities of a FAITH leader.

    a. Don't __Compartmentalize__.

    b. Cultivate __Integrity__.

    c. Resist __pride__.

    d. Practice __humility__.

    e. Learn from __Jesus__.

    f. Give God __control__.

    g. Be filled with the __Spirit__.

    h. Be willing to __grow__.

2. What steps have you taken in the past week to develop your leadership qualities?
    - ❑ Reread session 6
    - ❑ Completed the Home Study Assignments
    - ❑ Spent time each day asking God to search you and make you the leader He desires you to be
    - ❑ Surrendered control of your life to the Spirit each day
    - ❑ Hoped that something would change but didn't do much about it
    - ❑ Nothing

LEADERS ON LEADERSHIP

"A leader must be sure he is always growing. Continual growth is a key to effective leadership, and God is the key to growth." —Leroy Eims[1]

---

110 / *Growing as a FAITH Leader Facilitator Guide*

Questions to Be Answered

Many FAITH leaders have discovered, even after being involved in FAITH for several semesters, that they still have questions about practical skills they need as FAITH Team Leaders—questions like these:
- How can I help my Learners see the __big__ __picture__ of FAITH?
- How can I manage our __time__ better—each week and the whole semester?
- How do I __encourage__ my Learners during the week?
- How do I challenge my Learners to give their __best__?
- How do I deal with __personality__ __differences__ on my Team?
- How can I make sure my Learners have reached appropriate __goals__ by the end of the semester?

In this session we will answer these questions, all of which will bring into focus certain skills that are necessary for you to develop as a leader.

As a leader, you are concerned about helping your Learners memorize and begin sharing the FAITH outline. At the same time, you want to develop your Learners into future Team Leaders, who in turn will develop other future leaders. Why should you be concerned about how your Learners are developing as leaders? Consider the following characteristics of most persons who have completed their first FAITH semester.

> **CHARACTERISTICS OF FAITH BASIC GRADUATES**
> - They have memorized the FAITH outline, but it's very wooden. Their presentations are not yet natural and conversational.
> - They still have great fear, especially about sharing the outline on their own.
> - They have a once-a-week-soul-winner mentality. This develops because they participate in FAITH only one time a week and often don't think about it at other times.
> - They have a limited understanding of the connection between Sunday School and FAITH. Usually, they think FAITH is about evangelism, while Sunday School is about Bible study.
> - They have a program mind-set rather than a strategy mind-set. They think of FAITH and Sunday School as programs with definite starting and stopping times rather than ongoing, 24-7 ministries.
> - They are marginally prepared to be multipliers. This too relates to mind-set. Many say or think, "I've done FAITH," as if completing the initial semester is the end of their journey.

HEAR IT

Step 2 (5 mins.)

Direct participants to turn to page 111 in their Journals and to fill in the blanks as you present the material in "Questions to Be Answered." Use the computer presentation or overhead cel 34.

Questions to Be Answered

Handwritten margin notes:
* Multiply ones self into your learners
* How are you developing

If you've seen evidence of the truth of these statements, you know that many Learners are not ready to become leaders simply because they've memorized the FAITH outline. You are the key to helping your Learners become leadership quality by the time they graduate from their first semester of FAITH. Some leadership characteristics will come only with on-the-job training. However, you can take some steps to equip Learners to be ready to lead. As you work on improving the skills in your life, you can also help prepare your Learners for leadership.

Help Learners Catch the Vision

Before every team meeting a high-school football coach showed a photo of the school's football team that had won the state championship seven years ago. He reminded players that they weren't practicing and playing just for fun but to win each game and ultimately become the state champions. He was casting the vision by helping the team see the possibilities.

__Vision__ __casting__ is an important skill in leadership, especially for a FAITH Team Leader. This semester you have already discovered more about the big picture of FAITH—especially its connection with Sunday School. It is vital that you share this connection with your Learners, helping them see that FAITH is as much about discipleship (growing and multiplying) and ministry (caring) as it is about evangelism (sharing). True, the evangelism part of the strategy gets a lot of focus each week in FAITH, but that's only because most churches (and most Christians) find it easier to give attention to the other two areas.

As a FAITH leader, you should remind your Learners in every possible way that FAITH is an __ongoing__ __strategy__ rather than a once-a-week activity. Here are some ways to do that.

COMMUNICATING THAT FAITH IS AN ONGOING STRATEGY

- Let Learners know that you share your faith during the week, not just during Visitation Time.
- Lead your Team to visit a prospect on a different night from your usual visitation night.
- Share in Sunday School the results of your Team's visits and the way your Team helps the class fulfill its purposes.
- Let Learners know that you pray with your prayer partners for people you've visited.
- Emphasize multiplication in the FAITH ministry and remind Learners that their first semester is just the beginning.

Step 3 (5 mins.)

Ask participants to turn to page 112 in their Journals and to fill in the blanks as you summarize "Help Learners Catch the Vision." Use the computer presentation or overhead cel 35.

> Help Learners Catch the Vision

Manage Your Time Wisely

People who are being lazy often remark that they are just killing time. Those who use this expression may not realize that time is life. When people waste time, they are actually wasting their precious lives.

Why should you be concerned about time management? Because FAITH ministry is eternally important. Paul's words in Ephesians 5:15-16 remind us of the importance of time management: "Pay careful attention, then, to how you walk—not as unwise people but as wise—making the most of the time, because the days are evil."

One of Satan's most subtle traps is to deceive us into mismanaging time, especially during the FAITH semester. Here is what Satan will do if you are not careful. Arriving late to the church, you rush through Team Time and often run out of time before you can check Learners' homework, especially memorization of the FAITH outline. You linger in the building determining whom you will visit first and try to determine the best route to the home. You might talk with another person in the room whom you haven't seen in a while, or you might try to catch a staff member to discuss something. You get to the car and spend more time talking about where you are going or discussing issues that are not relevant to the visit. You drive casually, taking your time to get to your assigned visit. If the person is not home, you go back and sit in the car trying to determine whether you have enough time to make another assigned visit or whether you should go to your assigned street to do Opinion Polls. Rationalizing that you don't have enough time, you get back to church before most other Teams arrive. When this FAITH night is over, you and your Team members likely wonder why you don't see results from your involvement in the FAITH ministry.

Does any of this sound familiar? How can you improve your time-management skills to make the best use of your time?

Arrive __early__ *if possible.*
Get to Team Time early enough that you are well prepared and unhurried when your Learners arrive. If you cannot be early, at least be on time.

Delegate __previsitation tasks__ .
Delegate a Learner to arrive early, pick up the Team folder, and examine the visit(s) assigned. With your guidance this member can assess the priority of each visit and can get directions to the house.

Get to the __car__ *quickly after Teaching Time.*
When Teaching Time has concluded, you and Learners should make your way to the car without delay. Remind Learners of the purpose and value of the time allotted for visitation. If they need to talk with anyone,

---

Step 4 (5 mins.)

Direct participants to turn to page 113 in their Journals and to fill in the blanks as you present the main ideas in "Manage Your Time Wisely." Use the computer presentation or overhead cel 36.

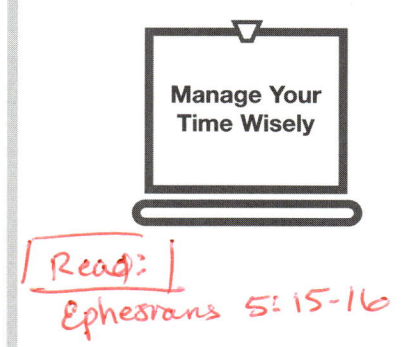

[Manage Your Time Wisely]

Read: Ephesians 5:15-16

Show them how, and when first

encourage them to do so at another time, perhaps after Celebration Time or on another day of the week.

Focus the Team on the _____visit_____.
When you are in the car, remind the Team of the persons you will visit and pray for them, even as someone is driving. While in the car, you can also ask Learners to practice the FAITH outline, or you can share elements of the FAITH strategy that will help their future leadership.

Maximize time between _____visits_____.
Review the previous visit and encourage your Learners. Direct a Learner to recite the outline or work on a difficult part of the outline. Already having decided where you are going allows you to maximize your time between visits. After your final visit, use travel time to discuss details for your Celebration Report.

Try one more _____door_____.
When your Team thinks it's time to go back to the church for Celebration Time because no one is home, <u>knock on one more door.</u> Teams that have done this were later able to share wonderful, life-changing testimonies.

Delegate _____postvisitation_____ _____tasks_____.
When you return to the church, instruct a Learner to fill out the Celebration Report. <u>Designate another Learner to replenish your visitation folder with tracts</u>, <u>ministry brochures</u>, <u>and other materials</u> you might need for the next week's visits.

Encourage Learners

Have you ever tried to teach a child to tie a shoelace? Often the child forgets which way to loop or wrap and can't make the knot, or the loops pull out when the child tries to finish the knot. Sometimes the child kicks off the shoe in frustration and dejectedly concludes, "I'll never learn to tie my shoe." Yet with some motivation the child will try again and will eventually succeed in tying the shoelace.

<u>The ability to encourage members of your FAITH Team is an important leadership skill.</u> Learners not only become fearful at the beginning of a FAITH semester but also get easily discouraged, especially if they watch a competent witness share the FAITH outline in a natural way. This fear and discouragement may continue throughout the semester if Learners don't receive adequate encouragement.

Step 5 (5 mins.)

Direct participants to turn to page 114 in their Journals and to fill in the blanks as you summarize "Encourage Learners." Use the computer presentation or overhead cel 37.

[Encourage Learners]

The Book of Hebrews emphasizes that believers should "encourage each another daily" (Heb. 3:13). Get in the habit of encouraging other believers, especially Learners on your FAITH Team. With ongoing encouragement, your Learners will realize how vital encouragement is to the FAITH process, and they will also keep pressing on, regardless of the obstacles they encounter. Here are ways to encourage Team members.

_____**Believe**_____ *in them.*
Believing in your Learners is a matter of attitude. If they sense that you lack confidence in them, they will be reluctant to continue and will fall prey to Satan's lie that they can't do all FAITH requires or that they don't need to be concerned about FAITH training.

[margin note: They will notice too!]

_____**Praise**_____ *them for their work.*
By this time in the semester Learners probably won't have the outline completely memorized and may have struggled when sharing in some parts of a visit. Still, they have probably worked hard and are doing some things well. Focus on the positive, emphasizing that they can continue to build on what they have already done.

_____**Contact**_____ *them during the week.*
Use notes, e-mails, or phone calls to let Learners know that you pray for them and recognize their progress. This encouragement is especially important if one member of your Team is struggling.

Let them _____**practice**_____ *the FAITH outline.*
Provide opportunities for Learners to practice sharing the outline with other members of your class or church so that they can build confidence in less stressful settings. You might occasionally arrange to stop by certain persons' houses if Learners need a comfortable place to practice.

_____**Point**_____ ___**out**___ *areas of concern.*
Bring areas of improvement to Learners' attention by showing them how it should be done without saying, "You did it wrong. You should have done this." Instead, you might say, "When you get to this point, it would probably flow more easily if you said. …" Also, asking Team members how they felt about a certain situation can open the door for your feedback. Often they already realize where they bungled the presentation or another aspect of the visit, and they want guidance for improving.

[margin note: Constructive criticism]

Step 6 (5 mins.)

Direct participants to turn to page 116 in their Journals and to fill in the blanks as you summarize "Use Modeling to Teach Skills." Use the computer presentation or overhead cel 38.

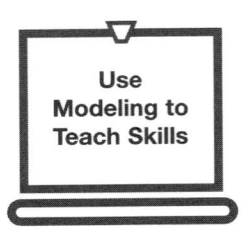

> Use Modeling to Teach Skills

Use Modeling to Teach Skills

Have you ever tried to learn to snow ski? Most likely you didn't learn by reading a book or by watching a video. Although those methods of instruction might help you understand the basics, the best way to learn to ski is to have a competent skier stand beside you, explain what to do, and show you the correct way to do it. After watching, you try it, and the person can demonstrate the skill again to ensure that you can get it right. This process works best for teaching someone a new skill.

You recognize the hypocrisy of someone who insists, "Do as I say, not as I do." People tend to learn more by what they see than what they hear, especially when the two things differ. Leading effectively is extremely difficult if you do not model the role of a FAITH Leader.

Have you ever seen a photocopy that had been made from another photocopy, which perhaps was several generations removed from the original document? The print was probably not as clear and clean as you desired. When you tried to make a copy from that document, you usually got a poor-quality copy because the quality of the master was poor.

The same is true for you as a FAITH Leader. If your leadership skills are not the best they can be, the result of your ministry will be less than the best, and this pattern will repeat itself if your Learners become leaders in the FAITH ministry. Make a commitment to the Lord right now and then share it with your accountability partner that from this point you will be the very best model you can be so that you produce high-quality FAITH graduates.

Here are a few tips for modeling the skills that you want Team members to learn.

Know the ___FAITH___ ___outline___.

Make sure you know the outline the way it is presented in *A Journey in FAITH Journal*. You would be surprised to know how many Learners comment that their Leaders do not know the outline. Early in the semester your Learners will ask questions about the flow and content of the outline, and your knowledge of it must be adequate to satisfy their answers. They need to learn the outline by the book, so you need to know it by the book. You will share the outline in a conversational manner while making a visit, but your thorough knowledge of it will build confidence in your Learners and will encourage them to learn it accurately.

Model effective ___time___ ___management___.

Practice the points in "Manage Your Time Wisely" on pages 113–14 of this session. When you make the best use of your time as you lead, your Learners will begin to do the same. Lead by example.

116 / Growing as a FAITH Leader Facilitator Guide

Discuss ___**visits**___.
After a FAITH visit, explain to your Learners why you did or said something that may have seemed unusual. Let them ask questions about your presentation. Discuss what you might have done differently. Let them see that you don't have all the answers and that you still struggle with certain issues during a visit. They will soon realize that their challenges are a normal part of learning.

Respond to Personality Differences

If you are around other people for very long, you will quickly discover that some of them are not like you in some ways. You may be quiet and reserved, while others are loud and outgoing. You may be a stickler for accuracy, while others allow a lot of room for error. You may like a lot of variety, while others prefer more routine. You may be very people oriented, while others are more task oriented. These differences sometimes cause friction between friends, spouses, colleagues, and neighbors, but as Christians we must recognize that God created everyone to be different, and we must seek to relate to them as God wants us to.

Throughout the Bible we see persons with different personality types. Consider the sisters Mary and Martha, whose differences caused friction one day when Jesus came to their house (see Luke 10:38-42). Or think about the difference between fiery-tempered Peter and even-tempered Barnabas. God used all of these and many others for His kingdom work, in spite of their differences. In the same way, God will use you and your Team members, even with your personality differences, to accomplish His work.

Perhaps you've already discovered personality differences among the members of your FAITH Team. Knowing how to build a Team with varying attitudes and personalities is a critical skill. These ideas may help.

Pray for ___**Team**___ ___**members**___.
This step sounds simple, but prayer is vital to the success of your Team. Satan would love nothing better than to create division among the members of a FAITH Team because of personality differences. You may hear other leaders or Learners say about another FAITH participant, "He rubs me the wrong way. We can't seem to get along." Because this common problem is spiritual in nature, it demands a spiritual response—prayer. As you pray, ask God to give you His heart for the person and to guide you to respond to him or her as God would.

Step 7 (5 mins.)

Ask participants to turn to page 117 in their Journals and to fill in the blanks as you present the main ideas in "Respond to Personality Differences." Use the computer presentation or overhead cel 39.

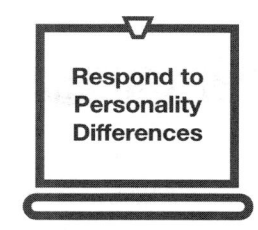

> Respond to Personality Differences

Session 7: Sharpening Your Leadership Skills / 117

Focus on ____**strengths**____.
Focus on the qualities you enjoy about the person rather than the traits that rub you the wrong way. You could say something like, "I appreciate the fact that you're talkative and outgoing. It's really a help during the INTRODUCTION when we meet a prospect." In addition, instead of focusing on your differences, focus on your common purpose of evangelism and ministry through the FAITH strategy.

Embrace ____**differences**____.
View the different personalities of your Team as an asset rather than a liability. During the visit you may discover that your prospect is very shy and would relate better to someone with the same personality. Guide the Team to understand ways different personalities complement each other, not only in FAITH but also in other areas of God's kingdom work.

Address ____**problems**____ *early.*
When a Team member becomes a distraction or creates other problems, address the issue early in the semester. If necessary, seek the guidance of your pastor or FAITH Director.

Go for the Goal

When basketball players shoot, they don't throw the ball up in the air without concern for what it hits. They aim at the goal with the desire that the ball goes in it. If anything else happens, they haven't reached their goal and must try again. The same is true in FAITH. As a Team Leader, set goals before the semester begins and work toward those goals. If anything else happens, you should not be satisfied but must continue working toward those goals.

Think about your Learners. Do you have any goals for them? You expect that they will be at a certain point in their FAITH development by this time in the semester, but what is that point? You can't reach a goal that you haven't already established.

Setting goals for your Learners will enable you to stay focused on the task of developing potential leaders. On the following page are sample goals you might set for Learners.

Step 8 (5 mins.)

Direct participants to turn to page 118 in their Journals as you summarize "Go for the Goal," using the computer presentation.

---

118 / *Growing as a FAITH Leader Facilitator Guide*

SAMPLE GOALS FOR LEARNERS IN FAITH BASIC

Week 3	Learners participate in the *Preparation* part of the outline. Ask them questions during the visit to draw them into the conversation even if they call for only a yes-or-no answer.
Week 4	Learners share their Sunday School testimonies.
Week 5	Learners share their evangelistic testimonies.
Week 6	Learners share both testimonies.
Weeks 7–11	Learners share all of the outline they have learned to this point.
Week 8	Learners recommit to finish the semester. This tends to be a critical point during a FAITH semester. At this point they should also begin praying about two new Learners they could enlist for the next semester.
Weeks 12–16	Learners lead the visit from beginning to end.
Week 15	Learners reveal names of the persons they have enlisted for the next semester.

Perhaps you have not yet mastered the art of setting goals for Team Learners. Or perhaps you're dissatisfied with your time management, encouragement, modeling, or another leadership skill. Start where you are and go from this point forward, doing the best you can and continually praying during the remainder of the semester. You will be amazed by what God will do in and through you and your FAITH Team members.

STUDY IT

Step 9 (5 mins.)

Overview the Home Study Assignments for session 7.

Transition to assemble with FAITH Teams to prepare for home visits. (5 mins.)

DO IT (110 MINS.)

Visitation Time

DO IT
1. Pray for sensitivity to the situations the Team will encounter in these visits. Always be open to enrolling someone in Sunday School.
2. During the INTRODUCTION listen for opportunities for you, your Sunday School class, or your church to minister. Be ready to develop a friendship and to offer to meet a need.
3. All Team members should know the FAITH presentation through A is for AVAILABLE. While visiting, invite Team members to support you up to the letter A.

Celebration Time

SHARE IT
1. Ask a Team member to take the lead in sharing the report.
2. Hear reports and testimonies.
3. Complete Evaluation Cards.
4. Complete Participation Cards.
5. Update visitation forms with the results of visits.

SHARE IT (30 MINS.)

---

[1] Leroy Eims, *Be a Motivational Leader* (Wheaton, IL: Victor Books, 1982), 18.

Home Study Assignments

Day 1: Your Relationship with God

Read Joshua 1:1-9. Review the characteristics of a FAITH Basic graduate presented on page 111. Even though you are a FAITH leader, you may relate to some of the statements. Check any of the following areas in which you still need improvement.
- ❏ Developing a natural and conversational outline presentation
- ❏ Overcoming fears about FAITH
- ❏ Making FAITH an ongoing part of your daily life
- ❏ Increasing your understanding of the FAITH/Sunday School connection
- ❏ Thinking of FAITH as a strategy
- ❏ Growing as a multiplier

Pray and ask God to help you grow as a FAITH participant and leader so that you follow His ways and do what He desires.

Day 2: Your Relationship with Your FAITH Team

Review the time-wasting scenario in the section "Manage Your Time Wisely" on page 113. How is this description like your or your Team's experience?
- ❏ We never waste time like that.
- ❏ We occasionally get sidetracked in these ways.
- ❏ That sounds exactly like us.

On a scale of 1 to 5, with 5 being the highest, how would you rate yourself in the following time-management actions?

Arrive early if possible.	1 2 3 ④ 5
Delegate previsitation tasks.	1 2 3 ④ 5
Get to the car quickly after Teaching Time.	1 2 3 ④ 5
Focus the Team on the visit.	1 2 3 ④ 5
Maximize time between visits.	1 2 3 ④ 5
Try one more door.	1 2 3 ④ 5
Delegate postvisitation tasks.	1 2 3 ④ 5

Record one thing you will do this week to encourage each member of your Team.

Call them to help them on their studies - help them w/ accountability.

Day 3: Your Relationship with Your Sunday School Class

Read Matthew 22:37-38; 28:18-20. Think about your Sunday School class experience. What evidence do you see that Sunday School class members have caught the vision of FAITH working with Sunday School?

_____

_____

Setting goals should include enlistment for next semester. Begin to pray for new FAITH participants from your Sunday School class. Set a personal goal to ask certain individuals by a certain date to become involved in FAITH. Write that date here.

_____

Challenge Sunday School class members to begin praying about their involvement next semester. Share your goals with your accountability partner and pray for each other over the phone today.

Day 4: Your Relationship with the Lost

Write the name(s) of one or two lost persons you are still praying for on a regular basis.

James - Washington meet on Tuesday 10/5

_____

Look back at the Home Study Assignment for day 4 of session 1 (p. 27). What goal did you set for growing in your relationship with lost persons during this semester of FAITH?

_____

_____

How are you progressing toward that goal? _____

_____

_____

Day 5: Your Relationship with Your Family and Your Church

Read Ephesians 5:15-16. How is Satan stealing time from your family?

_____

_____

What are you doing to manage your time wisely at home? *Set priorities*

_____

_____

What are some things your family is doing together in your home each week to develop spiritually?

_____

_____

List at least one goal for each family member you would like to see fulfilled in the next 12 months. Beside each goal, state what can you do to help each family member reach that goal.

- *praying together more*
- *Tyler becoming a Christian @ a young age*
- _____

_____

_____

_____

_____

_____

_____

FAITH TIP

Overcoming the Fear Factor

Many people in your church know about FAITH but don't participate. Often the reason is fear, though they might give you a number of other excuses. But fear isn't limited just to those who are not involved with FAITH. Most FAITH Learners, as well as many leaders, struggle with fear about a variety of things. Most relate to sharing the gospel.

Fear can manifest itself in one of the following ways.
- When the FAITH Team rings the doorbell during a prospect visit or Opinion Poll, a Team member thinks, *I hope no one is at home so that I don't have to share the FAITH outline*.
- When out on a FAITH visit and unable to find the assigned home, the FAITH Team drives around the entire time and perhaps never gets out of the car.
- When checking the folder for the visitation assignment, a Team member is relieved to find a ministry assignment rather than a prospect visit; now he or she won't have the pressure of sharing the FAITH presentation.

Such feelings are normal for a certain period of time, but Satan will use those feelings to his advantage to keep you away from a prospect who needs to hear the gospel or to delay you in making a visit. So what can you do?

1. Understand that because fear is a natural human emotion, everyone experiences it. Even so, remember that Jesus is Lord over all, including our emotions, so we don't have to live as slaves to fear. He tells us to " 'take courage! I have conquered the world' " (John 16:33).
2. Remember Paul's words to Timothy: "God has not given us a spirit of fearfulness, but one of power, love, and sound judgment" (2 Tim. 1:7). We can trust this promise from God's Word.
3. Pray for boldness. The apostles did this after the Jewish leaders ordered them to quit preaching and teaching about Jesus. As a result, "they were all filled with the Holy Spirit and began to speak God's message with boldness" (Acts 4:31).

As you teach your Learners to trust in God's power rather than their own, you will help extinguish Satan's flaming arrows of fear, and you will help your Learners become better prepared to be leaders themselves.

SESSION 8
The FACTS of Multiplication

In this session you will—

CHECK IT by engaging in Team Time activities;

KNOW IT by reviewing content from session 7;

HEAR IT by examining the biblical principle of multiplication and understanding its meaning for your ministry as a FAITH leader;

STUDY IT by overviewing Home Study Assignments;

DO IT by leading your Team in making visits;

SHARE IT by celebrating.

IN ADVANCE
- Overview content.
- Preview teaching suggestions. Prepare key points. Decide whether to use the session 8 computer presentation or overhead cels 40–43 (see pp. 310–13).
- Prepare the room for teaching.
- Pray for participants and for Teams as they prepare to visit.
- As Teaching Time begins, direct participants to open their Journals to page 128.

TEAM TIME

CHECK IT (15 MINS.)

If the computer presentation is used, display the agenda for Team Time. Add other points to the agenda as needed.

CHECK IT agenda:
- ✔ FAITH Visit Outline
- ✔ Session 7 Debriefing/Other Home Study Assignments
- ✔ Help for Strengthening a Visit

Leading Team Time

All Team members participate in Team Time. They are primarily responsible for reciting the assigned portion of the FAITH Visit Outline and for discussing other Home Study Assignments.

As you direct this important time of CHECK IT activities with your Team, keep in mind that Learners look to you as a role model, motivator, mentor, and friend. Team Time activities can continue in the car as the Team travels to and from visits.

Lead CHECK IT Activities

✔ *FAITH Visit Outline*
- ❑ Listen while each Learner recites all of **Preparation**; all of the outline points for the letters *F* (FORGIVENESS), *A* (AVAILABLE), and *I* (IMPOSSIBLE); key words for the letters *T* (TURN) and *H* (HEAVEN); and key words for the **Invitation**.
- ❑ Indicate your approval by signing or initialing Journals. Encourage Learners.
- ❑ Provide an opportunity for Learners to practice reciting the portions of the FAITH Visit Outline they have learned to this point.

✔ *Session 7 Debriefing/Other Home Study Assignments*
- ❑ God's forgiveness is available for everyone. Even the most hardened criminal or the most unloving person is the target of God's love and forgiveness. John 3:16 reminds us of the scope of God's love and forgiveness (" 'God so loved the world … that whoever' " [NKJV]). This same verse introduces us to the fact that God's forgiveness is not automatic (" 'whoever believes in him' " [NKJV]). This passage also focuses on the consequences of not accepting God's forgiveness (" 'perish' " [NKJV]). It is important to remember that many persons you visit will not understand that God's forgiveness is available to them, but it is not automatic.

✔ *Help for Strengthening a Visit*
- ❑ Many persons you seek to visit will indicate that they do not have much time for a lengthy visit. Some persons may not allow your Team to enter the house because of time or personal constraints. Your primary jobs are to seek to build relationships with people and to introduce them to the idea of enrolling in your Sunday School class or department. Indeed, you look for opportunities to ask the Key Question, hear responses, and share the FAITH gospel presentation. But also look for opportunities to build bridges with the person through Sunday School enrollment. God may be using you to plant

a seed. He may also be using you and your Team members to nurture relationships on His behalf and to prepare the harvest. Be sensitive to opportunities God is providing for you in the midst of visits.

Notes

_____
_____
_____
_____
_____
_____
_____
_____

Actions I Need to Take with Team Members This Week

_____
_____
_____
_____
_____
_____
_____
_____
_____

Transition to classrooms for instruction on the content of the session. (5 mins.)

TEACHING TIME

KNOW IT

Step 1 (5 mins.)

Direct participants to turn to "A Quick Review" on page 128 in their Journals and to follow the instructions to complete the activities. Use the computer presentation or overhead cel 40 to review the answers:
1. c, e, f
2. a. early, b. previsitation tasks, c. car, d. visit, e. visits, f. door, g. postvisitation tasks

Be careful not to exceed the five-minute time limit.

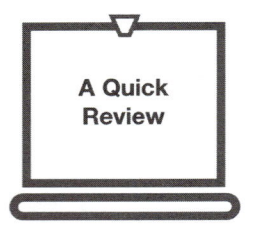

A Quick Review

A Quick Review

Session 7 focused on practical skills needed for effective Team leadership. Complete the following activities to check your learning.

1. Team Leaders are instrumental in helping FAITH Learners understand the big picture of FAITH. Check the actions you can take to help Learners catch the vision that FAITH is an ongoing strategy.
   - ❏ a. Emphasize FAITH as a program or an activity that belongs to a certain day of the week.
   - ❏ b. Don't mention sharing your faith during the week.
   - ❏ c. Visit at a different time from your normal Visitation Time.
   - ❏ d. Keep silent about FAITH during your Sunday School class.
   - ❏ e. Talk about praying with your prayer partners.
   - ❏ f. Emphasize the importance of FAITH multiplication.

2. Fill in the blanks to identify ways you can make the best use of your time during Team Time, Visitation Time, and Celebration Time.

   a. Arrive __early__ if possible.

   b. Delegate __previstation__ __tasks__.

   c. Get to the __car__ quickly after Teaching Time.

   d. Focus the Team on the __visit__.

   e. Maximize time between __visits__.

   f. Try one more __door__.

   g. Delegate __postvrostation__ __tasks__.

> **LEADERS ON LEADERSHIP**
>
> *"Wise leaders plan, from the very inception of their leadership, for the time when they will no longer be around."* —Bob Briner and Ray Pritchard[1]

128 / Growing as a FAITH Leader Facilitator Guide

Does Your Growth Strategy Add Up?

Have you ever remodeled your house by building an addition? Whether it's a family room, an expanded kitchen, or an additional bedroom, an addition can be beneficial. However, it can also cause problems. One is the mess, especially if you live in the house during construction. A second problem is the expense, which can cost tens of thousands of dollars. A third is the value, which in some cases can't be recovered when the house is sold because the asking price exceeds that of other comparable houses in the neighborhood. Addition also has drawbacks for Christians and churches.

An addition mentality undermines __life__ __change__. Some people understand the Christian faith as adding Jesus to their lives rather than a complete surrender to Christ as Savior and Lord. They think of Jesus being a part of their life rather than *being* their life.

The biblical concept of being born again refers to a new life, not a modified old life. This new life is described in the Book of Ephesians: "You took off your former way of life, the old man that is corrupted by deceitful desires; you are being renewed in the spirit of your minds; you put on the new man, the one created according to God's likeness in righteousness and purity of the truth" (Eph. 4:22-24). Paul also referred to the new life in Romans 12:2: "Do not be conformed to this age, but be transformed by the renewing of your mind." When we try to add Jesus to our lives, nothing really changes. This is why so many Christians are living defeated lives: there has been no life change.

An addition mentality thwarts __spiritual__ __growth__. Another pitfall of the principle of addition is evident when believers add elements to their spiritual development. Christians should practice many important disciplines, such as worship, praying, fasting, studying the Scriptures, giving, and witnessing. Unfortunately, some Christians try one of these disciplines for a while, then go to something else. They add an element to their spiritual lives for a season, then change to another, as if they are repainting a room in their homes. This approach to spiritual growth can be legalistic and devoid of meaning. God intends the spiritual disciplines to be natural, ongoing avenues for pursuing a living, deepening relationship with Him.

An addition mentality impedes __church__ __growth__. Because believers frequently understand church growth as addition, many are content to add people to the kingdom and to their church. The plateau and decline of the church have proved the ineffectiveness of this approach. A few people do all the work, and the other members

---

HEAR IT

Step 2 (5 mins.)

Ask participants to turn to page 129 in their Journals and to fill in the blanks as you use the content in "Does Your Growth Strategy Add Up?" to emphasize the pitfalls of an addition growth mentality. Use the computer presentation or overhead cel 41.

> Does Your Growth Strategy Add Up?

Step 3 (10 mins.)

Direct participants to turn to page 130 in their Journals and to fill in the blanks as you present the material in "Multiplication: Do the Math." Use the computer presentation or overhead cel 42.

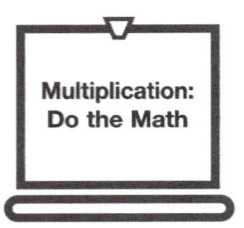

> Multiplication: Do the Math

---

are not trained as effective soul-winners. Although people sometimes accept Christ, they are not discipled in the basics of the Christian life and the necessity of evangelism. Thus, the soul-winners in the church have no one to take their place. Churches that operate by the principle of addition are only one generation away from extinction.

This session will introduce you to a more biblical approach to kingdom growth: the principle of multiplication. Then sessions 9–11 will help you apply the principle of multiplication to your FAITH Teams and Sunday School in practical ways.

Multiplication: Do the Math

How do children learn the basics of mathematics? They focus first on addition, which most children easily grasp. They can look at two cookies, add two more cookies, and recognize that they now have four cookies. Eventually, though, children must move on to multiplication. Although multiplication is important, most children find it more difficult than addition and therefore don't get excited about it.

A similar thing happens in some churches. Recognizing the importance of addition, members celebrate when people join their fellowship. If they learn about multiplication, however, they quickly discover that it is difficult and therefore don't get excited about it.

Even so, understanding and following the principle of multiplication is of vital importance for all Christians. Jesus gave us a commission to take the gospel to all the world. This task requires leaders; yet many leaders don't understand who they are or what they are to do.

What is a leader? Many people would respond that a leader is someone who has followers. A biblical leader, however, is more than that. Many followers, after their leader is no longer around, forget about the cause and go back to life as it was before the leader came along. This was the case with the followers of Theudas and Judas, who likely sought to overthrow the Roman government sometime before or around the birth of Christ (see Acts 5:36-37). The same is true in many organizations and even in some churches. A dynamic, charming, magnetic person can always attract a group, but because no human leader lives forever, eventually the attraction diminishes.

The best leaders, however, are those who reproduce themselves in the lives of others. This is the essence of biblical leadership. This principle, seen throughout the Bible, is probably best summarized in 2 Timothy 2:2: "What you have heard from me in the presence of many witnesses, commit to faithful men who will be able to teach others also." A biblical leader encourages others to follow his or her example but, at the same time, intentionally trains them so that they can naturally assume the position and responsibilities of a leader. Occasionally, a follower

---

130 / Growing as a FAITH Leader Facilitator Guide

replaces the leader, but most often followers go out and become leaders in their own right.

This is the focus of the FAITH strategy, and it fulfills the pattern of multiplication presented in 2 Timothy 2:2. Paul described the principle of multiplication in a letter to his protégé Timothy. You will recall from session 1 that Paul outlined the process of multiplication as follows.

__Receive__ *(learn): "what you have heard from me."*
Perhaps you can recall being in school when someone asked, "Do we have to know this?" Basically the person wanted to know whether the subject would be on a test, as if it would be memorized for the test, then quickly forgotten.

Unlike this type of "learning," growing as a FAITH leader requires that you continually receive. You are always in a position to learn, especially from God's Word. And it's not enough just to listen; you must put into practice what you've learned (see Luke 6:46-49; Jas. 1:22). You can never be satisfied in your Christian walk thinking that you have arrived. God wants you to experience Him daily. You must learn more about yourself and more about Him every day.

In addition to learning from God's Word each day, you should learn from other Bible-based material, as well. J. Oswald Sanders writes that "leaders should determine to spend a minimum of half an hour a day reading books that feed the soul and stimulate the mind."[2] FAITH Discipleship courses such as this one provide material that will help you learn and grow during the FAITH semester, but other resources, including books, tapes, and conferences, can also help you grow as a FAITH leader.

{growth step}

__Repeat__ *(teach): "commit to faithful men."*
In *Share Jesus Without Fear* William Fay explains why so many Christians do not share their faith with others. He says that even many long-time believers often claim, "I don't know enough." Fay insists that these people know plenty, but they keep taking in spiritual truth without sharing that truth.[3] As a FAITH leader, you recognize that the salvation you have received from God is not to be kept to yourself but shared with others. In the same way, you must share what you've learned with the Learners in your care.

__Reproduce__ *(train): "who will be able to teach others also."*
Throughout history master craftsmen have taken on apprentices who worked with them for little or nothing, not only doing menial tasks but also learning the trade and how to teach it to others. After a number of years these apprentices would go out on their own to earn a living and train their own apprentices. For centuries this process was repeated but, except in a few vocations, is rarely followed in occupations today.

> **Step 4 (10 mins.)**
>
> Ask participants to turn to page 132 in their Journals and to fill in the blanks as you summarize "Multiplication: Know the FACTS." Use the computer presentation or overhead cel 43.
>
> Multiplication: Know the FACTS

The same can be said of spiritual training. Although some believers still learn truth and share it with others, many don't guide other believers to train those who come after them. For example, in many large Sunday School classes a gifted teacher focuses more on telling than on reproducing those who can train others. Sharing the truth of the Word is important, but it is also important to prepare others to share the truth and to teach others to do the same.

Multiplication: Know the FACTS

It is a fact that 8 x 8 = 64. Once you learn this fact, you can use it again and again with the same results. In the same way, basic facts of spiritual multiplication are found throughout the New Testament. We will call these the FACTS of multiplication. The letters in FACTS stand for phrases that can help you remember the principle of multiplication.

F *is for* _____fruitful_____ _____results_____.
The parable of the sower (see Matt. 13:1-23) emphasizes this principle. The key idea of this parable is found in verse 8. Discussing the seed, Jesus said, " 'Still others fell on good ground, and produced a crop: some a hundred, some sixty, and some thirty times what was sown.' " In addition, verse 23 notes, " 'The one sown on the good ground—this is one who hears and understands the word, who does bear fruit and yields: some a hundred, some sixty, some thirty times what was sown.' "
  Through multiplication you will reap fruitful results that will benefit your church and the kingdom of God—a yield that is many times more than your original investment.

A *is for* _____amazing_____ _____growth_____.
In the parable of the mustard seed (see Matt. 13:31-32) Jesus said the seed is " 'the smallest of all the seeds, but when grown, it's taller than the vegetables and becomes a tree, so that the birds of the sky come and nest in its branches' " (v. 32).
  By following the principle of multiplication, you will see amazing growth that strengthens and enlarges your church so that it can benefit others and give glory to God.

C *is for* _____continuous_____ _____action_____.
Paul's directions to Timothy in 2 Timothy 2:2 don't apply to a one-time event. If that were the case, the initial messenger would pass along the message to another person, who passes it down the line like a bag of peanuts at a ballgame. The leader would never share the message again, nor would anyone else who heard it and passed it to one other person.

Instead, Paul's words emphasize that the messenger must continue to share the message with others, who also continue to share it with others, and so forth. The Bible doesn't identify a specific number of persons with whom you are to share. The idea is to keep sharing throughout your life with anyone who will listen. In this way your church's FAITH ministry will see multiplication in action as the number of people hearing the gospel message grows exponentially.

T *is for* **time** - **sensitive**.

The parable of the talents (see Matt. 25:14-30) says that when the master entrusted property to his servants, he expected them to multiply what they had been given. The servants didn't have an unlimited amount of time to accomplish the task he gave them. The master would come back and call the servants to give an account of what they had done.

In the same way, your time as a FAITH leader is limited, and the time others have to hear and share the message is also limited. Therefore, you must be faithful to use every opportunity to share the message so that it will multiply as much as possible before the Master returns.

S *is for* **Spirit** - **empowered**.

First Corinthians 3:1-9 points out the different roles of Paul and Apollos in sharing the message of salvation. Paul noted in verse 6, "I planted, Apollos watered, but God gave the growth." This verse reminds us of a very important fact about multiplication: it comes as a result of God's work, but we must also work with God to bring it about. Writing to the Ephesian Christians, Paul emphasized this partnership when he wrote that God "is able to do above and beyond all that we ask or think—according to the power that works in you" (Eph. 3:20).

In order to experience the principle of multiplication, you must allow the Holy Spirit to work in you as you minister through the FAITH strategy. As you do, you will witness God do far beyond what you can even imagine.

Multiplication: Witness the Miracle

Investment professionals want people to discover the "miracle" of compound interest. For example, a person who saves $2.74 each day ($1,000 a year), with an average interest rate of 10 percent, will have $486,851 after 40 years.[4] One wealthy man referred to compound interest as "the eighth wonder of the world."[5] It is truly incredible how such a small amount can grow into something so large.

Step 5 (10 mins.)

Direct participants to turn to page 133 in their Journals. Present the content in "Multiplication: Witness the Miracle," using the computer presentation. Have two volunteers read aloud 2 Kings 4: 1-7 and Matthew 14:13-21 as reminders of the way God works through multiplication.

Scripture depicts the way God can take a little of something and multiply it even more miraculously than compound interest occurs. In 2 Kings 4:1-7 a widow in deep debt told Elisha about her tragic situation. Obeying the prophet's instructions, the woman witnessed the miracle of multiplication as she filled up countless jars with oil from a single jar that had only a little oil in it. In Matthew 14:13-21 Jesus fed a crowd of more than five thousand people with only five loaves of bread and two fish. Verse 20 says, "Everyone ate and was filled. Then they picked up twelve baskets full of leftover pieces." Throughout the Bible we see evidence of the principle of multiplication. It was a priority in Jesus' ministry. In fact, one of His main purposes in training the twelve disciples was for them to take what they received from Him and not only share it but also use it to train others to share the gospel.

We live in an instant society of ATMs, microwaves, and instant messaging. Unfortunately, these things tempt us to think that everything should be quick and easy. Most things that are worthwhile, however, take time and effort to accomplish. The apostle Paul emphasized this in Galatians 6:9: "We must not get tired of doing good, for we will reap at the proper time if we don't give up." Multiplication in your FAITH ministry will take time, just as multiplication does in farming. Some FAITH Team Learners have dropped out after the first semester because they saw little, if any, visible results from their efforts. Some FAITH leaders are even thinking about quitting after this semester because their Sunday School class hasn't grown, they haven't seen many professions of faith, new believers haven't joined their church, few Sunday School class members have become involved in FAITH, and a number of other reasons. Remember that multiplication is in God's hands and occurs according to His time. After all, He is the one who brings the growth (see 1 Cor. 3:6).

Our churches need FAITH leaders who are committed to the Lord and to His work of multiplication. As you work with Him and utilize the principle of multiplication through the FAITH strategy, you will eventually experience an incredible harvest of new believers, classes, and churches that will produce renewed energy and excitement for going and making disciples.

Most people today want a fast food religion.

STUDY IT

Step 6 (5 mins.)

Overview the Home Study Assignments for session 8.

Transition to assemble with FAITH Teams to prepare for home visits. (5 mins.)

Visitation Time

DO IT

1. Be a good listener. You earn the right to share the good news by listening to the stories of the persons you visit. They may share with you some things that make you uncomfortable or may raise some questions you would rather not address—but listen. It is not necessary to be able to answer all of their questions, but it is necessary to care.
2. Are Team members becoming increasingly comfortable with making adjustments as the visit merits? Although your Team should plan in advance what is to happen and what responsibilities the various Team members will assume, the best visit is one in which visitors adjust to the needs of the situation.
3. Team Leader, affirm your Team Learners as they show increasing confidence and ease in sharing their testimonies and in using the FAITH Visit Outline.
4. At the Team Leader's cue, Learners should be able to share FORGIVENESS and AVAILABLE.

Celebration Time

SHARE IT

1. Ask a Team Learner to take the lead in sharing your Team's report.
2. Hear reports and testimonies.
3. Complete Evaluation Cards.
4. Complete Participation Cards.
5. Update visitation forms with the results of visits.

---

[1] Bob Briner and Ray Pritchard, *The Leadership Lessons of Jesus* (Nashville: Broadman & Holman Publishers, 1997), 126.
[2] J. Oswald Sanders, *Spiritual Leadership* (Chicago: Moody Press, 1994), 102.
[3] William Fay, *Share Jesus Without Fear* (Nashville: LifeWay Press, 1999), 24.
[4] Howard Dayton, *Your Money Counts* (Gainesville, GA: Crown Financial Ministries, 1996), 102.
[5] Ibid.

DO IT (110 MINS.)

SHARE IT (30 MINS.)

Home Study Assignments

Day 1: Your Relationship with God

Read 2 Timothy 2:2. Have you lived primarily by—
- ☑ the principle of addition?
- ☐ the principle of multiplication?

Are Christian disciplines that you practice—
- ☐ simply spiritual elements you have added to your life?
- ☑ a natural part of your spiritual growth in your relationship with God?

Check the spiritual disciplines that need to become a regular part of your spiritual life. Circle one to which you will give greater attention for the next month.
- ☐ Personal Bible study
- ☐ Personal worship
- ☐ Fasting
- ☐ Giving
- ☑ Prayer
- ☐ Being a life witness
- ☐ Serving others
- ☐ Fellowshipping with other believers

Day 2: Your Relationship with Your FAITH Team

Think of the FAITH Team Learners you have trained in the past.
How many are still involved in FAITH? _all_
How many are leading FAITH Teams? _N/A → youth_

How are they reproducing themselves in the lives of their Learners?

great assistant leaders — outgoing - get the job done

How could you have led your Learners differently after studying session 8?

More encouragement / accountability

Identify a way you are helping or have helped your FAITH Learners—

receive the message: _practice - examples_

repeat the message: _____

reproduce themselves in others' lives: _____

Day 3: Your Relationship with Your Sunday School Class

Draw a diagram to show the difference between the principles of addition and multiplication in kingdom growth. Try to illustrate the difference between training one person each semester and training two persons each semester who in turn train two more the following semester.

When it is time to begin enlistment for the next semester of FAITH, how can you use your diagram to inform your class about FAITH and to encourage greater interest?

_____

_____

Begin praying for additional Sunday School members to catch the vision of the FAITH Sunday School Evangelism Strategy® and to get involved next semester.

Day 4: Your Relationship with the Lost

Read Galatians 6:7-9. Give an example of one way you are practicing the principles of these verses in your life.

_____

In what ways are you sowing the seeds of the gospel outside FAITH?

_____

_____

Memorize Galatians 6:7-9 to help you prioritize the principle of multiplication. Ask God to encourage and strengthen you this week so that you will not grow weary in well doing.

Day 5: Your Relationship with Your Family and Your Church

Read Psalm 78:3-6. How are you sharing the gospel with your children or with those in the next generation?

_____

_____

_____

_____

Think of someone in your church (perhaps in your Sunday School class) of the same gender who has recently become a Christian. Which of the following actions have you taken this semester on behalf of that person?
❏ Tried to develop a relationship
❏ Invited to a fellowship in your home
❏ Offered to take to lunch
❏ Asked to join you for prayer or to study about growing as a Christian
❏ Other: _____

_____

Make a commitment to reproduce yourself in the life of this new believer by spending time together once a week. Ask your pastor or another church-staff member to recommend material you could use to disciple this person.

SESSION 9
Multiplying Your Team

In this session you will—

CHECK IT by engaging in Team Time activities;

KNOW IT by reviewing content from session 8;

HEAR IT by studying ways to multiply the ministry of your FAITH Team;

STUDY IT by overviewing Home Study Assignments;

DO IT by leading your Team in making visits;

SHARE IT by celebrating.

IN ADVANCE
- Overview content.
- Preview teaching suggestions. Prepare key points. Decide whether to use the session 9 computer presentation or overhead cels 44–48 (see pp. 314–18).
- Prepare the room for teaching.
- Pray for participants and for Teams as they prepare to visit.
- As Teaching Time begins, direct participants to open their Journals to page 142.

TEAM TIME

CHECK IT (15 MINS.)

If the computer presentation is used, display the agenda for Team Time. Add other points to the agenda as needed.

CHECK IT agenda:
- ✔ FAITH Visit Outline
- ✔ Other Home Study Assignments
- ✔ Session 8 Debriefing
- ✔ Help for Strengthening a Visit

Leading Team Time

All Team members participate in Team Time. They are primarily responsible for reciting the assigned portion of the FAITH Visit Outline and for discussing other Home Study Assignments.

As you direct this important time of CHECK IT activities with your Team, keep in mind that Learners look to you as a role model, motivator, mentor, and friend. Team Time activities can continue in the car as the Team travels to and from visits.

Lead CHECK IT Activities

✔ *FAITH Visit Outline*
- ❑ Listen while each Learner recites the FAITH Visit Outline: all of *Preparation* and *Presentation*, adding *T* is for TURN to the gospel presentation; plus the key words for *Invitation*. Be aware of time limits if two Learners are sharing; someone may need to recite in the car going to and from visits.
- ❑ Initial each Learner's work in his or her Journal.
- ❑ Practice other parts of the outline as time allows.

✔ *Other Home Study Assignments*
- ❑ Emphasize the importance of involving the Sunday School class in FAITH, whether by prayer support, in training, or in follow-up. Explain that in this session Sunday School will be the focus of building bridges to people.
- ❑ Ask: Do class/department members who are not participating in FAITH still see themselves as a part of this ministry? In what ways? Are you sharing prayer needs and results of visits with fellow class members? Are they praying for you and for people you and your Team will visit? Are your class, department, and church growing spiritually and numerically?
- ❑ Home Study Assignments and memorization are reaching their maximum. Make a special effort during the week to personally encourage Learners, especially those who may have fallen behind in memory work or home study.

✔ *Session 8 Debriefing*
- ❑ Some important theological truths are communicated in this part of the gospel presentation. Are Learners at ease and confident in sharing about both God's love and His justice? About their own sinfulness?
- ❑ Ask Learners to recall from their personal experience—
  - their need to be saved;
  - their inability to save themselves;

- God's saving initiative in their lives (their life-changing experience).

Doing so will help them continue to identify with the people they visit. All of us are sinners in need of God's grace. Some of us have been fortunate enough to receive and accept it, while others still need to know about God's forgiveness. Letting them know is a big part of what FAITH is all about.
- ❑ Overview ways to respond to a works answer to the Key Question.

✔ Help for Strengthening a Visit
- ❑ By this time most Team members have seen someone accept Christ during a home visit. Remind Team members of how such a visit should motivate them to continue in their efforts. If not, remind Team members that God is still working, even if they have not seen specific desired results.
- ❑ Call on the Assistant Team Leader, if your Team has one, to encourage other Team members; he or she may have had experiences in earlier FAITH training that can motivate others.
- ❑ As important as practice is, it is not the same as sharing the gospel in a home visit. Acknowledge that fact even as you encourage your Team to practice with one another and with other believers, as the opportunity allows.

Notes
_____
_____
_____
_____

Actions I Need to Take with Team Members This Week
_____
_____
_____
_____

Transition to classrooms for instruction on the content of the session. (5 mins.)

TEACHING TIME
KNOW IT

Step 1 (5 mins.)

Direct participants to turn to "A Quick Review" on page 142 in their Journals and to follow the instructions to complete the activities. Use the computer presentation or overhead cel 44 to review the answers:
1. *Receive:* learn from God's Word through teaching others. *Repeat:* share with others what you've learned. *Reproduce:* guide others to share what they've learned with still others, continuing the process.
2. fruitful results, amazing growth, continuous action, time-sensitive, Spirit-empowered

Be careful not to exceed the five-minute time limit.

A Quick Review

HEAR IT

Step 2 (5 mins.)

Present the content in "Get Others Involved," using the computer presentation on the CD-ROM.

A Quick Review

In session 8 you examined the principle of multiplication. Complete the following activities to review what you learned.

1. Below are the three actions Paul taught in 2 Timothy 2:2. Explain how each communicates the principle of multiplication.

   Receive: *learn — it is no enough to listen — we must do*
   Repeat: *teach — that we do know enough*
   Reproduce: *train — guide others to the place of leadership.*

2. Fill in the blanks to recall the FACTS of multiplication.

   F is for *fruitful* *results*
   A is for *amazing* *growth*
   C is for *continuous* *action*
   T is for *time* - *sensitive*
   S is for *Spirit* - *empowered*

> **LEADERS ON LEADERSHIP**
>
> "Leaders create and inspire new leaders by instilling faith in their leadership ability and helping them develop and hone leadership skills they don't know they possess." —John Maxwell[1]

Get Others Involved

A 10-year-old boy on a hiking trip with his scout troop got separated from the group in a heavily wooded area. The scout leaders contacted the boy's parents and the local authorities, and volunteers began searching for the boy. As sundown approached, a TV reporter interviewed the boy's mother, who pleaded for more people to help search for her son. Soon dozens of people were in the woods who, along with two helicopters in the sky, tried to find the boy. Even after dark the rescuers continued to search, aided by flashlights, bloodhounds, and walkie-talkies. Finally, just before midnight the word came that one of the groups had found the boy, who had fallen into a crevice and was hurt but was still alive. As the boy was being attended, the message quickly spread that the rescuers could stop searching because he was safe.

While a lost child in the woods creates great concern, many more children and adults are lost in our world but don't have anyone searching for them. As a FAITH leader, you are involved in the search-and-rescue mission, but surely you recognize that the task is too great for the small number of people who are working with you. More are needed to get involved in the task—many, many more.

In this session we will learn how to multiply FAITH Teams. Now that you understand the principle of multiplication, this session will help you discover ways you and your church can multiply the number of people involved in finding and rescuing the lost.

Recognize Hindrances to Multiplication

How do you know whether a tree is living? One clue is that the tree is growing. Healthy trees get taller and wider and produce new leaves and buds. When a tree is not growing, someone usually examines it to determine the problem.

Like a healthy tree, the FAITH Teams in your church should also grow. When Teams do not grow and multiply, we need to examine them to determine the problem. Here are some of the reasons FAITH Teams do not multiply.

The _____schedule_____ keeps new people from participating.
Churches sometimes find that new people cannot participate in FAITH because of the schedule. If, for example, Team Time begins at 5:30 on a weeknight, some people might be leaving work, while others have not yet finished their workday.

Church members lack _____knowledge_____ about FAITH.
In some churches, while the majority of members may have heard about the FAITH ministry, they know little about it. Often members lack knowledge because the teaching and visitation aspects of FAITH happen at a time when they are not at the church building to see or hear about them. Or their ignorance may be a result of selective listening: they perceive FAITH to be just another witness-training or outreach program. *[handwritten: what is the difference?]*

New Learners are not _____enlisted_____.
Every army needs new recruits to be prepared for battle. The same is true in the FAITH ministry. If new recruits are not enlisted, FAITH participation will be limited to the small number of people who normally come for any kind of outreach ministry.

Step 3 (5 mins.)

Direct participants to turn to page 143 in their Journals and to fill in the blanks as you present the material in "Recognize Hindrances to Multiplication." Use the computer presentation or overhead cel 45.

> Recognize Hindrances to Multiplication

Session 9: Multiplying Your Team / 143

Team Leaders do not ____return____.
As FAITH cannot grow without new Team Learners, it likewise cannot grow if Team Leaders do not return. If parents stop reproducing, there are no future generations. If Team Leaders do not return, Team Learners cannot be trained, and the FAITH ministry will not multiply.

The FAITH leadership is ____inconsistent____.
In any size church the FAITH strategy requires the cooperation of a number of people who carry out their responsibilities. Because people are different, their leadership styles are also likely to be different. While the leadership of the pastor may be exemplary, for example, a FAITH group Facilitator may lack enthusiasm or ability. Inconsistency among leaders tends to breed frustration and discontent among participants and may cause some to stop participating.

Learners are not adequately ____trained____ *to lead Teams.*
Most Learners are primarily focused on learning an outline and are not thinking about leading a Team someday. They may not realize that becoming a leader is one goal of FAITH training. Many people find themselves leading a Team because they were asked, but they did not receive adequate training to lead. If this dysfunction is never confronted, it continually causes problems.

Address the Problems

Have you ever been driving down the highway and suddenly heard your car make a strange noise? What did you do? Some people who hear such a noise pull over to the side of the road, open the hood, and look around in the engine compartment. Others may listen closely for a few more minutes. Then, if they don't hear it again, they assume that it was nothing. A few people might try to ignore the sound and keep driving.

When there is a known or suspected problem with a vehicle or with anything else, we would do well to address the problem so that it doesn't get worse. Especially with the FAITH strategy, ignoring a problem can greatly undermine its success in a church. Although many churches have experienced plateaus in their FAITH ministries, they have also discovered ways to address the causes and move on to a new period of growth. Here are some ways to address the problems that hinder multiplication.

Adjust the ____schedule____.
Your church may find that making schedule changes will increase participation, especially for new Learners. New Learners represent opportunities to develop new leaders who can start new Teams in the future. Some

---

Step 4 (5 mins.)

Ask participants to turn to "Address the Problems" on page 144 in their Journals and to fill in the blanks as you present the material. Use the computer presentation or overhead cel 46.

Address the Problems

churches have added additional meeting times, such as a morning FAITH session, while others have moved to a different day of the week, such as Sunday afternoon or evening instead of a weeknight. As a Team Leader, you may know persons who could participate if the schedule were different. If so, talk with your pastor or your FAITH Director about the way such changes might benefit your church.

Share personal __testimonies__.
Your church may need to increase its efforts to spread the word about FAITH throughout your church membership. While this can happen through conventional promotional efforts, the best information and motivation will come through those who are already involved. As a Team Leader, regularly share your FAITH testimony with others and make sure Team members talk about FAITH in their Sunday School classes. When asked by your church's worship leaders, share your own testimony or enlist participants to share benefits of FAITH in a worship-service setting.

Emphasize __reenlistment__ *and* __recruitment__.
Several times each semester the FAITH ministry should emphasize reenlistment, especially with current Learners. As a Team Leader, remind your Learners that a multiplying strategy requires not only new recruits to be Learners but also returning Learners to become leaders.

Nothing replaces the need for personal enlistment. Just as the vast majority of people attend church because a friend asked them to attend, the vast majority of FAITH participants become involved because friends asked them to participate. The most effective way to multiply your FAITH ministry is personal enlistment.

Challenge your Learners to begin praying now about becoming Team Leaders next semester and for God to show them someone in their Sunday School classes they could enlist to join them on FAITH Teams.

Encourage __quality__ *along with quantity.*
The number of people involved in your FAITH ministry is important. The more who are involved, the more visits that can be made. The more visits that are made, the more times the gospel is presented. Be careful, however, not to sacrifice the quality of your FAITH ministry as you focus on multiplication. Quality produces quantity. People are drawn to a ministry that is organized and led with a commitment to excellence. As a Team Leader, don't ever settle for mediocrity in your ministry, because you are involved in God's kingdom work!

Utilize FAITH __events__.
Your FAITH leadership can utilize two key events to multiply your FAITH ministry. A FAITH Kickoff Banquet is important not only

for enlistment but also for educating the church about the FAITH ministry and how it complements the church's vision. Your church members should get excited to hear testimonies about changed lives, inspirational music, and a challenging message about the need for all believers to be involved in witnessing to others.

In addition, an All on the Altar Sunday, scheduled just before a new semester of FAITH, challenges church members to give their all for Jesus Christ. The Sunday-morning worship service includes testimonies, music, and a message focused on every believer's responsibility to share the gospel. Two invitations are given after the sermon. The first is for people who want to enlist in the FAITH ministry to bring a FAITH Commitment Card to the altar. The second invitation offers people the opportunity to commit their lives to Christ or make other commitments.

Remember to ___pray___.
Jesus said, " 'The harvest is abundant, but the workers are few. Therefore, pray to the Lord of the harvest to send out workers into His harvest' " (Matt. 9:37). We must pray for more laborers in God's harvest field, because only a small number of believers are actually sharing their faith. The task is great, but we are involved in God's work, not just in sharing our faith but also in leading others to do the same. Don't underestimate the power that prayer can have in multiplying the FAITH Teams in your church.

Prepare Your Team to Multiply

When a couple learns that the wife is pregnant with their first child, they start getting ready for the baby. They tell their family and friends, discuss potential names, buy furniture, and prepare the room. No couple would wait until the baby arrives to make any needed changes. Rather, they make preparations from the time they learn about the pregnancy until the baby is born.

As a Team Leader, you can [need to!] do certain things to prepare your Team to multiply—not just before the next semester starts but during the course of the current semester. Because Learners are busy learning and sharing the FAITH outline, you do not need to tell them you are intentionally preparing them to become leaders. By taking steps like the following, you can give Learners the practice and confidence they need to be prepared to lead Teams so that multiplication can continue.

Offer constructive ___evaluation___.
Proverbs 27:5 states, "Better is open rebuke than hidden love." An effective Team Leader is not afraid to be honest when evaluating Team members. Because most Learners know they need help but are too afraid or too

---

Step 5 (10 mins.)

Direct participants to turn to page 146 in their Journals and to fill in the blanks as you summarize "Prepare Your Team to Multiply." Use the computer presentation or overhead cel 47.

> Prepare Your Team to Multiply

proud to ask for it, they will quickly and openly respond to your suggestions. They already have the expectation that you will help them become adequately trained soul-winners through FAITH. This cannot happen unless you give appropriate and careful constructive evaluation.

Provide increasing __ownership__.

Delegation is a difficult task for many leaders. An on-fire soul-winner may be so eager to lead people to Christ that he fails to remember his responsibility to train Team Learners. Satan may even tempt FAITH Team Leaders not to delegate because they want others to know that they led another person to Christ. Such pride is a sin that does not honor God. In addition, such leaders must remember that although they may plant and water a seed, God gives the growth (see 1 Cor. 3:6).

As a Team Leader, continually remind yourself that your job is to train others, who can train others. They will not be adequately trained unless you delegate responsibilities each week, starting small at first and increasing throughout the semester.

Confront Learners' __apprehensions__.

Many Learners have a natural fear of knocking on a complete stranger's door in a survey setting. Many Team Leaders and Learners have found, however, that using the Opinion Poll is the quickest way to gain competency in sharing the outline in a real setting (even if it's only a portion) and to become experienced in using the Opinion Poll. Lead your Team to begin using the Opinion Poll early in the semester. If you wait until the end of the semester, you will discover that future leaders will be inadequately prepared and fearful of using the Opinion Poll.

Schedule prearranged __visits__.

One way to ensure that Learners begin hearing the outline early in the semester is to occasionally prearrange a visit to a church member who allows them to present the outline. A friendly and familiar environment helps ease the tension when a new Learner is sharing the FAITH outline for the first time. Many FAITH Teams have seen God do amazing and unexpected things on such visits. (See the FAITH at Work testimony on p. 154 for an example.) Conduct this type of visit only rarely, however, so that your focus remains on prospects who need to hear the gospel.

Use some visits for __enlistment__.

While on ministry visits, you may be able to help multiply your Team by discussing with fellow Sunday School class members the value of participating in FAITH. Of course, the ministry need may preclude an enlistment discussion. You will find that persons who have been absent for short periods of time, rather than chronic absentees, are more open to a discussion of FAITH participation.

Nurture __Assistant__ *Team Leaders.*
Some Teams have Assistant Team Leaders who have completed FAITH Basic but are not ready to lead a Team. A Team Leader has a great opportunity to multiply the ministry of FAITH by reproducing himself or herself in this potential leader. The key lies in delegating total responsibility of leading the Team as soon as possible. The Assistant Team Leader will more than likely know the outline at the beginning of the semester. He or she may simply need confidence and direction in leading a Team once inside a home. As a Team Leader, you should model by example during the first few weeks, then delegate leadership responsibility soon thereafter. The Assistant should be completely leading the Team by week 6 or 7. Your role will then be to encourage and make needed suggestions for the remainder of the semester. Also remember to communicate to the Assistant Team Leader the importance of preparing Learners to be leaders.

Look to Your Group Leader for Guidance

Step 6 (5 mins.)

Direct participants to turn to "Look to Your Group Leader for Guidance" on page 148 in their Journals and to fill in the blanks as you present the material. Use the computer presentation or overhead cel 48.

> Look to Your Group Leader for Guidance

In businesses managers supervise the work of the other employees. These managers work under the supervision of directors, who often work under the supervision of vice-presidents. Usually, directors have been managers and can help the managers appropriately guide their people. When the manager has a problem, he or she looks to the director for help.

Similarly, the FAITH strategy employs different levels of leadership. If your church has more than a few FAITH Teams, you probably have (or should have) Group Leaders who oversee several FAITH Teams in addition to leading Teams. To cultivate a multiplying ministry, a FAITH Team Leader needs several types of support from the Group Leader.

Group Leaders offer __accountability__.
One of the Group Leader's responsibilities is to manage several other FAITH Teams and hold the leaders of those Teams accountable. He or she does that by checking each Team's FAITH Participation Cards each week. A Group Leader can learn whether a Learner is participating in the weekly visit and can notice a pattern of little or no participation even though a Learner is attending each week. If this is the case, the Group Leader should discuss this issue with the Team Leader and help the Team Leader know how to involve the Learner. When Team Leaders know that a Group Leader will hold them accountable, they will be more committed to keeping Learners involved and developing them to be future FAITH leaders.

Group Leaders offer _____**wisdom**_____.
A Group Leader is a valuable resource for every Team Leader. Often the Group Leader is a more experienced leader who can help identify and troubleshoot most problems that arise. The Group Leader may also be needed to help a Team Leader who has a Learner who is not willing to learn the material or participate in weekly visits.

Group Leaders offer _____**encouragement**_____.
Group Leaders encourage Team Leaders and Learners not only through their enthusiasm for winning souls but also through personal words of praise. A Group Leader's encouragement makes a difference, especially to first-timers and those who are frustrated, overwhelmed, or discouraged.

Group Leaders offer _____**consistency**_____.
While some FAITH leaders have a firm grasp of the FAITH strategy and are effective in their leadership, others may not be at the same level of understanding or effectiveness. Throughout the FAITH ministry a common vision and strategy must be implemented, beginning with the pastor and followed by the FAITH Director, Group Leaders, Team Leaders, and other participants. Group Leaders can help all their Team Leaders be consistent in their leadership so that Learners have a high-quality experience regardless of their leader. This is why a weekly Group Leaders' meeting is vital for consistency and multiplication in the FAITH ministry.

Some Team members you are mentoring may be potential Group Leaders. Your involvement in their lives helps develop them as leaders.

Carefully Pass the Baton

At the start of a relay race, one runner holds a metal cylinder when the starting gun fires, and the runner takes off around the track. At a certain point the runner approaches a teammate, who starts running and anticipates the handoff when the first runner passes the baton to him. After the handoff the first runner drops out of the race, and the second runner runs around the track anticipating the handoff to the third runner. This process continues until the fourth runner finishes the race. Often relay races are won or lost depending on how well the handoff is made, regardless of how fast the individual runners are.

The FAITH ministry is similar in some ways to a relay race, but it also has some differences. As a Team Leader, you are like a runner who leaves the starting block with the baton—the leadership of the FAITH Team. At a certain point, however, you will pass that baton to another person, who will race with it and eventually hand it off to someone else.

Step 7 (5 mins.)

Ask participants to turn to page 149 in their Journals. Summarize "Carefully Pass the Baton," using the computer presentation.

[Handwritten note: Once you pass it off - it is time to pick it up again and start all over. "ON GOING!"]

STUDY IT

Step 8 (5 mins.)

Overview the Home Study Assignments for session 9.

Transition to assemble with FAITH Teams to prepare for home visits. (5 mins.)

DO IT (110 MINS.)

SHARE IT (30 MINS.)

As in the relay race, your <u>efforts will be slowed down if the handoff is not made properly</u>. Unlike the relay runner, however, you will continue to run the race and hand off the baton to yet another person, who will do the same with someone else, and so on until the end of the race—the day when each of us running in the race receives from the righteous Judge "the crown of righteousness" (2 Tim. 4:8).

Visitation Time

DO IT

1. As you drive to your visit, discuss ways you are learning to reach out to persons you meet in everyday life. Suggest ways your Team's Sunday School class can begin to reach new persons for Christ.
2. In this session your Team Learners studied turning from the world to Christ. Discuss reasons people have difficulty doing this. Emphasize the need to consider the way a Christian witness is perceived by non-Christians.
3. As the Team returns to the church from its visits, the Team Leader should guide in an evaluation of what happened and what follow-through should be made by the Team and/or class/department. Discuss how the report should be presented during Celebration Time; be careful not to tell personal or sensitive details that surfaced during visits.
4. At the Team Leader's cue, Learners should be able to share IMPOSSIBLE.

Celebration Time

SHARE IT

1. Highlight the results of ministry visits as you debrief with your Team. Indicate the different types of Sunday School ministry visits and why certain topics were discussed in the different types of visits. What would Team members suggest as actions for follow-up?
2. Hear reports and testimonies.
3. Complete Evaluation Cards.
4. Complete Participation Cards.
5. Update visitation forms with the results of visits.

---

[1]John Maxwell, *Developing the Leaders Around You* (Nashville: Thomas Nelson Publishers, 1995), 11.

Home Study Assignments

Day 1: Your Relationship with God

Read Romans 12:1-2. Place an X on the continuum to indicate the extent to which God and the world influence your life.

God ━━━━━━━━━━━┼━━━━━━━━━━━▶ **World**

Name areas of your life in which you find yourself conforming to the world.

_____

_____

What do you need to do to renew your mind? _____

_____

Spend time in prayer, asking God to transform you by the renewing of your mind.

Day 2: Your Relationship with Your FAITH Team

Review "Prepare Your Team to Multiply" on pages 146–48 in this session. Then evaluate how well you are preparing your Team Learners for future Team leadership.

	Doing Well	Need Work
Offering constructive evaluation	❏	❏
Providing increasing ownership	❏	❏
Confronting Learners' apprehensions	❏	❏
Scheduling prearranged visits	❏	❏
Using some visits for enlistment	❏	❏
Nurturing Assistant Team Leaders	❏	❏

What are some things you need to start doing to help your Team multiply?

_____

_____

Pray and recommit to producing quality leaders. Contact your accountability partner and ask him or her to pray for you to carry out your commitment.

Day 3: Your Relationship with Your Sunday School Class

Evaluate the quality of your Sunday School class in the following areas.
1 = poor; 5 = excellent.

Greeting and nurturing guests	1 2 3 4 5
Arrangement and decor of your classroom	1 2 3 4 5
Follow-up with guests and absentees	1 2 3 4 5
Class fellowships (schedule, activities, prospects present)	1 2 3 4 5
Increasing enrollment	1 2 3 4 5
Increasing attendance	1 2 3 4 5

How can your FAITH Team enhance the quality of guests' Sunday School experience?

_____

_____

Day 4: Your Relationship with the Lost

Read Matthew 9:9-13. Jesus spent time with people the religious community excluded. Name some people you spend time with who may feel excluded by many Christians or churches.

_____

_____

Check ways you could connect with these and others like them.
- ❏ Party
- ❏ Sports league
- ❏ Hobby
- ❏ Parent-teacher group
- ❏ Civic club
- ❏ Internet chat room
- ❏ Neighborhood group
- ❏ Other: _____

Choose one of the ways you checked and ask God to show you how you can use it to connect with someone who has no relationship with Christ. Then try it this week!

Day 5: Your Relationship with Your Family and Your Church

List all of the ministries and other activities in which you are involved in your church.

_____

_____

_____

_____

Go back and circle those in which you have a leadership responsibility.

Evaluate the quality of your involvement and leadership in these ministries by answering the following questions.
Are you involved in too many things? ❑ Yes ❑ No
Are you overcommitted in leadership? ❑ Yes ❑ No
Is a ministry suffering because of your overcommitment? ❑ Yes ❑ No
Is your family suffering because of your overcommitment? ❑ Yes ❑ No

What changes do you need to make to enhance the quality of your ministry in your church and in your home?

_____

_____

_____

_____

_____

FAITH AT WORK

Many people might feel that a practice session of FAITH is a waste of time when there are real lost people in the world, but this testimony may change some minds.

The day had been full of activity in preparation for my husband's birthday dinner that evening. I was so tired that when it was time for dinner, I couldn't wait for everyone to leave so that I could collapse into bed. We had an enjoyable birthday dinner, our extended family members had just left, and we were cleaning up when the phone rang. It was our pastor, who shared that his FAITH Learners needed to practice the FAITH outline, but they had not found anyone at home that night. Because our house is close to the church building, he wanted to know if they could stop by to practice. My first thought was about the house—it was a wreck with dirty dishes and wrapping paper—but how do you refuse someone who is practicing to tell others about Jesus? So I said yes, that it would resemble a real visit because it was unexpected and the Team had never practiced in our home.

When the Team arrived, we went through a mock FAITH visit and were about to conclude when a car pulled into my driveway. It was my brother, who had been scheduled to work and therefore had not been able to come to dinner. But he had not had to work after all and had decided to drop by. I quickly told the Team that my brother desperately needed the Lord and that if they stayed, they would have a real opportunity to share the FAITH outline.

When my brother came in, we explained to him what the Team was doing at our house and asked if he would allow them to share with him. He agreed and listened to the FAITH presentation. To my surprise, at the end my brother prayed to receive Jesus as his Savior and Lord. I couldn't believe it. My brother's heart had been very hardened toward the Lord. This was truly a miracle!

I had my doubts that night about my brother's sincerity, but seeing how God has changed my brother's life during the past two years has shown me that if we have faith as small as a mustard seed, God will move mountains. God is doing that very thing in my brother's life. The mountains haven't been moved all at once as I would like, but in God's perfect timing they are moving one stone at a time, and our family has been changed forever.

Our God is an awesome God!

Lisa Lucas
Colonial Heights Baptist Church
Jackson, Mississippi

SESSION 10
Multiplying New Sunday School Units

In this session you will—

CHECK IT by engaging in Team Time activities;

KNOW IT by reviewing content from session 9;

HEAR IT by learning ways to multiply Sunday School units in your church;

STUDY IT by overviewing Home Study Assignments;

DO IT by leading your Team in making visits;

SHARE IT by celebrating.

IN ADVANCE
- Overview content.
- Preview teaching suggestions. Prepare key points. Decide whether to use the session 10 computer presentation or overhead cels 49–55 (see pp. 319–25).
- Prepare the room for teaching.
- Pray for participants and for Teams as they prepare to visit.
- As Teaching Time begins, direct participants to open their Journals to page 158.

Session 10: Multiplying New Sunday School Units / 155

TEAM TIME

CHECK IT (15 MINS.)

If the computer presentation is used, display the agenda for Team Time. Add other points to the agenda as needed.

CHECK IT agenda:
✔ FAITH Visit Outline
✔ Other Home Study Assignments
✔ Session 9 Debriefing
✔ Help for Strengthening a Visit

Leading Team Time

All Team members participate in Team Time. They are primarily responsible for reciting the assigned portion of the FAITH Visit Outline and for discussing other Home Study Assignments.

As you direct this important time of CHECK IT activities with your Team, keep in mind that Learners look to you as a role model, motivator, mentor, and friend. Team Time activities can continue in the car as the Team travels to and from visits.

Lead CHECK IT Activities

✔ FAITH Visit Outline
❏ Listen while each Learner recites all of the *Preparation* and *Presentation* content and key words for *Invitation*.
❏ Give opportunities for Learners to practice reciting the portions of the FAITH Visit Outline they have learned to this point.

✔ Other Home Study Assignments
❏ This may be a good time to discuss the benefits of keeping a weekly journal as part of FAITH training. Discuss some of the truths or understandings gained through the weekly Bible studies. Dialogue about how the reflective questions have influenced Learners' training experience.

✔ Session 9 Debriefing
❏ *T* is for TURN. This is the point in the gospel presentation when a person makes a significant choice—whether to receive salvation. To be forgiven, a person must turn from his sin and turn to Christ. He must trust Christ and Christ only. The imagery of turning is reinforced with the simple question, If you were driving down the road and someone asked you to turn, what would he or she be asking you to do? (*Change direction*) Most people can easily understand the idea of changing from one direction to another. The Bible uses the word *repent* to depict the same thing. The Bible is clear about the need for a person to repent of sin and to live for Christ (change direction) by committing to and trusting Him. Team members will need to remember the significance of the concepts behind the letter *T* to help explain and emphasize the how of the gospel.

✔ Help for Strengthening a Visit
❏ The illustration of changing directions in a car is the only dialogue that is planned as part of the actual gospel presentation. It is important to ask the person to share his or her answer to the question.

The response is predictable, but by asking the question, you call the person's attention to the gospel and increase his or her participation in the discussion. You might be talking with a child, a younger youth, or someone who obviously does not drive. If so, adapt the question to something like "If you were riding down the road and you asked the driver to turn, what would you be asking the driver to do?" Usually, it will be significant to use the word *repent* only after the question has helped you explain what the word means. Using the turning analogy to emphasize faith in Christ also helps clarify the meaning of *repent*. For many unsaved or unchurched people, *repent* is associated with religious or churchy terms; without a relevant, contemporary explanation, this word might lose much of its significance.

❑ Remind Team members to listen during each visit for ministry opportunities, as well as for things a person might say to help you identify with his or her spiritual journey.

❑ Discuss how, as a Team Leader, you communicate follow-up information to the appropriate age group/class/department when you encounter family members of different ages in a home visit.

Notes

_____
_____
_____
_____
_____

Actions I Need to Take with Team Members This Week

_____
_____
_____
_____
_____

Transition to classrooms for instruction on the content of the session. (5 mins.)

TEACHING TIME

KNOW IT

Step 1 (5 mins.)

Direct participants to turn to "A Quick Review" on page 158 in their Journals and to follow the instructions to complete the activities. Use the computer presentation or overhead cel 49 to review the answers:

1. a. evaluation, b. ownership,
   c. apprehensions, d. visits,
   e. enlistment, f. Assistant
2. c, e, f, h

Be careful not to exceed the five-minute time limit.

[A Quick Review]

HEAR IT

Step 2 (5 mins.)

Present "Answering Questions," using the computer presentation. State that this session will answer the following questions about multiplying new Sunday School units: What? Why? When? How? Where?

A Quick Review

In session 9 you learned ways to multiply FAITH Teams. Completing the following activities will help you review what you learned.

1. A Team Leader can take certain actions to equip a FAITH Team to multiply. Fill in the blanks below to identify these actions.
   a. Offer constructive _evaluation_.
   b. Provide increasing _ownership_.
   c. Confront Learners' _apprehensions_.
   d. Schedule prearranged _visits_.
   e. Use some visits for _enlistment_.
   f. Nurture _Assistant_ Team Leaders.

2. Check the actions a Group Leader can take to support FAITH Team Leaders.
   ❏ a. Chew out lazy Learners.
   ❏ b. Take visits the Team Leader doesn't want.
   ☑ c. Hold Team Leaders accountable.
   ❏ d. Publicly humiliate Team Leaders who are ineffective.
   ☑ e. Offer wisdom to help address problems on a Team.
   ☑ f. Provide encouragement.
   ❏ g. Take all the Teams out to dinner. — Mary!
   ☑ h. Help all Team Leaders be consistent.

> **LEADERS ON LEADERSHIP**
> "There is no limit to what God can do through one church if they are willing to follow Christ and fulfill the purposes of God in extending the kingdom."—Henry Blackaby and Melvin Blackaby[1]

Answering Questions

When was the last time a three-year-old asked you a question? Why do kids ask so many questions? Because they are learning! God placed in them a desire to learn and grow and discover their world. Sometimes you have to answer their questions honestly with "I don't know." Yet other times you delight in helping them learn what you've already discovered.

Questions are also important ways adults learn. A discussion of multiplying new Sunday School units is likely to produce a number of questions. In this session we will answer questions to discover ways to multiply Sunday School units.

158 / Growing as a FAITH Leader Facilitator Guide

What?

Question: What do we mean by new Sunday School units?
Answer: New units can fall into the following three categories.

Traditional Sunday School ____classes____
These are new classes that develop within the context of a church's traditional Sunday School structure, perhaps like the class you are involved in now. You likely meet in a classroom on Sunday morning at the church campus at the same time as most or all of the other Sunday School classes. These classes usually precede or follow a corporate worship service.

Nontraditional Bible-study ____groups____
These groups don't reflect the traditional Sunday School class in terms of location or target group. Instead, they may meet in a home during the week and may not refer to themselves as Sunday School classes. Or they may consist of a narrow group of people, such as those who work in the same office building and meet before work or those who meet for Bible study after a workout at the gym. Regardless of their meeting place or the persons targeted, these groups should reflect the strategy of their Sunday School siblings in that they exist for the same purpose. (Review session 2 for the definition of *Sunday School* and a discussion of its purpose.)

New ____churches____
These include churches that start either as a Bible-study group or as a worship service but eventually include both small groups (whether traditional Sunday School or otherwise) and corporate worship.

Regardless of the structure or focus of your current class or church, you as a FAITH Team Leader can help multiply any or all of these new units. Later in this session you will discover how you can get involved.

Why?

Question: Why should we start new Sunday School units?
Answer: Because the church is a body, and it must function like a body.

For a more extensive answer it is helpful to think about an analogy Paul used to refer to the church—that of the body (see Rom. 12:4-5; 1 Cor. 12:12-27; Eph. 5:29-30). It's not much of a stretch for Christians to think about the different members of the church as different parts of the body. But because the church is the living, breathing body of Christ, we should expect it to have certain other characteristics of a human body, as well. Primary among those characteristics is the cell structure. A human

---

Step 3 (5 mins.)

Direct participants to turn to page 159 in their Journals and to fill in the blanks as you present the material in "What?" Use the computer presentation or overhead cel 50 to help participants understand the variety of units that can be multiplied.

Step 4 (10 mins.)

Direct participants to fill in the blanks in "Why?" in their Journals as you present the material. Use the computer presentation or overhead cel 51.

Session 10: Multiplying New Sunday School Units / 159

body consists of many cells, which naturally create other cells. In the same way, the cells in a church—the small groups—should naturally be creating other cells. The desired result of reproduction is the same in the church—multiplying believers to keep the body healthy and growing.

When Sunday School classes do not reproduce, we have reason for concern. Maybe the class is too small and thus is not ready to reproduce. More often, however, the problem is that the class has a maintenance focus rather than a multiplication focus. With a maintenance focus the class spends the majority (if not all) of its time looking inward, attending to class members' needs and wants.

Because you are a FAITH Team Leader, you are instrumental in helping your class and your church catch the vision of starting new Sunday School units as a natural function of the body. Your class should be involved in multiplying new units for several reasons.

New units create **excitement**.

People like new things, such as cars and TVs, and get excited about them. The excitement is even greater about a new baby; the family gets excited, and so do friends. And when a multiple birth occurs, like the McCaughey septuplets born in Iowa in 1997, the excitement extends even to strangers. New Sunday School units create excitement for the entire church as people are won to Christ and become involved in Bible study.

New units are generally more **aggressive** in evangelism and ministry.

This is particularly true if the units are started by persons involved in the FAITH strategy. If only a few leaders are in the new unit, they will likely be more hungry for new people to get involved and will be more intentional about caring for those who are part of the group—both members and prospects. In contrast, when a class already has a lot of people on its membership roll and prospect list, it's like your body after Thanksgiving dinner—you're full, you're not interested in anything else, and you want just a comfortable place to relax.

New units make it easier to develop **relationships**.

Many new people who are invited to established classes often find it difficult to fit into units where people already know and love one another. Because new units have not developed these established relationships, it's easier for newcomers to get in on the ground floor of building the fellowship.

New units provide more opportunities for **service**.

In many established Sunday School classes some members feel that they are not needed, because other people are doing the things they were gifted and called to do. Because they are not serving as God designed them,

[Handwritten notes in margin:]
- *If we spend all of our time looking to the inside we are going to miss what is on the outside.*
- *New Units will always grow faster then (old) ones { Excitement is key! }*

they are not experiencing the fulfillment that comes from serving the Lord. In contrast, new units provide many opportunities for newcomers, as well as for members who are not currently serving, to minister as God desires.

New units generally ___grow___ more quickly.
Just as a human body rapidly grows in the first few years of life and later slows down, so does a new Sunday School unit. It's important not only to know about the principles and process of multiplication but also to be aware of the potential of multiplication. John McClendon gives this example. Imagine that your class averages about 12 persons on Sunday and has an enrollment of 24 members and 24 prospects. You presently have a secretary, an outreach-evangelism leader, and 4 ministry leaders. Let's say that your class stays together for 10 years and grows to an average attendance of 30, with 60 enrolled and 60 prospects, and you have a secretary, an outreach-evangelism leader, and 10 ministry leaders. Today this might be perceived as a very successful class.

But imagine that your class commits to start one new unit every two years during that 10-year period. You must train a teacher for each new class. That's five new classes started directly from your class in 10 years. If each new teacher trained another new teacher and started a new class every 2 years, your class would have helped start as many as 16 new units in 10 years!

Let's say that each class averages 12 persons, has 24 members and 24 prospects at the end of 10 years, and has a teacher, an apprentice (teacher in training), an outreach-evangelism coordinator, and 3 ministry coordinators. The numbers are staggering. More than 350 would attend 16 classes. The result from one class would be 744 members, 744 prospects, and 217 leaders who made a commitment to grow by multiplying. Even if you were only 50 percent successful, what could God do through one class whose leaders and members were willing to make this commitment? Imagine the results if all adult classes in our more than 40,000 Southern Baptist churches made the same commitment! What an impact on kingdom work![2]

When?

Question: When should we start new Sunday School units?
Answer: When one or more of the following are true.
1. A wide __age__ __range__ exists in the class—10 or more years.
2. The class enrollment is between 25 and 40.
3. The meeting place is full of people.
4. __Ministry__ __needs__ are neglected.
5. Many new adults in the community are in the same age group.

Emphasize the potential that comes with multiplication, as presented in the example by John McClendon.

Step 5 (5 mins.)

Direct participants to turn to page 161 in their Journals and to fill in the blanks as you present the material in "When?" Use the computer presentation or overhead cels 52–53. Emphasize that these factors are not equal in weight; yet all indicate that it may be time to start a new class. Remind participants that the time to begin planning for a new class is before the listed factors develop.

When?

6. New church members are being enrolled in other classes.
7. Many active class members have no __**responsibility**__ in the class.
8. The number of prospects is greater than the number of members.
9. Attendance is less than __**40**__ percent of enrollment.
10. Too many attend for members to get to know one another.
11. Active members are not missed when they are absent.
12. Class leaders can't __**recall**__ who attended the previous week.

Although the items on the list are not of equal weight (for instance, neglected ministry needs are far more serious than new church members being enrolled in other classes), all of these factors must be evaluated when considering whether it is time to start a new unit. Often classes wait until one or more of these concerns arise, then start wondering what to do. By that time their proposed solutions often include finding a larger space or dropping a lot of inactive members from the roll.

Instead of being reactive, your class should be proactive in considering when to start new units. The time to start planning a new unit is when you detect even one of the previous symptoms.

As a FAITH Team Leader, help other class leaders (and perhaps especially the teacher) understand that multiplication is healthy and beneficial. Ways to do this include—
- mentioning this as a prayer concern during class;
- talking about the possibility during leadership meetings;
- emphasizing the need with members of your FAITH Team;
- sharing the concern with your pastor or other church staff.

Often, if God has shown you the need for and the potential of starting new units, He has also placed in others the same concerns, and they may be waiting for someone to bring up the subject.

How?

Step 6 (5 mins.)

Direct participants to page 162 in their Journals and ask them to fill in the blanks as you summarize "How?" Use the computer presentation or overhead cels 54–55. Point out that the FAITH Tips at the ends of sessions 3 and 10 provide additional information on starting new units.

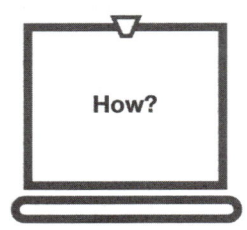

Question: How do we start a new Sunday School unit?
Answer: Follow a proven strategy like this one (always working through your pastor and minister of education or Sunday School director).
1. Share the multiplication __**vision**__ with class members and leaders.
2. Talk further with church staff and other leaders about plans.
3. Recast the vision on a regular basis but in different ways.
4. Seek "missionaries" who will help start a new unit.
5. Allow the missionaries to be __**apprentices**__ for current leadership positions.
6. Identify the birthday for the new unit.
7. Regularly meet with new class leaders for __**prayer**__ and __**coordination**__.

162 / Growing as a FAITH Leader Facilitator Guide

8. Seek prospects through Opinion Polls, inactive lists from other classes, and other sources.
9. Plan a _____**fellowship**_____ before the new unit begins, inviting all prospects.
10. Visit prospects.
11. Conduct the first meeting of the new unit.
12. Hold regular _____**leadership**_____ _____**meetings**_____ to evaluate, update, and plan.
13. Keep in touch with the sponsor (the class or group that helped start the new unit).
14. Continually pray for God's _____**leadership**_____.

Once established, a new unit must actively fulfill the purposes God has planned for it. In addition, the new unit should be conditioned from the start to have a multiplication mind-set so that multiplying new units becomes as natural as breathing. For additional ideas on how to multiply new units, see the FAITH Tip at the end of this session (p. 169) and at the end of session 3 (p. 59).

Where?

Question: Where can we start new Sunday School units?
Answer: Wherever a place is available!

For years committed people have started new units—Sunday School classes, Bible-study groups, and churches—in a variety of creative places. Of course, the most likely place to start may be an empty room on your church property. But without remodeling your current church facility or building additional ones, you can find a variety other places to meet that others have previously used.
- Converted rooms in the church building, such as storage rooms, staff offices, media libraries, choir rooms, and so on
- Portable buildings brought onto the church property (in compliance with zoning regulations)
- Off-site space, such as nearby members' homes, community rooms in members' apartment complexes, members' offices or workplaces (such as a doctor's office waiting room or a break room at a local factory), schools, health clubs, and others

Have you ever participated in a team challenge course? This exercise challenges teams to work together to bring about individual achievement and team advancement. Talk of multiplying new units is like a challenge course that frightens most church members. As a FAITH Team Leader, you must assume the role of the challenge-course instructor, guiding and encouraging these members, especially in your Sunday School class, to realize the need for multiplying new units and to help establish them.

Step 7 (5 mins.)

Present the material in "Where?" using the computer presentation.

Close by challenging participants to let God use them to multiply new units.

STUDY IT

Step 8 (5 mins.)

Overview the Home Study Assignments for session 10.

Transition to assemble with FAITH Teams to prepare for home visits. (5 mins.)

DO IT (110 MINS.)

To learn more about multiplying new Sunday School units, see the Adult Sunday School portion of the CD-ROM provided in *Essentials for Excellence: Connecting Sunday School to Life* (LifeWay Press, 2003).

Visitation Time

DO IT

1. Think about being an ambassador to the persons you visit. Your goal is to share God's message of reconciliation through Jesus Christ. Your enthusiastic attitude reflects your deep conviction about the truth you share. Make sure you fulfill your responsibility as an ambassador by speaking and acting in a way that honors Christ.
2. On the drive, discuss what it means to have heaven here and now.
3. All Team members should know the FAITH presentation through *H* is for HEAVEN. While visiting, invite Team members to support you throughout the presentation. Tell them that next week they will be expected to lead the gospel presentation.

Celebration Time

SHARE IT (30 MINS.)

SHARE IT

1. Ask a Team member to take the lead in sharing reports.
2. Hear reports and testimonies.
3. Complete Evaluation Cards.
4. Complete Participation Cards.
5. Update visitation forms with the results of visits.

---

[1] Henry T. Blackaby and Melvin D. Blackaby, *Experiencing God Together* (Nashville: Broadman & Holman Publishers, 2002), 242.
[2] Adapted from John McClendon, *Beyond the Walls: Multiply Your Adult Ministry* (Nashville: LifeWay Press, 2002), 13–14. Out of print.

Home Study Assignments

Day 1: Your Relationship with God

Read Isaiah 54:2-3. What concerns do you have about multiplying new Sunday School units? Be honest!

_____

_____

_____

How might God respond to your concerns? _____

_____

_____

Day 2: Your Relationship with Your FAITH Team

Record the names of your FAITH Team members and their leadership gifts or strengths. Then list ways they could be involved in multiplying a new Sunday School unit.

_____

_____

If your Team Learners asked why you would want to start a new Sunday School unit, which of the following statements would you use to answer their question?
- ❏ New units create excitement.
- ❏ New units are generally more aggressive in evangelism and ministry.
- ❏ New units make it easier to develop relationships.
- ❏ New units provide more opportunities for service.
- ❏ New units generally grow more quickly.

If Learners asked why they should be involved in starting new Sunday School units, how would you respond?

_____

Day 3: Your Relationship with Your Sunday School Class

Read the following list and check the statements that are true of your class.
- ❏ A wide age range exists in the class—10 or more years.
- ❏ The class enrollment is between 25 and 40.
- ❏ The meeting place is full of people.
- ❏ Ministry needs are neglected.
- ❏ Many new adults in the community are in the same age group.
- ❏ New church members are being enrolled in other classes.
- ❏ Many active class members have no responsibility in the class.
- ❏ The number of prospects is greater than the number of members.
- ❏ Attendance is less than 40 percent of enrollment.
- ❏ Too many attend for members to get to know one another.
- ❏ Active members are not missed when they are absent.
- ❏ Class leaders can't recall who attended the previous week.

Go back and circle the three issues you consider to be most serious. What will you do to share with your class the importance of these factors and steps that need to be taken?

___

Day 4: Your Relationship with the Lost

Read Isaiah 61:1-3. Think about persons in your community or city who have needs that are not being met, such as immigrants, migrant workers, and jobless people. Name that group. ___

How could a new Sunday School unit be used to meet the needs of this group of people, especially their spiritual needs?

___

Where could a new Bible-study group be started (away from the church building) that might attract these people?

___

Who has an interest in that group of people or something in common with them and could help start the new group?

___

Day 5: Your Relationship with Your Family and Your Church

Spend time praying with your family this week (or with concerned members of your church family) about the need to multiply new Sunday School units. Share with them your vision for expanding God's kingdom in this way and the possibilities that exist for doing so.

Check out the One in a Million tab at the North American Mission Board's Web site at *www.namb.net*. Make an appointment to talk with your pastor about ways your church can be involved in multiplying new units to impact one million people in the next few years. Write some preliminary ideas here.

_____

_____

_____

_____

_____

_____

_____

FAITH AT WORK

In 1992 my wife, Dawn, and I were asked to consider teaching a class for young married adults. We were very hesitant at first because we loved the Sunday School class we had joined only eight months earlier. Though we hated to leave so many new friends, we knew we had been called to serve others rather than merely enjoy the comforts of our class, and we accepted the opportunity.

Over the past 10 years Dawn and I have started five young-married Sunday School classes. Although we have had to sacrifice in many ways and have had to separate from close friends to form these new units, God has always blessed our classes and has provided us with many new friends and co-laborers each time we have followed His direction.

God has blessed our efforts because we have followed His pattern. Jesus trained His disciples not only to encourage and to have fellowship with one another but also to reach a lost and dying world. Although encouragement and fellowship are extremely important in Sunday School, a class can become inwardly focused. Class members can get so comfortable with friendships in their classes that they become complacent about forming new relationships with guests. I once heard someone compare visiting a Sunday School class full of established relationships to attending a family reunion of someone else's family. The guest doesn't feel like part of the group. Each time I hear people say how much they love their Sunday School class, I think about how I might feel as a guest in that class. The danger of forming such a close-knit group of friends in a Sunday School class is that newcomers often feel neither wanted nor needed.

The best way to ensure that a class does not become inwardly focused, complacent, and satisfied is to set a goal to reproduce the class within a reasonable period of time. A class grows fastest when its members feel the urgency of inviting others. It's hard to create this urgency when the class is full.

Over the years Dawn and I have accumulated a variety of ideas and strategies for multiplying Sunday School units, which are presented in the FAITH Tip that follows.

Kelon Hall
Mobberly Baptist Church
Longview, Texas

FAITH TIP

Ideas for Multiplying Sunday School Units

Following are specific steps to use in preparing for and beginning a new Sunday School class.

Articulate class goals.
Discuss plans to multiply your class. Begin with the goal of reproducing the class within 18 to 24 months.

Aggressively recruit leaders.
Involve as many people as possible in the current class's ministry. Ask members for their input. If they contribute ideas, give them positions of responsibility in the class. Training leaders is vital, so give members opportunities to discover and use their spiritual gifts.

Reproduce leaders.
As a class grows in size and before you begin a new class, double-staff or rotate class leaders so that enough people become familiar with the particular responsibilities of each leadership position. Ultimately, a new class will be started with a core leadership team. Having positions double-staffed will prevent vacancies when leaders depart for the new unit. It is equally important that the old class continue to thrive, so leave it with adequate leadership.

Send out experienced leaders.
The more experienced leaders should lead the new class, while the less experienced or new leaders lead the established class. Traditionally, church leaders have asked members who have never taught to begin teaching a fledgling class. This approach is like trying to navigate without a map or a compass. Although the established class will still present a challenge, the leaders will already have a pattern, and the learning curve will not be as steep.

Make a clean break.
If possible, do not locate the new class next door to the old class. Allow it to develop its own identity. People tend to move when they feel a void. If they continue to cling to the relationships in the old class, they will not be nearly as motivated to invite people to the new class and to form new relationships. If the church has multiple Sunday School hours, consider changing to a different time, at least for the first six months.

Allow time for new classes to grow.
Other church leaders can support those who agree to start a new class by not enlisting the leaders of the new class to work in other areas of the church, such as child care, for a period of time. The main attraction of a new class is its people. When guests come, they need to meet the class leaders, and they need to be greeted and made to feel welcome.

The following ideas can help you grow a new Sunday School class.

Be organized.
Maintain a class organization chart, recognize class leaders, and encourage accountability.

Create the right image.
Publish a newsletter even if you don't have much to report or even if it is not weekly. The newsletter could include just a map to your classroom, a list of class leaders, and a calendar of upcoming events.

Create the right atmosphere.
Don't ever have a humdrum class meeting. Play music, stand up until class begins, have mixers, and so forth.

Plan a social each month.
Always having an upcoming event to announce creates a good impression on members and visitors.

Kelon Hall
Mobberly Baptist Church
Longview, Texas

SESSION 11
The Process of Multiplication

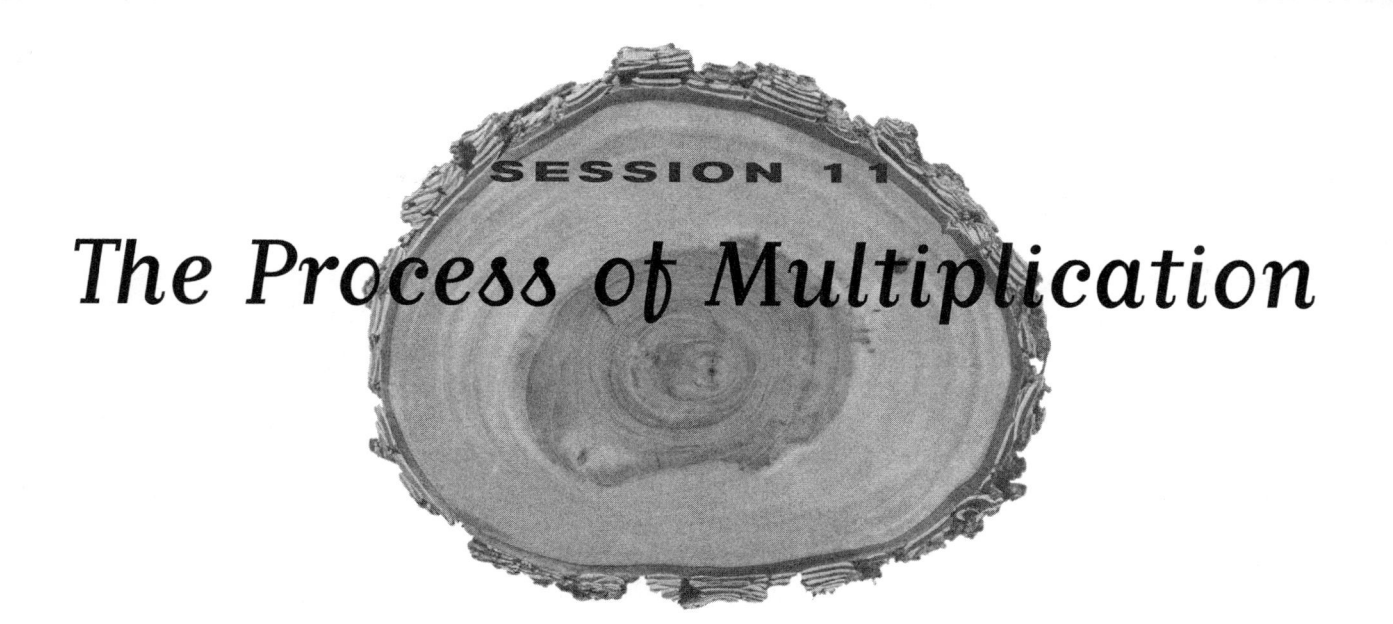

In this session you will—

CHECK IT by engaging in Team Time activities;

KNOW IT by reviewing content from session 10;

HEAR IT by learning a biblical process for multiplication;

SAY IT by practicing the *Invitation* portion of the FAITH Visit Outline;

STUDY IT by overviewing Home Study Assignments;

DO IT by leading your Team in making visits;

SHARE IT by celebrating.

IN ADVANCE
- Overview content.
- Preview teaching suggestions. Prepare key points. Decide whether to use the session 11 computer presentation or overhead cels 56–60 (see pp. 326–30).
- Prepare the room for teaching.
- Pray for participants and for Teams as they prepare to visit.
- As Teaching Time begins, direct participants to open their Journals to page 174.

TEAM TIME

CHECK IT (15 MINS.)

If the computer presentation is used, display the agenda for Team Time. Add other points to the agenda as needed.

CHECK IT agenda:
- ✔ FAITH Visit Outline
- ✔ Session 10 Debriefing
- ✔ Help for Strengthening a Visit

Leading Team Time

All Team members participate in Team Time. They are primarily responsible for reciting the assigned portion of the FAITH Visit Outline and for discussing other Home Study Assignments.

As you direct this important time of CHECK IT activities with your Team, keep in mind that Learners look to you as a role model, motivator, mentor, and friend. Team Time activities can continue in the car as the Team travels to and from visits.

Lead CHECK IT Activities

✔ *FAITH Visit Outline*
- ❏ Listen while each Learner recites the FAITH Visit Outline beginning with HOW and including all of the **Invitation**. Indicate any notes for improvement.
- ❏ Make sure Team members know the correct sequence in using *A Step of Faith* in making a transition from the gospel presentation to leading someone to declare commitments to Christ as Savior and Lord, to enroll in Sunday School, and to publicly acknowledge new faith in Jesus. Since several Home Study Assignments dealt with the use of *A Step of Faith*, you may not need additional review of session 10 assignments.
- ❏ Make certain Team members are able to lead a person to pray to receive Christ and to pray for Christian growth. Also, be certain Team members are comfortable in leading a person to record commitment(s) they have made and to provide the information the church needs.

✔ *Session 10 Debriefing*
- ❏ Heaven HERE and Heaven HEREAFTER are fundamental beliefs of the Christian. Do Learners demonstrate a sense of comfort in sharing their joy in Christ and their assurance of eternal life in God's presence?
- ❏ H also stands for HOW. This becomes the hinge on which a Learner is able to clarify for another person how a person can have God's forgiveness, heaven and eternal life, and Jesus as personal Savior and Lord. Make sure the person is becoming increasingly comfortable in using the picture on the cover of *A Step of Faith* to identify with the need for God's forgiveness. You received earlier training to help your Team know what to do if *A Step of Faith* is not available.

✔ Help for Strengthening a Visit

- ❑ Remind Team members that they are seeing the Holy Spirit at work as they make themselves available for visitation. Recall examples of ways you have seen the Holy Spirit at work when a person has heard the FAITH gospel presentation.
- ❑ One of the great privileges and responsibilities in FAITH training is to encounter family members of someone you are assigned to visit. Although your Team is focusing on persons from your Sunday School department or class, you quickly learn that there are many opportunities to minister to and share the gospel with persons of other age divisions. Dialogue about ways to meaningfully include preschoolers, children, youth, and adults in a visit who would not be assigned to your department or class.
- ❑ Indicate that next week's practice session is a good way to improve skills and increase confidence. Share schedule adjustments.

Notes

_____
_____
_____
_____
_____

Actions I Need to Take with Team Members This Week

_____
_____
_____
_____
_____
_____

Transition to classrooms for instruction on the content of the session. (5 mins.)

TEACHING TIME

KNOW IT

Step 1 (5 mins.)

Direct participants to turn to "A Quick Review" on page 174 in their Journals and to follow the instructions to complete the activities. Use the computer presentation or overhead cel 56 to review the answers:
1. a. classes, b. groups, c. churches
2. The correct order is 6, 10, 5, 7, 11, 13, 1, 8, 4, 9, 12, 14, 3, 2.

Be careful not to exceed the five-minute time limit.

A Quick Review

SAY IT

Step 2 (5 mins.)

Ask accountability partners to practice sharing the *Invitation* portion of the FAITH Visit Outline with each other.

A Quick Review

In session 10 you learned practical ways to multiply Sunday School units in your church. Recall what you learned as you complete the following.

1. Fill in the blanks to name the three types of new Sunday School units that can be started.

   a. Traditional Sunday School *classes*

   b. Nontraditional Bible-study *groups*

   c. New *churches*

   Place a check mark beside the one you would like to be involved in starting within the next six months.

2. Read the following steps for starting a new Sunday School unit. Arrange the steps in the correct sequence from 1 to 14.
   - *6* Identify the birthday for the new unit.
   - *10* Visit prospects.
   - *5* Allow the missionaries to be apprentices for current leadership positions.
   - *7* Regularly meet with new class leaders for prayer and coordination.
   - *11* Conduct the first meeting of the new unit.
   - *13* Keep in touch with the sponsor (the class/group that helped start the new unit).
   - *1* Share the multiplication vision with class members and leaders.
   - *8* Seek prospects through Opinion Polls, inactive lists from other classes, and other sources.
   - *4* Seek "missionaries" who will help start a new unit.
   - *9* Plan a fellowship before the new unit begins, inviting all prospects.
   - *12* Hold regular leadership meetings to evaluate, update, and plan.
   - *14* Continually pray for God's leadership.
   - *3* Recast the vision on a regular basis but in different ways.
   - *2* Talk with church staff and other leaders about plans.

LEADERS ON LEADERSHIP

"Multiplying leaders delegate responsibility to disciples." —Avery Willis and Henry Blackaby[1]

---

174 / *Growing as a FAITH Leader Facilitator Guide*

Focus First on Following

Mark 1:17 records Jesus' words: " 'Follow Me, … and I will make you into fishers of men!' " The process of multiplication is intricately woven into this verse. In this session you will discover that if you want to be successful at multiplication, especially filling up the new Sunday School unit you have committed to start, you must follow the formula Jesus provided. The first step is to focus on following Him.

Follow ____Jesus____.
Do you remember playing Follow the Leader as a child? One person was the leader, and the other children did exactly what the leader did—march around the room, turn around, jump off a chair, and so on. In the same way, multiplication begins with believers following Jesus. Though this is not a game, the goal is the same as in Follow the Leader—to do exactly what our Leader did when He lived on earth. Because He came " 'to seek and to save the lost' " (Luke 19:10) and give abundant life (see John 10:10), our priorities must be the same. Becoming a multiplier first requires staying focused on our Leader so that our ministry will align with His will.

Let Jesus make you the ____disciple____ *He wants.*
The purpose of the FAITH strategy is not to produce converts to Christ but to produce followers of Christ. Following Christ means that believers strive to grow in all the disciplines of faith, such as praying, studying the Bible, fellowshipping, worshiping, giving, fasting, witnessing, and serving. Following Christ positions believers to hear what God says and to do what He desires. Following Christ also leads believers to understand the vital necessity of sharing their faith with others. FAITH then equips believers to share when they have opportunities.

Through discipleship we become the kind of example and mentor God can use to multiply believers and to make other disciples.

Become a ____fisher____ *of* ____men____.
The reason multiplication has often failed in many churches is that new believers have not been immediately encouraged to learn how to share their faith. This is a big mistake. As new believers are involved in sharing their faith, they develop an outward vision rather than an inward vision. They focus on others rather than on themselves. This outward focus is essential for anyone to be involved in multiplication.

The most likely candidate to become a Team Learner in FAITH is a new believer. New believers who have had a life-changing experience are enthusiastic about their new relationship with Christ and want to tell others. They also know many friends and family members who do not know the Lord, so they can identify many new prospects for FAITH

HEAR IT

Step 3 (10 mins.)

Ask participants to turn to "Focus First on Following" on page 175 in their Journals and to fill in the blanks as you present the material, using the computer presentation or overhead cels 57–58. Emphasize that following Jesus must be the priority of our lives if we want to be effective multipliers.

Focus First on Following

Session 11: The Process of Multiplication / 175

> READ
> • Mark 2:13-17

Teams. And when they are involved as FAITH Learners, they have opportunities to lead others to the Lord.

This process is seen in the events recorded in Mark 2:13-17:

> Jesus went out again beside the sea. The whole crowd was coming to Him, and He taught them. Then, moving on, He saw Levi the son of Alphaeus sitting at the tax office, and He said to him, "Follow Me!" So he got up and followed Him. While He was reclining at the table in Levi's house, many tax collectors and sinners were also guests with Jesus and His disciples, because there were many who were following Him. When the scribes of the Pharisees saw that He was eating with sinners and tax collectors, they asked His disciples, "Why does He eat with tax collectors and sinners?" When Jesus heard this, He told them, "Those who are well don't need a doctor, but the sick do need one. I didn't come to call the righteous, but sinners."

When Levi (Matthew) decided to follow Christ, he realized that he knew a number of other people who needed to hear the gospel. So he threw a party and invited these prospects, along with Jesus and His disciples. Levi was instrumental in introducing others to Jesus, though he had been following Jesus for only a short time.

Think of the possibilities for your church and your FAITH ministry if the Levi process were the norm.

THE LEVI PROCESS

1. New believers begin __following__ __Christ__ in order to be more like Him.
2. New believers identify new __prospects__ because they want others to know about Christ.
3. New believers want to __share__ with others about their new life.
4. New believers become FAITH __Learners__ to learn how to share Christ with others.
5. New Learners want to teach others how to lead people to __Christ__.
6. New Learners become new __leaders__ in FAITH.
7. New leaders mentor __new__ __Learners__ in FAITH, continuing the multiplication process.

You know that your FAITH ministry will not multiply if you do not have new leaders. However, you will not need new leaders if you do not have new Learners. Furthermore, you will not have new Learners if you do not have new believers who are following Christ and are encouraged soon after coming to Christ to learn how to share their faith. Therefore, this pattern of following Christ must be instilled early in a believer's life. The implications are great for your church, your FAITH Team, and the kingdom of God.

Reject Substitutes for Jesus

When was the last time you made a cake, a pie, or cookies? You probably followed a recipe, even if it was memorized, and used ingredients others had used in making the same thing. But what if you had decided to use salt instead of sugar? The results would not be the same!

In the same way, substituting something for Jesus is another reason multiplication fails in many churches. Jesus said, " 'Follow Me!' " (Mark 2:14). Because the emphasis is on *Me*, Jesus Christ is the goal, the One you are to follow. But for many Christians, following Jesus is not the goal. Though they claim to follow Him, Satan has deceived them into following something else.

Don't follow **self** *instead of Jesus.*
What if you saw a man walking in a small circle and asked him why? It would be ridiculous if he answered, "I'm following myself." Though following self is abnormal and spiritually unhealthy, that is what we do when we focus on personal plans, goals, comfort, or needs. Jesus taught us to place God above self and other values in life (see Mark 12:30).

Don't follow **religion** *instead of Jesus.*
Many Christians find themselves spiritually dry and defeated because they are in churches that have been doing the same things for years and don't know why they are doing them. Going through the functions of religion as they are told, these believers become like robots in automatic mode rather than disciples who continually learn and grow. God's desire is that we enjoy a living relationship with Him through His Son, not adhere to empty ritual that does not satisfy.

Don't follow **people** *instead of Jesus.*
Some believers are so influenced by family, friends, or coworkers that they focus their lives on pleasing others rather than on pleasing Christ. Eventually, they realize that they have no joy in what they are doing, or they experience spiritual trauma when these persons let them down. Centering our lives on another human is idolatry.

When we follow anything other than Jesus Christ, we eliminate the potential for multiplication because we do not know His will and

---

Step 4 (10 mins.)

Direct participants to turn to page 177 in their Journals and to fill in the blanks as you present the material in "Reject Substitutes for Jesus." Use the computer presentation or overhead cel 59.

Reject Substitutes for Jesus

Session 11: The Process of Multiplication / 177

do not share with others the necessity of following Him. In addition, we rob Him of the rightful glory that is due to Him. Conversely, when we follow Jesus, He receives all the glory. When Jesus is the object of our following, others see Him and are drawn to Him, and that begins the multiplication process.

Trust Jesus to Do His Part

When a task seems impossible, most people are hesitant even to try it. Because of past failures they may have become conditioned to refuse an assignment that appears unattainable, regardless of the potential benefits. The process of multiplying and making disciples of all nations (see Matt. 28:19) probably seems like an impossible task to most new believers and to many long-time believers. Even starting one hundred thousand new Sunday School units each year throughout the Southern Baptist Convention probably seems an impossible undertaking. So how can it be done?

When you look again at Mark 1:17, you discover another important phrase: " 'I will make you.' " Jesus' words indicate that He is the multiplying agent. You can trust Jesus to do His part if you do your part—follow—and stay focused on Him. Notice three truths about Jesus' words.

Jesus' ___desire___ is to make believers into multipliers. Jesus wants Christians to be soul-winners who work with Him to develop other believers into mature Great Commission Christians (see His words in Matt. 28:18-20 and Acts 1:8). In Mark 1:17 when Jesus said, " 'I will make you,' " His words are personal and individual for every believer. We need only look at the cross to hear Jesus say from His heart, "I did this for you and others, and I want you to tell others what I have done for them."

Jesus' ___will___ is for believers to become multipliers. Some believers try to excuse themselves by saying, "I'm not gifted to be a soul-winner or a multiplier. I'm not against evangelism, you understand, but it's for someone else, not me." Nothing could be further from the truth. In fact, it is a common strategy Satan uses. The word *you* in Mark 1:17 could be applied to every believer.

Jesus' ___power___ enables believers to become multipliers. Transformation cannot happen apart from the power of Jesus Christ. Believers can say and do a lot of good things, but they can never produce the harvest. Neither can believers make others into soul-winners. Jesus promised He could and would. Paul discovered that the key to becoming a multiplier was found in giving his weaknesses to Christ so that God could demonstrate His power through him (see 2 Cor. 2:1-10).

Step 5 (5 mins.)

Direct participants to page 178 in their Journals. Ask them to fill in the blanks as you summarize "Trust Jesus to Do His Part." Use the computer presentation or overhead cel 60.

[Trust Jesus to Do His Part]

As a FAITH Leader, you are the key to helping believers, especially new believers, understand that the Lord can make them into the multipliers He expects them to be in order to accomplish the task He has given to all believers. Remind new believers, Sunday School class members, and others in your church about the priority of following Jesus alone and the importance of trusting Him to do what only He can do.

Experience the Expected Result

When you want to get fire from a match, what do you do? First you take the match and strike it across the rough surface of the box or book. Then you get a flame. It's the expected result, and it will happen as planned, assuming nothing is wrong with the matches or with the striking surface.

Jesus concluded His statement in Mark 1:17 by saying, " 'I will make you into fishers of men.' " When we follow Christ, we keep growing in Him to the point that we tell others about Him. This is the expected result, and when we follow the process He gave us, it will happen as planned.

Note that the expected result is fishers, not men. Our focus must be on the fishing, not on the catch. Many believers get frustrated because things aren't happening as they expect, and they aren't seeing many people come to Christ. Thus, they conclude that the multiplication process will never be fulfilled.

Remember that people are at different stages in their spiritual journeys. While some are on the threshold of faith, others are miles away. You've likely realized this in FAITH visits when you've offered people the opportunity to make a commitment to Christ. The different responses people give can be seen in Jesus' parable of the sower in Matthew 13:1-23. Jesus explained the different responses to the gospel in verses 18-23:

> "You, then, listen to the parable of the sower: When anyone hears the word about the kingdom and doesn't understand it, the evil one comes and snatches away what was sown in his heart. This is the one sown along the path. And the one sown on rocky ground—this is the one who hears the word and immediately receives it with joy. Yet he has no root in himself, but is short-lived. When pressure or persecution comes because of the word, immediately he stumbles. Now the one sown among the thorns—this is one who hears the word, but the worries of this age and the pleasure of wealth choke the word, and it becomes unfruitful. But the one sown on the good ground—this is one who hears and understands the word, who does bear fruit and yields: some a hundred, some sixty, some thirty times what was sown."

Step 6 (5 mins.)

Ask participants to turn to page 179 in their Journals. Summarize "Experience the Expected Result," using the computer presentation. Remind them that believers must focus on fishing and leave the results to the Lord. Point out that when we don't worry about the catch, we experience more joy in fishing.

STUDY IT

Step 7 (5 mins.)

Overview the Home Study Assignments for session 11.

Transition to assemble with FAITH Teams to prepare for home visits. (5 mins.)

DO IT (110 MINS.)

SHARE IT (30 MINS.)

One emphasis of this parable is that believers need to be faithful in planting the seeds of the gospel and leave the results to the Lord. This takes all the pressure off us and infuses evangelism with joy and passion.

Becoming a fisher of men is the natural result of being a follower of Christ. As you follow this process, you will experience great blessings in your Sunday School, your church, and the kingdom of God. The Lord Himself developed this process of multiplication, and He will use it to accomplish His will in order to bring glory to Himself.

> To learn more about the biblical process of multiplying believers, see *MasterLife 4: The Disciple's Mission* (LifeWay Press, 1997).

Visitation Time

DO IT

1. As you visit, view the lost persons you meet with the same sense of urgency you would have for your own family members.
2. On the way to visit, ask Team members what they felt and thought when they looked at the *Step of Faith* picture.
3. Part of your discipling role is to turn over the responsibility to Learners. All Team members should know the FAITH presentation through ***Invitation***. Prepare them to take the lead and present most if not all of the presentation.

Celebration Time

SHARE IT

1. Ask a Team member to take the lead in sharing reports.
2. Hear reports and testimonies.
3. Complete Evaluation Cards.
4. Complete Participation Cards.
5. Update visitation forms with the results of visits.

---

[1]Henry T. Blackaby and Avery T. Willis, Jr., *On Mission with God* (Nashville: Broadman & Holman Publishers, 2002), 213.

Home Study Assignments

Day 1: Your Relationship with God

Read Mark 1:17 and memorize this verse.

Read again the section "Focus First on Following" on pages 175–76 in session 11. Then look at the list below. Check any of the items that cause you difficulty as you seek to live this verse.
❏ Following Jesus—seeking to do what He did
❏ Letting Jesus make you the disciple He wants you to be
❏ Fishing for men as a part of your daily life

To which of these areas do you need to give greatest attention? Write it here.
_____

Make a fresh commitment to the Lord today to truly follow Christ, grow as His disciple, and be a multiplying witness.

Day 2: Your Relationship with Your FAITH Team

Circle a number on the scale to indicate how well you see the process of multiplication being carried out in your church through the FAITH ministry.

Low   1   2   3   4   5   6   7   8   9   10   *High*

Name some new believers who became new Learners and then new Leaders.
_____
_____

How are you helping your FAITH Team Learners focus on following Jesus?
_____
_____

Ask God to give you the names of people in your church whom you could encourage to join your Team or get involved in FAITH next semester.

Day 3: Your Relationship with Your Sunday School Class

Read Mark 2:13-17. Who are new believers in your Sunday School class who might be willing to host a party to which they can invite their lost friends and some of their Sunday School class members?

_____

Read the following ideas you could use in your area to meet those who would be the modern-day equivalent of "tax collectors and sinners" (Mark 2:16). Then check ideas your class could try.
- ❑ Prayer survey in your community
- ❑ Community health fair at your church
- ❑ Home buyer's seminar
- ❑ Sports league for community teams
- ❑ Auto-repair clinic
- ❑ Financial-planning seminar
- ❑ Community work day in a neighborhood nearby
- ❑ Job seeker's data bank
- ❑ Other: _____

Make a copy of your potential ideas and challenge your class leaders to consider them at your next leadership meeting.

Day 4: Your Relationship with the Lost

Think about your life for the past week. Beside each day listed below, write one way you sought to plant the seed of the gospel in the lives of persons who may not know Christ.
Sunday: _____
Monday: _____
Tuesday: _____
Wednesday: _____
Thursday: _____
Friday: _____
Saturday: _____

What emotions do you experience as you share the gospel with others?

_____

Ask God to help you overcome any fear you still have in sharing the gospel. Pray specifically for one or two lost persons and ways you can plant seeds.

Day 5: Your Relationship with Your Family and Your Church

In what ways can you help family members or close friends at church focus first on following Jesus?

_____

_____

_____

Write the name of at least one person in your family you are praying will trust Christ as Savior and Lord.

_____

How have you sought to plant the seed of the gospel in that person's life?

_____

_____

_____

What practical steps can you take to mentor believers in your family and help them become fishers of men?

_____

_____

_____

FAITH TIP

Keep the Oil Flowing

This material may be used in a training session with leaders and adult class leaders to motivate them to practice the multiplication process. (For more information see *Essentials for Excellence: Connecting Sunday School to Life*, LifeWay Press; also see session 8, p. 125.) Purchase one mason jar to display or a small one for each group member. Read 2 Kings 4:1-7, emphasizing the portion stating that when all the jars were full, the oil stopped flowing. Say:

A woman sought Elisha, whose reputation as a man of God was well known. She explained that her husband had just passed away and left her and her two sons with a debt that had to be paid. If the debt was not paid, her creditors would enslave her sons. She told Elisha that the only thing of value in her home was a jar containing a small quantity of oil. Elisha instructed her to take her sons and go around their community collecting as many empty jars as they could find. When they had gathered the jars, Elisha directed them to go inside their house, shut the door, and pour oil from their jar into the other jars. As long as there were jars to fill, the oil continued to flow miraculously from the one jar. But when all the jars were full, the oil stopped.

Explain that the jar represents the Sunday School class and the oil represents new people who attend. Explain that as long as there is room and needs are being met, the oil will keep flowing. But when the room is full or the class is too large, the oil will stop flowing. Ask the group to imagine what might have happened if the woman had gathered even more jars. Make the following applications.

- *God begins with us where we are.* Each member of each class is unique and important to God. He desires the best for members and for the class. We may not see how our class can begin a new unit, but God knows how.
- *God expects us to be involved in the process.* Just as the woman was invited to become involved in the miracle of the oil by gathering jars, God invites us to be part of kingdom work by gathering lost people, building leaders, and creating new units.
- *God has no limits.* We place limits on ourselves. The woman placed limits on the amount of oil she received by the number of jars she gathered.

Lead the group to consider ways it limits God's plan for growth by limiting the number of "jars" the class gathers. Explain that the class might reach a point at which it is full and the oil of new believers—and possibly even new spiritual growth in their own lives—might stop flowing. Explain that a new unit or class start is like another jar that God desires to fill.

Display the mason jar or give one to each learner and challenge participants to consider ways they can help the class begin a new unit.

Topper Reid, "The Miracle of the Oil Presentation for Starting New Units," Adult Sunday School Ministry portion of CD-ROM in *Essentials for Excellence: Connecting Sunday School to Life* (LifeWay Press, 2003).

SESSION 12
Practicing FAITH

In this session you will—

CHECK IT by spending the entire time in extended Team Time/ practice activities;

STUDY IT by overviewing Home Study Assignments;

DO IT by making visits in which a Team member may take the lead;

SHARE IT by celebrating.

IN ADVANCE
- Decide whether you wish to help Teams practice by reviewing previously viewed video segments of the FAITH Visit Outline from *A Journey in FAITH*.
- Pray for Team members as they begin taking the lead in visits.

TEAM TIME

CHECK IT (60 MINS.)

If the computer presentation is used, display the agenda for Team Time.

CHECK IT agenda:
✔ FAITH Visit Outline

Leading Team Time

All Teams remain together during this session for an extended Team Time. All Team members participate in Team Time. They are primarily responsible for reciting the assigned portion of the FAITH Visit Outline and for discussing other Home Study Assignments.

As you direct this important time of CHECK IT activities with your Team, keep in mind that Learners look to you as a role model, motivator, mentor, and friend. Team Time activities can continue in the car as the Team travels to and from visits.

Lead CHECK IT Activities

✔ FAITH Visit Outline

Neither the Team Leaders nor the Team Learners have Teaching Time this week. Instead, Leaders will spend the entire time with Team members, leading them to practice the FAITH Visit Outline. Here are some suggestions for the best use of this time.

1. Begin with prayer. Take about five minutes to pray for a productive practice session, for Learners to have accurate recall of the outline, and for a complete understanding of how to use the *Step of Faith* tract.
2. Allow each Learner to share in a conversational fashion the FAITH gospel presentation, beginning with the Key Question.
3. Provide feedback that encourages Learners for the parts they have learned and point out areas in which they need to do more work.
4. Guide Learners through the *Step of Faith* tract. Then allow each person to use the tract as if you were the person with whom he or she is sharing.
5. Consider rehearsing appropriate approaches to take in strengthening the skills and confidence of Learners in leading the visit. It may be helpful to suggest that the Team role-play several situations your Team or others have encountered during FAITH training.
6. Conclude with prayer about tonight's visit. Pray for a divine appointment. Pray that at least one of the Learners will have an opportunity to share the good news. Pray for God to remove all fear and to provide boldness in sharing Christ.

This practice session can be a valuable time to disciple your Learners if you take advantage of this opportunity to instruct them in the effective use of the outline.

FAITH Visit Outline

Preparation

INTRODUCTION
INTERESTS
INVOLVEMENT

Church Experience/Background
- Ask about the person's church background.
- Listen for clues about the person's spiritual involvement.

Sunday School Testimony
- Tell general benefits of Sunday School.
- Tell a current personal experience.

Evangelistic Testimony
- Tell a little of your preconversion experience.
- Say: "I had a life-changing experience."
- Tell recent benefits of your conversion.

INQUIRY

Key Question: In your personal opinion, what do you understand it takes for a person to go to heaven?

Possible Answers: Faith, works, unclear, no opinion

Transition Statement: I'd like to share with you how the Bible answers this question, if it is all right. There is a word that can be used to answer this question: FAITH (spell out on fingers).

Presentation

F is for FORGIVENESS

We cannot have eternal life and heaven without God's forgiveness. *"In Him [meaning Jesus] we have redemption through His blood, the forgiveness of sins"—Ephesians 1:7a, NKJV.*

A is for AVAILABLE

Forgiveness is available. It is—

AVAILABLE FOR ALL

"For God so loved the world that He gave His only begotten Son, that whoever believes in Him should not perish but have everlasting life"—John 3:16, NKJV.

BUT NOT AUTOMATIC

"Not everyone who says to Me, 'Lord, Lord,' shall enter the kingdom of heaven"—Matthew 7:21a, NKJV.

I is for IMPOSSIBLE

It is impossible for God to allow sin into heaven.

GOD IS—
- LOVE
  John 3:16, NKJV
- JUST
  "For judgment is without mercy"—James 2:13a, NKJV.

MAN IS SINFUL
"For all have sinned and fall short of the glory of God"—Romans 3:23, NKJV.

Question: But how can a sinful person enter heaven, where God allows no sin?

T is for TURN

Question: If you were driving down the road and someone asked you to turn, what would he or she be asking you to do? (change direction)
Turn means *repent*.

TURN from something—sin and self
"But unless you repent you will all likewise perish"—Luke 13:3b, NKJV.

TURN to Someone; trust Christ only
(The Bible tells us that) *"Christ died for our sins according to the Scriptures, and that He was buried, and that He rose again the third day according to the Scriptures"—1 Corinthians 15:3b-4, NKJV.*
"If you confess with your mouth the Lord Jesus and believe in your heart that God has raised Him from the dead, you will be saved"—Romans 10:9, NKJV.

H is for HEAVEN

Heaven is eternal life.

HERE
"I have come that they may have life, and that they may have it more abundantly"—John 10:10b, NKJV.

HEREAFTER
"And if I go and prepare a place for you, I will come again and receive you to Myself; that where I am, there you may be also"—John 14:3, NKJV.

HOW
How can a person have God's forgiveness, heaven and eternal life, and Jesus as personal Savior and Lord?

Explain based on leaflet picture, FAITH (Forsaking All, I Trust Him), Romans 10:9.

Invitation

INQUIRE
Understanding what we have shared, would you like to receive this forgiveness by trusting in Christ as your personal Savior and Lord?

INVITE
- Pray to accept Christ.
- Pray for commitment/recommitment.
- Invite to join Sunday School.

INSURE
- Use *A Step of Faith* to insure decision.
- Personal Acceptance
- Sunday School Enrollment
- Public Confession

Visitation Time

DO IT
1. Throughout FAITH you have been preparing your Team members to take the lead in a visit. Make sure Team members are informed that they will take the lead in specific visits.
2. As always, be prepared to assist, but do everything you can to encourage Team members to lead the entire visit. Encourage and support them when they make mistakes.

Celebration Time

SHARE IT
1. Ask a Team member to take the lead in sharing reports.
2. Hear reports and testimonies.
3. Complete Evaluation Cards.
4. Complete Participation Cards.
5. Update visitation forms with the results of visits.

STUDY IT
Overview Home Study Assignments for session 12. (5 mins.)

Transition to prepare for home visits. (5 mins.)

DO IT (110 MINS.)

SHARE IT (30 MINS.)

Home Study Assignments

Day 1: Your Relationship with God

Read Matthew 22:34-40. Describe how you are loving God with all your—

heart: _____

soul: _____

mind: _____

Recall the goal you set after session 1 for growing in your relationship with God this semester (see Home Study Assignments, day 1, p. 26). How are you progressing toward that goal?

_____

What will you do in the next four weeks to ensure that you meet your goal?

_____

Day 2: Your Relationship with Your FAITH Team

Read Luke 8:1-3; 9:1-6; 10:1-12. How did Jesus practice multiplication in—

Luke 8:1-3? _____

Luke 9:1-6? _____

Luke 10:1-4? _____

How are you following Jesus' example on your FAITH Team?

_____

_____

Pray for each Team member today. Contact Learners and let them know you are praying for them for the rest of the semester. Ask how they are doing in sharing the gospel during the week, other than in FAITH Visitation Time.

Day 3: Your Relationship with Your Sunday School Class

What percentage of your Sunday School class members would you estimate are actively sharing their faith on a regular basis?

   5%   10%   25%   35%   50%   65%   75%   95%   100%

Check the last time you shared a testimony in your class about witnessing to someone outside the FAITH ministry.
❏ Last week ❏ Last month ❏ Last year ❏ Five years ago ❏ Never

Recall the goal you set after session 1 for growing as a Sunday School leader this semester (see Home Study Assignments, day 3, p. 27). How are you progressing toward that goal?

_____

What will you do in the next four weeks to ensure that you meet your goal?

_____

Day 4: Your Relationship with the Lost

Read Acts 16:1-10. In what ways have you experienced God guiding you to specific lost persons who needed to hear the gospel?

_____

_____

Write the name of the lost person(s) you have been praying for since the beginning of this semester (see Home Study Assignments, session 1, day 4, p. 27).

_____

How have you shared the gospel with this person in the past 12 weeks?

_____

What has been the result of your fishing for men?

_____

Day 5: Your Relationship with Your Family and Your Church

Read Joshua 4:1-9. How do you initiate and take advantage of teachable moments in the lives of your children (or children in your church) to share with them the message of Jesus Christ?

_____
_____
_____
_____
_____
_____

Write a prayer for your family members. Ask God to guide you as you influence them to become faithful followers of Christ who share His message with others.

_____
_____
_____
_____
_____
_____
_____

SESSION 13
Growing as a Ministry Leader

In this session you will—

CHECK IT by engaging in Team Time activities;

KNOW IT by reviewing content from session 11;

HEAR IT by studying ways to minister to your Sunday School class members, new members, and community;

STUDY IT by overviewing Home Study Assignments;

DO IT by leading your Team in making visits;

SHARE IT by celebrating.

IN ADVANCE
- Overview content.
- Preview teaching suggestions. Prepare key points. Decide whether to use the session 13 computer presentation or overhead cels 61–65 (see pp. 331–35).
- Prepare the room for teaching.
- Pray for participants and for Teams as they prepare to visit.
- As Teaching Time begins, direct participants to open their Journals to page 196.

TEAM TIME

CHECK IT (15 MINS.)

If the computer presentation is used, display the agenda for Team Time. Add other points to the agenda as needed.

CHECK IT agenda:
- ✔ FAITH Visit Outline
- ✔ Session 11 Debriefing
- ✔ Help for Strengthening a Visit

Leading Team Time

All Team members participate in Team Time. They are primarily responsible for reciting the assigned portion of the FAITH Visit Outline and for discussing other Home Study Assignments.

As you direct this important time of CHECK IT activities with your Team, keep in mind that Learners look to you as a role model, motivator, mentor, and friend. Team Time activities can continue in the car as the Team travels to and from visits.

Lead CHECK IT Activities

✔ FAITH Visit Outline
❑ Listen while each Learner recites the FAITH Visit Outline. Because there is no new memory work, it may be best to ask Learners to recite the segment they have the most difficulty sharing during a visit.

✔ Session 11 Debriefing
❑ Because session 12 was a practice session with no new material, debrief session 11. Session 11 focused on the important time when a person is given the opportunity to personally accept God's forgiveness and salvation, so it is important that Team members be well trained. It is even more important that they grow in their sensitivity to the Holy Spirit's prompting during visitation.
❑ Discuss ways Team members are finding *A Step of Faith* helpful in prompting discussion in a visit. If time permits, allow Team members to practice the **Invitation**, using *A Step of Faith*.

✔ Help for Strengthening a Visit
❑ Discuss difficulties the Team has encountered in leading someone to hear and consider the FAITH gospel presentation. Evaluate ways the Team responded to selected experiences and identify appropriate ways to improve responses. Indicate that although most visits go smoothly, next week's session will help all Team members better handle challenges in a visit. Difficulties are things that happen or are said that could keep you from sharing the gospel and leading someone who is ready to respond to make a commitment to Christ. Principles for dealing with difficulties relate primarily to building bridges of relationships with the person, dealing with questions and objections, and working through the obstacles and distractions that take place.
❑ As you talk with Team members during the week, share ways you are seeking to take advantage of your daily-life witnessing opportunities. Also talk with them about opportunities they have to share the gospel during the week with persons they encounter.

Notes

Actions I Need to Take with Team Members This Week

Transition to classrooms for instruction on the content of the session. (5 mins.)

TEACHING TIME

KNOW IT

Step 1 (5 mins.)

Direct participants to turn to "A Quick Review" on page 196 in their Journals and to follow the instructions to complete the activities. Use the computer presentation or overhead cel 61 to review the answers:
1. b, f, g, h, i
2. To become fishers of men

Be careful not to exceed the five-minute time limit.

A Quick Review

A Quick Review

In session 11 you learned a biblical process of multiplication based on Mark 1:17; 2:13-17. These activities will test your learning.

1. Check the actions that are part of the Levi (Matthew) process.

   ❏ a. New believers start serving in ministry.

   ☑ b. New believers begin following Christ.

   ❏ c. New believers quit spending time with their old friends.

   ❏ d. New believers spend a lot of time learning about the Bible before they do anything else.

   ❏ e. New believers begin thinking about their needs and wants.

   ☑ f. New believers identify prospects who need to know Christ.

   ☑ g. New believers want to tell others about their new life.

   ☑ h. New believers become FAITH Learners.

   ☑ i. New Learners graduate to become Team Leaders.

2. What is the expected result of the process suggested by Mark 1:17?

   To become fisher of men

LEADERS ON LEADERSHIP

"It is not enough to keep learning more and more. We must act on what we know and practice what we claim to believe." —Rick Warren[1]

---

196 / *Growing as a FAITH Leader Facilitator Guide*

A Dual-Purpose Instrument

Have you ever used a ballpoint pen that also had a highlighter on the opposite end? This pen allows you not only to write notes about what you're reading but also to highlight important words and phrases.

FAITH is also a dual-purpose instrument a church can use to fulfill the Great Commission. Doug Williams, who with Bobby Welch originated the FAITH Sunday School Evangelism Strategy®, has a double-billed cap he sometimes wears in conferences to emphasize the dual-purpose strategy of FAITH. On one side of the cap is printed *Evangelism,* while on the other side is printed *Ministry.* Williams puts on the cap with *Evangelism* facing the front to emphasize to conferees that he may be on a prospect visit when he discovers a ministry need. At that point it becomes a ministry visit, he explains, and turns the cap around so that *Ministry* faces the front. Likewise, he says he may be on a ministry visit that presents an evangelistic opportunity. He then turns the cap back around so that the *Evangelism* side faces conferees.

To this point the primary focus of *Growing as a FAITH Leader* has been on evangelism, especially on reproducing leaders to carry out the Great Commission. In your church it's likely that most visits you make are prospect visits, whether from an assignment or because of a divine appointment when using the Opinion Poll. It is vital, however, that you also recognize the importance and benefits of ministry visits, which provide you the opportunity to care for the needs of others. This session will focus on ministry in the context of FAITH Sunday School, as well as ministry that can open the door to evangelism in your community.

Minister to Current Class Members

In an episode of *The Andy Griffith Show* several stray dogs of different breeds and sizes ended up at the courthouse. Barney finally took the dogs into the country and left them where they could run free. But Opie, after hearing the thunder of an approaching storm, was concerned about the dogs, especially one small dog that he called a trembler. Barney tried to explain to Opie that he didn't have to worry, because dogs take care of their own. In Barney's typical reasoning he tried to reassure Opie by explaining that dogs aren't like giraffes, which are selfish and unconcerned about one another. After all his talk he finally convinced himself of the need to go back and rescue the dogs from the coming storm!

HEAR IT

Step 2 (5 mins.)

Direct participants to turn to "A Dual-Purpose Instrument" on page 197 in their Journals. Using the computer presentation, discuss the two purposes of the FAITH strategy that Teams must not neglect.

Step 3 (10 mins.)

Ask participants to fill in the blanks in "Minister to Current Class Members" in their Journals as you summarize the material, using the computer presentation or overhead cel 62. Remind participants of the words of 1 John 3:18, "Little children, we must not love in word or speech, but in deed and truth."

> Minister to Current Class Members

Although it may not be true that dogs take care of their own, it should be a reality for every Sunday School class. As you discovered in session 2, ministry is one purpose of the church, and it is carried out through a church's small groups—the Sunday School. Ministry isn't just a good idea—it is biblical. Look at the words of Acts 2:42-47:

> They devoted themselves to the apostles' teaching, to fellowship, to the breaking of bread, and to prayers. Then fear came over everyone, and many wonders and signs were being performed through the apostles. Now all the believers were together and had everything in common. So they sold their possessions and property and distributed the proceeds to all, as anyone had a need. And every day they devoted themselves to meeting together in the temple complex, and broke bread from house to house. They ate their food with gladness and simplicity of heart, praising God and having favor with all the people. And every day the Lord added those being saved to them.

The early believers didn't just say to their fellow members, "I hope things work out for you." They did whatever their fellow believers needed. Why is ministry so important for a Sunday School class?

Ministry communicates love to   class   members   .
While most Christians recognize that the world needs to experience God's love, many often forget that those sitting in their classes and those who are enrolled (even if they rarely or never attend) need to be shown God's love, as well. Ministry to members shows that you really care about them.

Ministry demonstrates concern for   prospects   .
Prospects who visit your class see God's love in action and come to understand—hopefully through words backed up by actions—that God loves them. They are more likely to come back if they feel that class members are concerned about them.

Ministry motivates ministry to   others   .
People who have been in need know the benefits of having others help them. Many realize that without friends who cared about them they would have been helpless and hopeless. Often members are more willing to minister to others when they have been the beneficiaries of ministry.

Ministry reconnects people to the   Lord   and His   church .
This is especially true with FAITH ministry visits. You may have experienced this truth in your church. People become disconnected for many reasons. All reasons must be taken seriously and every effort made to help those who may be struggling in their walk with the Lord.

Ministry encourages involvement in __**FAITH**__.
Several members of your class may already be involved in ministering to others and could easily understand the purpose of ministry visits carried out by a FAITH Team. Most people are usually stronger, or at least more willing to participate, in ministry than they are in evangelism. You can encourage them to develop balance in their spiritual development by growing in evangelism through the FAITH ministry.

Session 4 emphasized that God has called you to be a minister. Because you are a FAITH Team Leader, you must also be a ministry leader, not only on your Team but also in your class. One phone call, ministry visit, or act of ministry may make a tremendous difference in someone's life. In addition, like the early Christians' ministry described in Acts 2:42-47, your ministry can be like a magnet to draw people to the Lord.

Minister to New Members

Imagine a family with four children that adopted six more children. After a year, however, the family could account for only seven children. Once the story was made known, the family would be covered up with media, police, and other authorities. Everyone would want to know what had happened. Even if the family could account for nine of the children, there would still be great concern that one family member was missing! Many churches are like this hypothetical family. Every year they bring new people into the family; yet after a year the churches cannot account for some of their new family members. What can be done to minister to new members in a way that ensures their full involvement in the body of Christ?

Use an __**assimilation**__ *process.*
Some churches have initiated a formal assimilation process requiring new members to complete a class or seminar before they can become official members. These requirements are intended to make church membership meaningful by teaching people the reason the church exists, the meaning of church membership, and the obligations and blessings that belong to members of the body of Christ.

Involve new members in __**Sunday School**__.
It is vital that your church help new members connect with the body of Christ through a Sunday School class. In session 3 you discovered a variety of ways to help people get connected and stay connected to your class. Recall or review the importance of these measures:
• Station a class greeter at the door.
• Wear name tags.

Step 4 (5 mins.)

Direct participants to "Minister to New Members" on page 199 in their Journals and to fill in the blanks as you present the material. Use the computer presentation or overhead cel 63.

```
Minister
to New
Members
```

Session 13: Growing as a Ministry Leader / 199

- Enlist good neighbors.
- Assign new members to care groups.
- Utilize fellowship.
- Take the lead as a FAITH Team Leader.

Encourage participation in ___ministry___.
In addition to making new members feel welcome and included, encouraging them to participate in ministry will help them develop connections with people and will jump-start their spiritual growth. Most new members who come to a church, especially new Christians, don't know what is expected of them. If they get accustomed to sitting in a class and doing nothing, breaking this habit will be difficult. But if they get involved in ministry soon after they join the church, they may establish a lasting habit of service that will benefit them and the church. In addition, new members can develop lifelong relationships with others—those for whom they have cared and those with whom they have ministered.

New members may have become a part of your class or church as a result of ministry actions by your class. Those who have received ministry are often most willing to minister to others in need.

Minister to Your Community

Robert Lewis, in *The Church of Irresistible Influence*, describes the problem the church in America faces today: "As the church engages a third millennium, it ... looks across a terrifying—and ever-widening—chasm:
- Between first-century authority and postmodern skepticism;
- Between a bold proclamation of God's love and unmet human needs;
- Between the selfless vision of Christ and the self-obsessed reality of our world;
- Between the truth of God's laws and the moral compromise of our culture;
- Between those who believe and those who don't."[2]

Lewis goes on to assert, "The church must rediscover its essential role and craft as a bridge builder. For the world's sake. For the church's sake. For God's sake. We can no longer simply afford to stand on one side of the Great Chasm and shout to those on the other side. We must connect. Otherwise, the greatest unbridged chasm will remain the gap between the stunning vision of Jesus Christ and the ever-receding influence of the contemporary church in the world."[3]

Ministry through the Sunday School class is an important way you can be involved in developing bridges to your community. Jesus taught in the Sermon on the Mount, " 'You are the light of the world' " (Matt. 5:14).

Step 5 (5 mins.)

Ask participants to turn to page 200 in their Journals and to fill in the blanks as you summarize "Minister to Your Community." Use the computer presentation or overhead cel 64.

Minister to Your Community

He went on to command, " 'Let your light shine before men, so that they may see your good works and give glory to your Father in heaven' " (Matt. 5:16). With these words the Lord emphasized the tremendous impact believers can have on society through their good works—tangible expressions of God's love. The ultimate impact comes when those who see or receive ministry actions give glory to God.

<u>Your vision of the possibilities and your leadership on your FAITH Team and in your Sunday School class are critical if your church is going to make an impact on the world.</u> Many people will no longer respond just to what they hear. They want to see appropriate actions that accompany a Christian's words. Your class can show caring actions through **ministry evangelism**, which connects ministry and the gospel. <u>The drawback to what has become known as the social gospel is that sometimes people focus on social ministry with little or no mention of the gospel.</u> Many churches and denominations that have plunged down this dangerous slope have become little more than social agencies. On the other side, however, are churches that "just want to get people saved" without any concern for their basic human needs.

There must be a healthy balance between the two approaches, as seen in the life of Jesus, who not only traveled around "telling the good news of the kingdom of God" (Luke 8:1) but also "went about doing good" (Acts 10:38). As a FAITH leader, you have the opportunity to lead members of your FAITH Team and your Sunday School class, along with other believers in your church, to minister to people in your community in practical ways, building bridges that earn you the right to share the gospel. In this way, you prepare the soil for the seed of the gospel.

This is the method many missionaries use to open the doors for evangelism in other countries. Their ministries include sharing agricultural techniques, meeting medical needs, teaching people how to read and write, and many other actions.

<u>The opportunities for you and your church to participate in ministry evangelism are limitless.</u> You can begin by looking around your community to see the variety of needs that exist, including housing, food, literacy, employment, and so forth. But ministry evangelism doesn't stop with these basic human needs; it can also provide for felt needs like recreation or soft drinks and include unpleasant but necessary activities like washing windows or cleaning gutters. Here are a few ideas for ministering to your community in Jesus' name.

- Establish a **partnership** with an adopted school and enlist church members to read to children or to help with ongoing activities or special events.
- Offer community **events** such as a July 4 picnic and fireworks; a health fair providing a variety of free tests and evaluations such as cholesterol, vision, or blood pressure; or a free car-care clinic with oil changes and tune-ups for cars of single mothers.

(Matthew 5:14-17)

- Sponsor __**sports**__ and __**recreational**__ activities such as a soccer-skills clinic, a 10K fun run, or a wild-game dinner.
- Work with community __**agencies**__ to build houses for low-income individuals or go door to door in your community collecting canned food for a local food bank.

Community events and activities such as these must be planned in advance, but sometimes ministry must be carried out quickly, with no advance planning. For instance, when a natural disaster strikes a community, your class and your church can take immediate action to help those who have experienced losses. And although ministry in these circumstances may be more long-term, the benefits can also be greater as you develop relationships with and care for people in need.

When people see your care for them, their needs, and their community, they will want to know what motivates you to love them in practical ways. Some will ask, opening the door for you to share a testimony. Others may not ask, but by building bridges through ministry, you can ask them the __**Key**____**Question**__ and perhaps share the FAITH outline with them. Sharing Christ through ministry evangelism resembles the approach of Paul, who reminded the believers in Thessalonica, "We cared so much for you that we were pleased to share with you not only the gospel of God but also our own lives" (1 Thess. 2:8).

Emphasize Enrollment

When you minister to persons who are not members of your Sunday School class, you build bridges over which the gospel can cross. In a FAITH visit after you share the FAITH outline with a prospect, regardless of the response, you should ask whether you can enroll the person in your Sunday School class. In the same way, after you minister to a person and maybe share the gospel, regardless of the response, you should try to connect the person to your Sunday School class. Here are some approaches you can use.

Refer to your class's __ministry__ __list__.
Instead of asking whether you can enroll the person in your class, ask whether you can add the person to your class's ministry list. Some persons respond more favorably to being on a ministry list than to being on a class roll, although they are the same thing.

Emphasize that no __risk__ *is involved.*
When you ask people about adding them to your ministry list, explain that it won't require anything from them; rather, it will place the requirement on your class to minister to them. Although you should share the

---

Step 6 (5 mins.)

Direct participants to turn to page 202 in their Journals and to fill in the blanks as you present "Emphasize Enrollment," using the computer presentation or overhead cel 65.

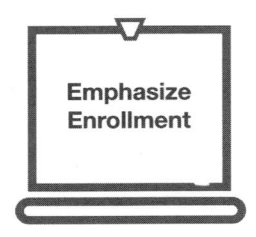

Emphasize Enrollment

benefits of your class through a Sunday School testimony, emphasize that if they decide to attend the class, no one will put them on the spot to read from the Bible, answer questions about it, or pray.

Get essential <u>information</u>.
Be sure to record the prospect's name, address, phone, and birthday for use in ministry.

Remember to <u>follow</u> <u>through</u>.
<u>Remember that your class must minister to the prospects.</u> Add them to a care group and get others involved in their lives so that they can establish a relationship with the body of Christ and, more importantly, with Christ Himself.

Become a <u>life</u> <u>minister</u>.
One goal of the FAITH strategy is for you to become a life witness, sharing the message of Christ in your daily life. A complementary goal is that you become a life minister, sharing the love of Christ in tangible ways in your daily life. When the two, witnessing and ministering, work hand in hand, the impact on God's kingdom is incredible!

Deal with Special Situations

Sometimes your FAITH Team may discover ministry needs that go beyond a one-time visit, for example, someone who is receiving treatment for cancer but has no family and no one else to help. If ongoing ministry is needed, bring together others in your class or church to provide ministry to help meet the person's ongoing need.

While on a ministry visit, your FAITH Team may also discover someone with a need that calls for a trained professional. If you discover persons dealing with addiction, struggling with depression, or mentioning suicide, talk and pray with them and strongly encourage them to talk with your pastor. As you silently pray for guidance, offer to talk with your pastor and to come back with him if necessary.

Most ministry visits won't require you to be a counselor but a conduit for the Counselor—the Holy Spirit—to bring wholeness to mind, body, and soul.

> To learn more about ministry evangelism, see *Meeting Needs, Sharing Christ: Ministry Evangelism in Today's New Testament Church* (LifeWay Press, 1995).

Step 7 (5 mins.)

Summarize "Deal with Special Situations," using the computer presentation.

STUDY IT

Step 8 (5 mins.)

Overview the Home Study Assignments for session 13.

Transition to assemble with FAITH Teams to prepare for home visits. (5 mins.)

DO IT (110 MINS.)

SHARE IT (30 MINS.)

Visitation Time

DO IT
1. As you make visits with your Team, look for opportunities to connect lost persons with Sunday School classes that can love and minister to them.
2. This week Learners have learned how to live FAITH in daily life. Share with them how this happens in your life.
3. Learners should have memorized the entire FAITH Visit Outline. Provide opportunities to let them share in FAITH visits.

Celebration Time

SHARE IT
1. Ask a Team member to take the lead in sharing reports.
2. Hear reports and testimonies.
3. Complete Evaluation Cards.
4. Complete Participation Cards.
5. Update visitation forms with the results of visits.

---

[1] Rick Warren, *The Purpose-Driven Life* (Grand Rapids: Zondervan, 2002), 231.
[2] Robert Lewis, *The Church of Irresistible Influence* (Grand Rapids: Zondervan, 2001), 27.
[3] Ibid., 28.

Home Study Assignments

Day 1: Your Relationship with God

Read James 2:15-17; 1 John 3:16-18. Mark each statement *T* for *true* or *F* for *false*.
___ 1. Ministry to fellow believers is a necessary element of the Christian faith.
___ 2. I don't have to be concerned about Christians who lack food and clothing.
___ 3. A Christian without compassion is difficult to imagine.
___ 4. My relationship with God is revealed by actions that accompany my words.
___ 5. Faith without corresponding actions can be a living faith.
___ 6. I should show my love rather than just talk about it.
___ 7. God doesn't want me to risk my life in service to others.

Review "Identify the Characteristics of God's Call" (pp. 66–69, session 4). Check the characteristics that are evident in your life as you minister to others.
❏ God prepared me for ministry. ❏ God called me to a life of sacrifice.
❏ God initiated His call. ❏ God called me to a unique role.
❏ God called me to a relationship. ❏ God expects obedience from me.
❏ God has done extraordinary things through me.

Pray that God will remind you of your calling to be a minister and that He will show you daily opportunities to build bridges for the gospel through ministry.

Day 2: Your Relationship with Your FAITH Team

Place an X on the line to indicate where you are in your relationship between participating in evangelism and participating in ministry through FAITH. Place an O to indicate where your FAITH Team members would place you.

Evangelism ○───────────────┼───────────────● **Ministry**

How have you communicated to Team members the importance of ministry visits?

_____

If the scale above indicates that you are one-sided, what can you do to be more balanced in practicing evangelism and ministry?

_____

Commit to make at least one ministry visit before the semester ends.

Day 3: Your Relationship with Your Sunday School Class

Read Acts 2:42-47. Rate your Sunday School class on how well your class demonstrates each action below. 1 = poor; 5 = well.

We prioritize Bible study.	1	2	3	4	5
Members are devoted to the fellowship.	1	2	3	4	5
We spend time praying for one another.	1	2	3	4	5
We see evidence of God's miraculous work.	1	2	3	4	5
We provide for those in need.	1	2	3	4	5
We spend time eating together.	1	2	3	4	5
Joy and gladness permeate our fellowship.	1	2	3	4	5
We give priority to worshiping God.	1	2	3	4	5
Nonmembers respect us.	1	2	3	4	5
New believers join our class.	1	2	3	4	5

Think about each member of your class who has needs. What is a practical way you can lead your class to help meet those needs?

_____

Think about class members who are disconnected from the class or the Lord. Ask God for wisdom to meet needs and to lovingly reconnect those persons.

Day 4: Your Relationship with the Lost

Does your class build bridges to lost persons in your community? ❑ Yes ❑ No

Which of the following ministries could your Sunday School class use to open the door for evangelism? Check one.
❑ Free car wash
❑ Move-in assistance for college students
❑ Free morning coffee
❑ Free oil changes
❑ Free yard "sale"
❑ Sports-skills-improvement clinic
❑ Smoke-detector-battery replacement
❑ Neighborhood health fair
❑ Community canned-food collection
❑ Wrapping packages at Christmas

Discuss the idea you checked with others in your church who are concerned about lost people. Then set a date and prepare for the event. Decide when and how you can connect the gospel to lost persons to whom you minister.

Day 5: Your Relationship with Your Family and Your Church

Read 1 Timothy 5:8. What does this verse say about caring for your family?

_____

_____

Is it enough to provide for the physical needs of family members without concern for spiritual and emotional needs?   ❑ Yes   ❑ No

Who in your family or church needs your ministry? _____

_____

_____

What can you do for that person? _____

_____

_____

Ask God to make you sensitive to the needs of your family and fellow church members so that you will not neglect those who are closest to you.

Answers to the true/false activity on page 205: 1. T, 2. F, 3. T, 4. T, 5. F, 6. T, 7. F

FAITH AT WORK

Several years ago I missed an opportunity to share Jesus with Mary, a woman I saw regularly. However, I discussed a business opportunity with her, explaining that more money would improve her life. Shortly after, Mary died suddenly and unexpectedly. I was ashamed.

God used that incident to open my heart to the people around me. I had always known I needed to be a witness, but I had never given much thought to how I could help bring people to Jesus. As I became involved in FAITH, I began to realize how many opportunities God gives us to share Jesus. I've discovered that the opportunity to share Jesus may begin with a kind word or a controlled reaction. We are called to action. People are watching. Whether or not they know we are Christians, they take notice of how we live. And that opens doors—opportunities to plant a seed, to bring in a harvest, or to nurture a fragile plant as we come alongside and encourage a fellow believer.

FAITH has equipped me to be intentional in sharing Jesus. It has given me a logical way to present God's plan of salvation to others. But it has also opened my eyes to needs among believers. The beauty of FAITH is that it is not just about evangelism but also about ministry. The abundant life Jesus promised in John 10:10 does not guarantee that a Christian's life will be easy. New believers and mature Christians face struggles, heartaches, sin, and great personal need.

Ministry is a key part of the FAITH strategy. Sunday School provides an environment for developing and strengthening godly friendships. Something happens when people pray, worship, and study God's Word collectively. As their hearts knit together, it becomes easier to know when someone has a need. The class can rally around the person, giving support and encouragement. Thus, the class members become to one another a physical reminder of Jesus' love for us and His care for and involvement in every aspect of our lives.

As my former Sunday School class got bigger and bigger, God laid it on our hearts for me and my husband to make a change. After much prayer and a period of waiting, we helped start a new class with a few other like-minded couples. Through this new class God has especially given us the desire and wisdom to minister to other believers effectively. And God has blessed our ministry. We are making a difference in one another's lives. And this knowledge strengthens us to make a difference in our world.

Amy Hall
Colonial Heights Baptist Church
Jackson, Mississippi

SESSION 14
Benefits of Leadership

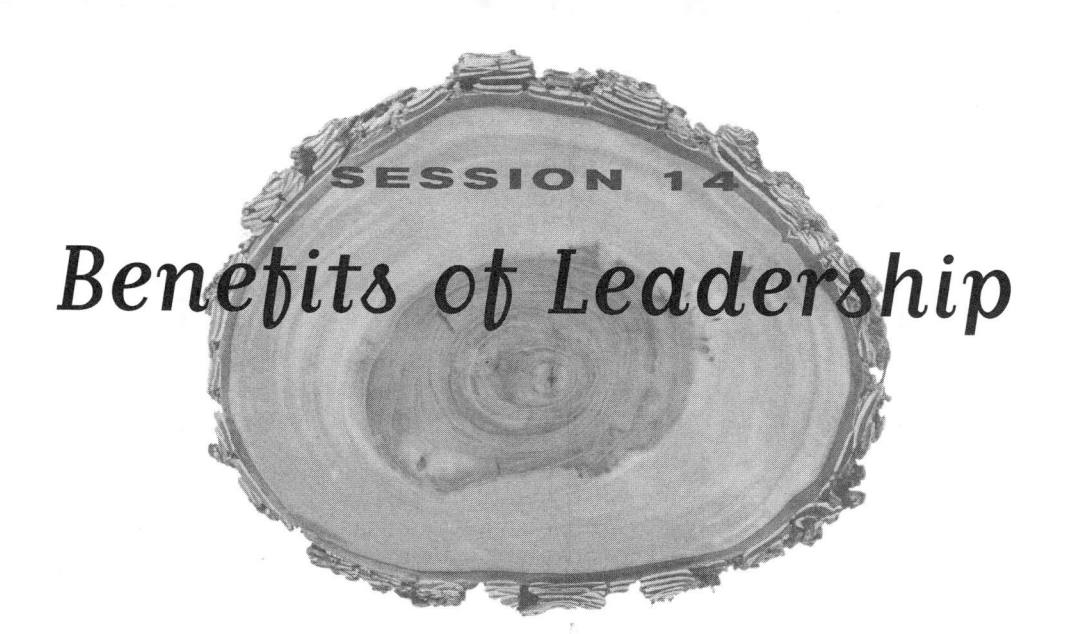

In this session you will—

CHECK IT by engaging in Team Time activities;

KNOW IT by reviewing content from session 13;

HEAR IT by examining the personal, church, and kingdom benefits of leadership;

STUDY IT by overviewing Home Study Assignments;

DO IT by leading your Team in making visits;

SHARE IT by celebrating.

IN ADVANCE
- Overview content.
- Preview teaching suggestions. Prepare key points. Decide whether to use the session 14 computer presentation or overhead cels 66–70 (see pp. 336–40).
- Prepare the room for teaching.
- Pray for participants and for Teams as they prepare to visit.
- As Teaching Time begins, direct participants to open their Journals to page 212.

TEAM TIME

CHECK IT (15 MINS.)

If the computer presentation is used, display the agenda for Team Time. Add other points to the agenda as needed.

CHECK IT agenda:
- ✔ FAITH Visit Outline
- ✔ Session 13 Debriefing
- ✔ Help for Strengthening a Visit

Leading Team Time

All Team members participate in Team Time. They are primarily responsible for reciting the assigned portion of the FAITH Visit Outline and for discussing other Home Study Assignments.

As you direct this important time of CHECK IT activities with your Team, keep in mind that Learners look to you as a role model, motivator, mentor, and friend. Team Time activities can continue in the car as the Team travels to and from visits.

Lead CHECK IT Activities

✔ *FAITH Visit Outline*
- ❑ Listen while each Learner recites as much of the FAITH Visit Outline as time allows. Make sure each person has a turn. It may be best to ask Learners to recite the segment they have the most difficulty sharing during a visit.
- ❑ As time permits, allow for additional practice on any part of the visit presentation, sequence, and materials (*A Step of Faith*, for example).

✔ *Session 13 Debriefing*
- ❑ Review: The FAITH Sunday School Evangelism Strategy® is designed to help equip the Sunday School member and leader to share the gospel and minister to prospects and members. A strength of this evangelism training is that participants learn a simple yet direct approach to talking with people about the message of the gospel when visiting with a Team of three. Another wonderful benefit is that someone who learns to share the gospel becomes more aware of witnessing opportunities during encounters throughout the week. Remind Team members that, as they continue training, they will become more aware of opportunities to share both a verbal and a lifestyle witness with people whose lives they intersect.

✔ *Help for Strengthening a Visit*
- ❑ Discuss some of the difficulties Teams have encountered in leading someone to hear and consider the FAITH gospel presentation. Call attention to the fact that this session formally introduces Learners to ways to deal with difficulties and distractions. At the same time, Team Leaders and other participants will learn other ways to help their Teams respond appropriately.
- ❑ As time allows, consider sharing a copy of the Witness Awareness Quotient (from *Building Bridges Through FAITH*, pp. 197–200) for Team members to use at their convenience. Or discuss some things

you learned as a result. Briefly help Team members see the impact of increasing their awareness of witnessing opportunities. It is one way to focus attention on strengthening both lifestyle and verbal opportunities to witness.

Notes

Actions I Need to Take with Team Members This Week

Transition to classrooms for instruction on the content of the session. (5 mins.)

TEACHING TIME

KNOW IT

Step 1 (5 mins.)

Direct participants to turn to "A Quick Review" on page 212 in their Journals and to follow the instructions to complete the activities. Use the computer presentation or overhead cel 66 to review the answers:
1. evangelism, ministry
2. 1. d, 2. b, 3. e, 4. a, 5. c
3. Subjective response

Be careful not to exceed the five-minute time limit.

A Quick Review

A Quick Review

Recalling what you learned in session 13 about ministry, complete the following review.

1. What are the dual purposes of FAITH?

   __evangelism__ and __ministry__

2. Why is ministry so important for a Sunday School class? Select the words in the column on the right that correctly complete the sentences in the left column. Then write the corresponding letter in the blank on the left of each statement.

   __d__ 1. Ministry communicates love to _____ _____.
   __b__ 2. Ministry demonstrates concern for _____.
   __e__ 3. Ministry motivates ministry to _____.
   __a__ 4. Ministry reconnects people to the _____ and His _____.
   __c__ 5. Ministry encourages involvement in _____.

   a. Lord, church
   b. prospects
   c. FAITH
   d. class members
   e. others

3. What is a ministry-evangelism activity your class or church can use to build bridges for the gospel?

   _____
   _____
   _____

LEADERS ON LEADERSHIP

"There is no greater experience for leaders than rejoicing with those who have matured in their faith as a result of their leader's faithfulness."
—Henry and Richard Blackaby[1]

212 / Growing as a FAITH Leader Facilitator Guide

Is It Worth the Effort?

Have you ever asked yourself, *Why am I doing this?* You've likely asked that question about an activity you were involved in, whether it was pulling weeds in a flower bed that seemed hopelessly overgrown or teaching a class of children who seemed to forget (or ignore) everything they had been taught. A similar question can be asked about what you've been learning and doing throughout your study of *Growing as a FAITH Leader:* are developing as a leader and seeking to multiply leaders worth the effort? Whether your answer is positive or negative, you can learn and grow from your experiences. Every challenge or opportunity you experience is valuable if you seek God's perspective.

If you are wondering whether leadership development is worth the difficulty, and especially if you are questioning whether leadership has any benefits, then this session is for you. You will discover the benefits of spiritual leadership that are evident in several areas of your ministry.

In *Kingdom Principles for Church Growth, Revised and Expanded*, Gene Mims presents a 1•5•4 Principle that applies to every church:

> ### THE 1•5•4 PRINCIPLE OF CHURCH GROWTH
> *1 driving force:*
> - The **Great Commission**
>
> *5 essential functions of the church:*
> - **Evangelism**
> - **Discipleship**
> - **Fellowship**
> - **Ministry**
> - **Worship**
>
> *4 results:*
> - Numerical **growth**
> - Spiritual **transformation**
> - Ministry **expansion**
> - Kingdom **advance** [2]

When a church remains focused on the Great Commission and carries out the five functions God has assigned, it will experience four results. The church can't accomplish its task without **leadership**. As you carry out your leadership responsibility through the FAITH Sunday School strategy in your church, you will discover the 1•5•4 Principle in action. The results are benefits for you, your church, and God's kingdom.

HEAR IT

Step 2 (5 mins.)

Ask participants to turn to page 213 in their Journals and to fill in the blanks as you present "Is It Worth the Effort?" Use the computer presentation or overhead cel 67.

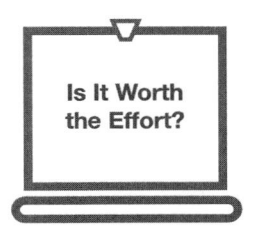

Is It Worth the Effort?

Step 3 (15 mins.)

Direct participants to turn to "Discover the Personal Benefits" on page 214 in their Journals and to fill in the blanks as you present the material. Use the computer presentation or overhead cel 68.

Discover the Personal Benefits

Discover the Personal Benefits

Sometimes when people hear the word *personal*, they equate it with something that is not meant to be shared, such as a personal-size pizza, or with an attitude that values the individual more than the team. Often they equate the word with selfishness; yet something that is personal doesn't always have to be sinful.

Personal benefits can come to a person as a result of an unselfish activity that is not motivated by the benefits. This is especially true with spiritual leadership. When you seek to accomplish God's will, you don't do it to be rewarded; yet you experience certain rewards that accompany your labor for the Lord. Likewise, when you focus on your leadership tasks, others in the body of Christ also experience personal benefits that spill over from your rewards.

Just as the H in FAITH relates to both the here and hereafter aspects of heaven, the rewards of leadership apply both in this life and in the life to come. You already know about many of the rewards you will receive hereafter, like a crown of righteousness (see 2 Tim. 4:8), treasures (see Matt. 6:20), an inheritance (see Col. 3:24), a dwelling place in God's house (see John 14:2), and many others. However, you may not recognize the rewards or benefits you experience here on earth as a result of your leadership. Consider these personal benefits.

The satisfaction of obeying God's __commands__
There is joy in doing what God has said to do. Perhaps the greatest joy comes from your obedience in making disciples and multiplying yourself in the lives of others. This is a primary focus of your leadership in the FAITH ministry.

The satisfaction of accomplishing God's __will__
There is excitement in doing what you were called and gifted to do. When you realize that God has a unique purpose for you, it energizes you to do what only you can do. Your task isn't complete until your life is over on this earth. That is why you must continue making disciples through your involvement in the FAITH Sunday School strategy.

The satisfaction of influencing another __generation__
There is encouragement in touching the life of someone who is considerably younger than you, especially your children and grandchildren. When this happens, you recognize that Christianity will continue because the torch has been passed. A part of your leadership focuses on your family and on those in God's family—your church—whom you impact through your leadership.

The satisfaction of seeing God work through __you__
There is amazement in recognizing that you are a tool in the hands of the Creator of the universe. Despite the fact that you came from dust, you have tremendous spiritual power when God works through you. You may have discovered this as God has worked through you in your FAITH Sunday School ministry.

The satisfaction of experiencing spiritual __transformation__
There is gratitude in realizing that you are not what you used to be, nor are you what you will be. Yet this change didn't come about because of your own efforts but because of God's work in you as you allowed Him to mold you into what He called you to be—a leader who is committed to fulfill the Great Commission.

The following personal benefits not only come as rewards directly to you but also bless others.

The satisfaction of seeing __growth__ *in others' lives*
It is exciting to discover what happens when people walk more closely with the Lord. They become more dedicated in practicing disciplines of the Christian faith like prayer, Bible study, witnessing, worship, ministry, fasting, and giving. They grow in their relationships with children, spouses, friends, and others. They grow in their influence in the church and community.

John referred to this satisfaction when he stated, "I have no greater joy than this: to hear that my children are walking in the truth" (3 John 4). As you lead others to follow Christ through the FAITH Sunday School Evangelism Strategy®, you experience the joy that comes from watching others mature in their relationships with the Lord.

The satisfaction of seeing __humility__ *develop in others' lives*
The longer believers spend time looking at the Lord instead of themselves, the more like Christ they become. They realize that what they are doing is for Christ and that He alone deserves the glory. They humble themselves as they follow Christ's example, denying their own interests and putting others ahead of themselves (see Phil. 2:3-8).

Paul saw humility in the life of Timothy, who Paul said would "genuinely care about [the] interests" (Phil. 2:20) of the believers in Philippi. Timothy did not seek his own interests as did so many other believers (see v. 21). As you encourage others on your FAITH Team or in your Sunday School class to humble themselves and put others' interests ahead of their own, you experience a great deal of satisfaction.

The satisfaction of seeing others gain __focus__
As believers allow the Holy Spirit to have more control of their lives, they begin to develop a warrior mentality. They recognize the scope

Session 14: Benefits of Leadership / 215

of the battle and the enemy they are fighting. Ephesians 6:12 takes on new meaning: "Our battle is not against flesh and blood, but against the rulers, against the authorities, against the world powers of this darkness, against the spiritual forces of evil in the heavens." They see the devastation and havoc Satan has caused and recognize that Jesus Christ is the only answer. Their burning desire is to lead others to know and experience God in a transforming way. They are not satisfied to stay in the safety zone but want to be on the front lines, in the thick of the battle.

Paul, who obviously had this focus, saw it develop in the life of Epaphroditus. Writing to the Philippians, Paul called him "my brother, co-worker, and fellow soldier" (Phil. 2:25). As you continue to lead others through the FAITH Sunday School Evangelism Strategy® to sharpen their focus on Christ, you experience the fulfillment that comes from helping develop "a good soldier of Christ Jesus" (2 Tim. 2:3).

Discover the Church Benefits

If you discovered that you had high cholesterol and began trying to lower it, would you be taking those steps just for your heart? Although you might realize that lowering your cholesterol would benefit your heart, you would ultimately be concerned about your whole body, which might not be around much longer if your heart were defective. Yet to do something that benefits the heart also benefits the entire body because the two have an interconnected relationship.

In the same way, an interconnected relationship exists between individuals and the church. Individual believers make up the body of Christ, with Jesus as "the head of the body" (Col. 1:18). As previously noted, personal benefits come to you because of your spiritual leadership even when your focus is not on yourself but on Christ and His church.

When you give leadership to fulfilling the Great Commission through the five functions of the church, you experience the joy of seeing God do incredible things in your church in the following four areas.

Numerical growth
Through your leadership in the FAITH Sunday School Evangelism Strategy®, you help bring more people to Christ, connect them to your church, and lead them to become active in Sunday School.

Spiritual transformation
Through your leadership in the FAITH Sunday School Evangelism Strategy®, you help believers become more like Christ as they grow in love, trust, and obedience to God and His Word.

Step 4 (10 mins.)

Direct participants to "Discover the Church Benefits" on page 216 in their Journals and ask them to fill in the blanks as you present the material. Use the computer presentation or overhead cel 69.

Discover the Church Benefits

Facilitator Guide

Ministry _____**expansion**_____
Through your leadership in the FAITH Sunday School Evangelism Strategy®, you help open up new opportunities to meet needs and reach people through means your church already uses or may not currently use. Many of these were mentioned in previous sessions, from starting new Sunday School units to sponsoring a health fair.

Kingdom _____**advance**_____
Through your leadership in the FAITH Sunday School Evangelism Strategy®, you guide people to develop a greater concern for God's global purpose by becoming more involved in missions. This includes not only local involvement but also involvement in your state, in your country, and around the world. This is God's plan as outlined in Acts 1:8.

As a result of your leadership in the FAITH Sunday School Evangelism Strategy®, your church will have a pool of new leaders who can assume responsibilities beyond the ministry of FAITH to influence each of the areas just described. In fact, the leaders who are best equipped to lead your church, regardless of the ministry area, are FAITH-trained leaders. They understand the big picture—the Great Commission. They realize that decisions in your church should be made not only for those who currently attend but also for those who do not yet attend. They understand the urgency to reach as many people as possible while time remains. They have a sense of excitement and anticipation that is contagious as they help lead the church to move forward under the direction of the Lord.

Discover the Kingdom Benefits

As a spiritual leader, you receive personal benefits that are by-products of the benefits to your church. Yet your ultimate concern must always be the same as that of Jesus. In teaching His disciples to pray, Jesus included the phrase " 'Your kingdom come' " (Matt. 6:10). The __**kingdom**__ was Jesus' ultimate concern. He knew that the kingdom of God comes when God rules in the __**hearts**__ of people.

As a result of your leadership on a FAITH Team and in your church, you can advance God's __**kingdom**__. This happens when people from "every tribe and language and people and nation" (Rev. 5:9) come to know God as Savior and obey Him as Lord. This is God's desire, and it was Christ's focus when He gave us our orders in Matthew 28:19-20. Through your continuing leadership in the FAITH strategy and in your church, you can help fulfill God's desire.

The benefits of leadership are worth the struggles, heartaches, and sacrifices. The benefits are numerous, not only for you but ultimately for God's kingdom. The task is not complete, so don't stop now! May

---

Step 5 (5 mins.)

Ask participants to fill in the blanks on page 217 in their Journals as you summarize "Discover the Kingdom Benefits." Use the computer presentation or overhead cel 70.

Discover the Kingdom Benefits

STUDY IT

Step 6 (5 mins.)

Overview the Home Study Assignments for session 14.

Transition to assemble with FAITH Teams to prepare for home visits. (5 mins.)

DO IT (110 MINS.)

your prayer echo that of Paul: " 'I count my life of no value to myself, so that I may finish my course and the ministry I received from the Lord Jesus, to testify to the gospel of God's grace' " (Acts 20:24).

> To learn more about kingdom results, see *Kingdom Principles for Church Growth, Revised and Expanded* (LifeWay Press, 2002).

Visitation Time

DO IT

1. All Team members should know the entire FAITH presentation. Are they ready to take the lead in a visit? Are they growing in their faith and in their capacity to share their faith? Are they learning to recognize when the FAITH Visit Outline needs to be adjusted in visits? Are they helping to establish bridges of relationship between the community and your Sunday School? Use your leadership role to challenge them to take the lead in visits and to offer support.
2. Share with Learners the importance of making ministry visits in order to strengthen their Sunday School and to connect members with a loving fellowship. Help them make the transition from asking, "How can I meet my needs?" to asking "How can I meet someone else's need?"
3. How far have Team members come since session 1? Have you taken the time to affirm them for their progress and to thank God for this mentoring experience?

Celebration Time

SHARE IT

SHARE IT (30 MINS.)

1. Ask a Team member to take the lead in sharing reports.
2. Hear reports and testimonies.
3. Complete Evaluation Cards.
4. Complete Participation Cards.
5. Update visitation forms with the results of visits.

---

[1]Henry and Richard Blackaby, *Spiritual Leadership* (Nashville: Broadman & Holman Publishers, 2001), 276.
[2]Gene Mims, *Kingdom Principles for Church Growth, Revised and Expanded* (Nashville: LifeWay Press, 2002), 6.

Home Study Assignments

Day 1: Your Relationship with God

Check benefits you have personally received as a result of your leadership.

❑ The satisfaction of obeying God's commands
❑ The satisfaction of accomplishing God's will
❑ The satisfaction of influencing another generation
❑ The satisfaction of seeing God work through you
❑ The satisfaction of experiencing spiritual transformation
❑ The satisfaction of seeing growth in others' lives
❑ The satisfaction of seeing humility develop in others' lives
❑ The satisfaction of seeing others gain focus

Spend time evaluating your leadership, especially your motives. Pray the words of Psalm 139:23-24 and listen to God as He searches your heart. Close your prayer time by praying for God's kingdom to advance and for His name to be exalted throughout the earth as a result of your leadership.

Day 2: Your Relationship with Your FAITH Team

How have your Team members benefited from your leadership this semester?

_____

_____

_____

As a Team Leader, what changes do you need to make for next semester?

_____

_____

_____

_____

Day 3: Your Relationship with Your Sunday School Class

Think of the members of your Sunday School class. Who has the potential to become a significant spiritual leader?

_____

What are you doing to help that person develop as a leader? _____

_____

_____

Spend time in prayer for that person today, asking that God will work in him or her. Also pray that God will work in you to develop that person into the leader He wants and needs.

Day 4: Your Relationship with the Lost

Read Acts 24:24-25. What are some ways people have responded when you shared the gospel with them? Check all responses that apply.
- ❑ Trusted Christ
- ❑ Became angry
- ❑ Changed the subject
- ❑ Asked questions
- ❑ Challenged your words
- ❑ Became convicted
- ❑ Delayed making a decision
- ❑ Struggled to understand
- ❑ Insisted that they didn't need Christ
- ❑ Became emotional

How are you dealing with these responses differently now than when you first started in FAITH?

_____

Do you have a warrior mentality—a sense of engaging in spiritual warfare?
❑ Yes ❑ No Do you find yourself being on the defensive or on the offensive when witnessing? ❑ Defensive ❑ Offensive

Ask God to help you move your eyes from the physical, flesh-and-blood battlefield to the spiritual battlefield.

Day 5: Your Relationship with Your Family and Your Church

Review the elements of the 1 •5 •4 Principle (see p. 213).

List evidence that your church is focused on the Great Commission.

_____

_____

_____

_____

_____

_____

List evidence that your church is carrying out each of the following purposes.

- Evangelism: _____

_____

_____

- Discipleship: _____

_____

_____

- Fellowship: _____

_____

_____

- Ministry: _____

_____

_____

- Worship: _____
  _____
  _____

List evidence that your church is seeing the following results.

- Numerical growth: _____
  _____
  _____

- Spiritual transformation: _____
  _____
  _____

- Ministry expansion: _____
  _____
  _____

- Kingdom advance: _____
  _____
  _____

SESSION 15

Where Do We Go from Here?

In this session you will—

CHECK IT by engaging in Team Time activities;

KNOW IT by reviewing content from session 14;

HEAR IT by considering the next steps you can take to influence others through FAITH;

STUDY IT by overviewing Home Study Assignments;

DO IT by leading your Team in making visits;

SHARE IT by celebrating.

IN ADVANCE
- Overview content.
- Preview teaching suggestions. Prepare key points. Decide whether to use the session 15 computer presentation or overhead cels 71–73 (see pp. 341–43).
- Be prepared to answer questions about next week's schedule.
- Prepare Preenlistment Cards and FAITH Force Multiplier Commitment Cards like the ones shown on page 228 and 231 or make copies of the cards from the file provided on the CD-ROM (inside the back cover of this Facilitator Guide). Put cards at every participant's place.
- Use the file provided on the CD-ROM (inside the back cover of this Facilitator Guide) to prepare copies of the evaluation form for participants to complete before session 16. Or plan to have participants use the evaluation form on pages 279–80 in their Journals.
- Prepare the room for teaching.
- Pray for participants and for Teams as they prepare to visit.
- As Teaching Time begins, direct participants to open their Journals to page 226.

TEAM TIME

CHECK IT (15 MINS.)

If the computer presentation is used, display the agenda for Team Time. Add other points to the agenda as needed.

CHECK IT agenda:
- ✔ FAITH Visit Outline
- ✔ Session 14 Debriefing
- ✔ Other Home Study Assignments
- ✔ Help for Strengthening a Visit

Leading Team Time

All Team members participate in Team Time. They are primarily responsible for reciting the assigned portion of the FAITH Visit Outline and for discussing other Home Study Assignments.

As you direct this important time of CHECK IT activities with your Team, keep in mind that Learners look to you as a role model, motivator, mentor, and friend. Team Time activities can continue in the car as the Team travels to and from visits.

Lead CHECK IT Activities

✔ FAITH Visit Outline
- ❑ Listen while each Learner recites as much of the FAITH Visit Outline as time allows. It may be best to ask Learners to recite the segment they seem to have the most difficulty sharing during a visit.
- ❑ As time permits, allow for any additional practice that is needed on the visit presentation and sequence.

✔ Session 14 Debriefing
- ❑ Briefly talk about distractions Team members have encountered in earlier visits.
- ❑ While reminding Team members that most visits go smoothly, help them begin to recognize principles and actions for handling difficulties. As you model ways to handle difficult situations during visits, explain what you did and why. Deal appropriately with difficulties that could take place at any time during visits. Difficulties are things that happen or are said during the visit that could keep you from sharing the gospel and leading a person who is ready to respond to make a commitment to Christ. Principles for dealing with difficulties relate primarily to building bridges of relationship with the person, dealing with any questions and objections, and working through the obstacles and distractions that take place.

✔ Other Home Study Assignments
- ❑ Remind the group of the assignment, due next week, to write a testimony describing what FAITH has meant personally.

✔ Help for Strengthening a Visit
- ❑ Remind Team members to listen during each visit for ministry opportunities and for ways to follow up appropriately.
- ❑ If you have shared the Witness Awareness Quotient with Team members (from *Building Bridges Through FAITH*, pp. 197–200), reemphasize as follows.

- The greater the number of Unsaved identified, the greater the potential for sharing a witness. The greater the number of Yes responses, the more someone is taking advantage of witnessing opportunities.
- If No responses are higher than Yes responses, then someone can consciously strengthen awareness of opportunities to share the gospel. If Yes responses are higher, then a witness can comfortably model for others the significance of sharing FAITH during daily-life opportunities.

Notes

Actions I Need to Take with Team Members This Week

Transition to classrooms for instruction on the content of the session. (5 mins.)

TEACHING TIME

KNOW IT

Step 1 (5 mins.)

Direct participants to turn to "A Quick Review" on page 226 in their Journals and to follow the instructions to complete the activities. Use the computer presentation or overhead cel 71 to review the answers:
1. Great Commission; evangelism, discipleship, fellowship, ministry, worship; growth, transformation, expansion, advance
2. The satisfaction of obeying God's commands, accomplishing God's will for your life, influencing another generation, seeing God work through you, experiencing spiritual transformation, seeing growth in others' lives, seeing humility develop in others' lives, seeing others gain focus

Be careful not to exceed the five-minute time limit.

A Quick Review

A Quick Review

In session 14 you studied the benefits of leadership. Complete the following activities as a review of what you learned.

1. What are the elements of the 1•5•4 Principle of church growth?

    1 driving force:

    - The _Great_ _Commission_

    5 essential functions of the church:

    - _evangelism_
    - _discipleship_
    - _fellowship_
    - _ministry_
    - _worship_

    4 results:

    - Numerical _growth_
    - Spiritual _transformation_
    - Ministry _expansion_
    - Kingdom _advance_

2. What are personal benefits you can experience from leadership?

    _____
    _____
    _____
    _____
    _____

LEADERS ON LEADERSHIP

"It's not the first but the last step in the relay race, the last shot in the basketball game, the last yard with the football into the end zone that makes the difference, for that is where the game is won." —John Maxwell[1]

Make the Decision

Have you ever been almost paralyzed over a decision you had to make? You may have weighed your options and written out a list of pros and cons, but they came out about even. Or you may have known the right thing to do but didn't want to do it. When faced with a difficult decision, some people have said, "I've decided not to decide." Yet in doing so, they've made a decision!

FAITH is greatly concerned with decisions—and not just those that come as a result of sharing the FAITH Visit Outline. Everyone who participates in FAITH must decide whether to continue in FAITH. Although this may not seem like an important decision, it can have life-changing consequences.

Your Team Learners in FAITH Basic are considering enlistment and reenlistment in session 15. Some have already decided not to participate in FAITH again next semester or perhaps ever again, despite the fact that you may have discussed with them the importance of reenlistment. In considering reenlistment, others have already determined, "I may come back, but I don't know enough to be a Team Leader."

While your Learners struggle with their decisions, it's possible that you, as a Team Leader, may also be struggling with a decision. For a variety of reasons you may have thought about not being involved in FAITH next semester. What are some of the reasons Team Leaders give for not returning the following semester?
- "There were more leaders than Learners this semester."
- "I didn't see any results."
- "I wasn't a very good leader."
- "I'm involved in too many other things."

Consider a response to each argument before you decide whether to be involved next semester.

Increase __enlistment__ *efforts.*
Some Team Leaders do not feel that they are needed. They argue, "We had more leaders than Learners this semester." Sometimes a church seems to have too many Team Leaders, but it's better than having too few! If leaders decide not to return because they didn't have Learners to train, a pattern will develop that will eventually harm the church.

The solution is to increase enlistment efforts for new Learners. Start with fervent prayer. Then take these steps to find new recruits for FAITH.
1. Think about new Christians your Team led to Christ this semester. Remind them of the importance of learning to share their faith.
2. Consider your prayer partners, who were initiated into the FAITH strategy as you met with them each week and shared victories and joys of participating in FAITH.

HEAR IT

Step 2 (15 mins.)

Direct participants to turn to "Make the Decision" on page 227 in their Journals and to fill in the blanks as you summarize the content. Use the computer presentation or overhead cel 72.

Make the Decision

Point out the Preenlistment Card at every place. State that the card helps participants focus their thinking on persons who might be open to FAITH enlistment efforts. Give participants a moment to complete the card.

3. Look in your Sunday School class for members who have not become involved in FAITH.

Personally ask two persons from any of these categories to become part of your FAITH Team next semester.

PREENLISTMENT CARD

Name _____

Sunday School department _____

List two persons in your Sunday School class or department for whom you will begin to pray to become FAITH Learners in the next semester of FAITH.

_____

_____

If someone has not yet come to mind, pray for the Lord to place a name on your heart.

Leave the results to ___God___.
Team Leaders sometimes comment, "I didn't see any results." Although their FAITH Teams have been faithful every week to visit and conduct Opinion Polls, they have become discouraged because no one has made a profession of faith.

The solution is to keep going and sharing and leave the results to God. You learned in session 11 that your focus must be on the fishing, not on the catch. God's Word promises, "We will reap at the proper time if we don't give up" (Gal. 6:9). Remember too that your work of discipling another believer (a Team Learner) is of great importance to the kingdom, so you haven't failed even if you've seen no professions of faith. Bobby Welch, who along with Doug Williams initiated the FAITH strategy, said, "I would do FAITH for no other reason than because of how it strengthens and grows the members we already have!"[2]

Learn from the ___past___.
Some FAITH Team Leaders made mistakes early in the semester or faced situations they didn't know how to handle. Unfortunately, they have allowed these situations to affect them for the remainder of the semester, and they have concluded, "I wasn't a very good leader."

228 / *Growing as a FAITH Leader Facilitator Guide*

The solution is to learn from the past. You are not the first to make a mistake. All leaders do it at some time, even the best FAITH Team Leaders. Sometimes the best education you can get is learning from your experiences. So keep growing as a leader and have faith "that He who started a good work in you will carry it on to completion" (Phil. 1:6).

Evaluate all of your **activities**.
Sometimes society seems to be traveling at the speed of light. Your schedule is probably full of many good activities. Too often, however, people are unwilling to sacrifice the good for the best. Other times they may be unable to say no and thus take on too many responsibilities. Faced with the decision of whether to lead a Team next semester, some Team Leaders say, "I'm involved in too many other things."

The solution is to evaluate all of your activities. Are they all of equal importance? Will your participation in them make a difference 5 years from now or 25 years from now? If your many tasks are church related, has God called you to do all of them? If not, you need to stop doing someone else's task. If God has called you to do all of them, He will give you all you need to complete the tasks He has given you.

You may recall from *Building Bridges Through FAITH* the detrimental effect that the loss of just one Team Leader can have on a church and the kingdom. Through a reverse-multiplication process, in fewer than 2.5 years it is possible that 243 fewer people would be available to make evangelistic or ministry visits. FAITH is one generation away from extinction if there are no new recruits or returning leaders next semester.

Join the FAITH Force

[Handwritten note: This is what our church needs!]

The Special Operations Forces of the United States Army consist of individuals who are Force Multipliers. These small units of approximately 12 highly specialized and trained individuals go into a country and train nationals for special military missions. Their training has given them the skills and attitude necessary to reproduce themselves in others, building a powerful fighting force.

This same strategy can be implemented in the FAITH Sunday School Evangelism Strategy® of your church. With the involvement of your pastor—a key leader in FAITH—your church can develop FAITH Force Multipliers to make the strategy more effective. A FAITH Force Multiplier has the skills and attitude necessary to help move FAITH to the next level. This soldier—
- works to develop a healthy Sunday School that engages people in evangelism, discipleship, fellowship, ministry, and worship to accomplish the purposes of the church;

Step 3 (15 mins.)

Ask participants to turn to page 229 in their Journals and to fill in the blanks as you summarize "Join the FAITH Force." Use the computer presentation or overhead cel 73.

Join the
FAITH Force

- passionately leads a FAITH Team, especially when it includes persons he or she has personally enlisted;
- works to equip, encourage, and mobilize individuals and churches to accomplish the Great Commission.

A FAITH Force Multiplier influences <u>**individuals**</u>.

If you stop and think about your spiritual development, you can probably recall individuals who made a significant difference in your life. They took time to invest in you the spiritual truths they learned from someone else. More than likely, your most significant mentor was someone who spent time with you one-to-one. That person's influence may not have come as much through words as it did through actions. You caught it. You must now influence others the same way. Think of individuals who would respond to your influence and leadership. Make a commitment today to be a FAITH Force Multiplier in their lives.

A FAITH Force Multiplier influences other <u>**churches**</u>.

The greatest power of influence is one friend persuading another friend. You may know members of other churches who have not heard about FAITH. To encourage them to begin FAITH in their churches, share your testimony of the way FAITH has changed your life and your church. Ask them to attend your next FAITH Kickoff Banquet to experience the excitement of what God is doing through FAITH.

With the agreement of both pastors, you can become a FAITH Force Multiplier by helping another church establish the FAITH strategy. Perhaps the church is in a rural area or an inner city. Of course, the pastor of the newly involved church must be trained in and committed to FAITH, but you could offer to lead two Learners in the church's first semester of training. God may allow you the time to lead a FAITH Team in your church and in another church. You might help beyond the first semester by teaching FAITH Advanced or a FAITH Discipleship course.

You could make an eternal difference by expanding the influence of FAITH to other churches. Although God may not call you as a missionary overseas, He may call you as a missionary in your own backyard.

A FAITH Force Multiplier influences another <u>**state**</u> or <u>**country**</u>.

As the Army's Special Operations Forces go to other countries, you can help meet tremendous needs by going to strategic cities in the United States and to other countries, either as a short-term missions volunteer or career missionary. Billions of people all over the world have never heard of Jesus Christ. Christians in these areas also need support.

Imagine living in a country run by a dictator and despot who has suppressed his citizens. They want to be liberated but have no hope and no help. Imagine the joy when one day Special Operations Force

Multipliers arrive and begin the process of liberation. Now imagine living in a country and praying for years that someone, just one person, would come and help you reach your fellow citizens with the gospel. Imagine the joy and relief when a spiritual Force Multiplier arrives.

Are you willing to enlist as a FAITH Force Multiplier? Examine this commitment card. Use it to express your commitment to be a FAITH Force Multiplier through your church to advance God's kingdom.

FAITH FORCE MULTIPLIER COMMITMENT CARD

With God's help I commit myself to become a FAITH Force Multiplier through _____ Church. I commit to talk with the following persons about participating with me in FAITH next semester.

_____

_____

I am committed to fulfilling the Great Commission through the FAITH Sunday School Evangelism Strategy®. I also commit to being a FAITH Force Multiplier by (check all that apply)—
❏ sharing the message of FAITH with believers in other churches as I have opportunities;
❏ assisting another church with FAITH;
❏ serving as a short-term volunteer in another state or country;
❏ serving as a career missionary in another state or country.

Signed _____ Date _____

Encourage participants to complete the FAITH Force Multiplier Commitment Card at their places.

Keep Advancing

Major General William G. Boykin, who commands the U.S. Army's John F. Kennedy Special Warfare Center and School, gave a challenging message to participants in a FAITH Institute. Emphasizing the nature of the battle that all FAITH participants will face, Boykin said, "Anyone who puts on the armor of God becomes a target for Satan. Be ready. He will be coming. He'll try to stop you from doing what God wants you to do." Boykin went on to add, "When you stepped into the FAITH arena, you said, 'Here am I. Send me.' … You volunteered to be a part of this

Step 4 (5 mins.)

Direct participants to "Keep Advancing" on page 231 in their Journals. Present the material, using the computer presentation. Challenge participants to keep pressing forward, following their Commanding Officer into the battle that He has already won.

Distribute copies of the evaluation form and instruct participants to complete it during the week and to return it to you in session 16. Or you may choose to ask participants to complete the evaluation form on pages 279–80 in their Journals, tear it out, and return it to you in session 16.

STUDY IT

Step 5 (5 mins.)

Overview the Home Study Assignments for session 15.

Transition to assemble with FAITH Teams to prepare for home visits. (5 mins.)

DO IT (110 MINS.)

SHARE IT (30 MINS.)

battle. When you took that step into the FAITH ministry and made that commitment, God had a plan for you. He has the plan, and your job is to stay faithful and to get up every day and put on that armor. Endure and wait to see what God has for you in this life. Endure!"[3]

We hope that the training you have received this semester has equipped you to be a FAITH Force Multiplier who can reproduce yourself in the lives of others and who endures. God wants to use you to build a mighty force that is ready to engage the enemy in spiritual battle. Satan has taken too much ground. It is time for God's people to put on the full armor of God and to rescue those who are in bondage and darkness.

Visitation Time

DO IT

1. As you drive, ask Team members to recall persons who are frequently absent from Sunday School. These persons may be facing crises. Ask Learners to think about what they can do to reinvolve these persons through caring ministry and loving fellowship.
2. Remember that this is the last week to visit before the final review. By now your Learners should be accepting responsibility for the visit. You should participate as a prayer partner on the FAITH Team. Take responsibility to deal with distractions like the baby, dog, phone, and so on. Always be ready to step in if Learners need assistance.
3. As you travel, talk about whom Team members have enlisted to be on their Teams for the next semester of FAITH. If they have not enlisted their Team members, encourage them to do so this week.

Celebration Time

SHARE IT

1. Ask a Team member to take the lead in sharing reports.
2. Hear reports and testimonies.
3. Complete Evaluation Cards.
4. Complete Participation Cards.
5. Update visitation forms with the results of visits.

---

[1] John C. Maxwell, *The 17 Essential Qualities of a Team Player* (Nashville: Thomas Nelson Publishers, 2002), 146.
[2] David Fleming, "FAITH: A Marriage Made in Heaven," *The Sunday School Leader,* January 2003, 6.
[3] Polly House, "FAITH strategy celebrates 5 years of evangelism via Sunday School," *Baptist Press,* 6 February 2003.

Home Study Assignments

Day 1: Your Relationship with God

Read Isaiah 6:1-8. Imagine that you are in God's throne room, witnessing the events Isaiah saw. Spend time in worship, confessing your sins and praising God.

Review the FAITH Force Multiplier Commitment Card you completed during session 15. Did you make every commitment God wanted you to make?
❏ Yes ❏ No Go back and make changes to the card if God leads you to change or add something.

Contact your accountability partner and share your commitment with him or her. Pray that God will empower the commitment you have made to Him in order to advance His kingdom.

Day 2: Your Relationship with Your FAITH Team

Considering where your Learners are at the end of this semester, what else could you have done to reproduce yourself in your Team members?

_____

_____

Look back in this session at the reasons Team Leaders give for not reenlisting in FAITH (p. 227). Which of these have you wrestled with at some point in your involvement in FAITH?
❏ "There were more leaders than Learners this semester."
❏ "I didn't see any results."
❏ "I wasn't a very good leader."
❏ "I'm involved in too many other things."
❏ Other: _____

How did God work in you to change your attitude about reenlisting?

_____

Ask for a few moments in your Sunday School class this week to emphasize the positive qualities you see in the members of your Team. Focus on the qualities that would make them FAITH Force Multipliers.

Day 3: Your Relationship with Your Sunday School Class

At your next class leadership meeting, introduce the need for a strategy to multiply your class. Look at the immediate future, but also develop a plan for two or more years ahead. Consider these elements:
- Increasing class members' involvement in FAITH
- Equipping members for ministry
- Starting a new class
- Sending out missionaries to help other classes or churches

Share the principles you have learned this semester with a leader from another class that did not have any members participating in FAITH this semester but has the potential to multiply within the next year. Offer to help that class prepare for multiplication.

Day 4: Your Relationship with the Lost

Read Romans 10:14-15. In your own words describe the strategy in these verses.

_____

_____

_____

_____

_____

_____

How could God use you as a FAITH Force Multiplier in a strategic city in the United States or in another country? Ask your pastor or another church-staff member about possible missions opportunities or contact the International Mission Board (*www.imb.org*) or the North American Mission Board (*www.namb.net*).

Ask God to introduce you to someone who does not know Him. Spend time with them in social settings so that you can multiply yourself in them. Let them hear and see the way Christ has changed your worldview. Pray that God will let them see the difference Christ has made in your life.

Day 5: Your Relationship with Your Family and Your Church

Call, e-mail, write, or talk with your Christian family members and friends who are members of other churches and ask whether their church is using the FAITH strategy. If not, share with them the benefits FAITH has brought to you, your church, and God's kingdom. If some of these churches are within a reasonable driving distance, talk with your pastor about the possibility of hosting a FAITH awareness meeting.

Ask your pastor or your FAITH Director whether they know of churches that are already utilizing FAITH that could benefit from your help. Seek two or three FAITH participants in your church who could join you in assisting another church.

FAITH TIP

Step Up to the Next Level of FAITH

No matter how long you have been involved in FAITH, you can always benefit from additional training. A National FAITH Institute offers four days of learning and sharing about FAITH and presents ideas for using FAITH to revolutionize your Sunday School. FAITH Institutes are specifically designed to help experienced FAITH churches improve their FAITH processes and Sunday Schools and to introduce FAITH to churches that have not yet experienced it.

FAITH Institutes offer three tracks for training FAITH Teams.

FAITH Basic Track
New FAITH trainees in the FAITH Basic Track receive training that qualifies them to begin FAITH in their churches. Participants have opportunities to interact with churches that currently use FAITH. Senior pastors must attend this track if they have not previously attended a FAITH Training Clinic.

FAITH Veterans Track
The FAITH Veterans Track is for persons who have attended a FAITH Training Clinic or have completed at least one semester of FAITH. Pastors, FAITH Directors, FAITH records secretaries, Sunday School leaders, and others involved in FAITH learn how to strengthen the Sunday School foundation that makes FAITH work. The veterans track offers—
- skill-development workshops;
- intentional efforts to build a national network of FAITH practitioners;
- heart-warming testimonies of transformed lives through FAITH;
- spirit-lifting messages pointing FAITH leaders to an expanded mission through FAITH;
- a forum for sharing ideas and strategies with other FAITH churches.

Training in FAITH is a prerequisite for all participants in the Veterans Track. Senior pastors must attend a FAITH Clinic before enrolling in this track.

POR FE Track
A POR FE Track runs simultaneously with the FAITH Basic and Veterans Tracks. This track includes complete training in using POR FE (Spanish FAITH) materials.

To learn more about National FAITH Institutes or to register, visit the LifeWay Web site at *www.lifeway.com/faith*. The LifeWay Web site is also a source of information about area meetings that equip leaders to further strengthen FAITH in their church.

SESSION 16
Final Review

In this session you will—

CHECK IT by engaging in Team Time activities;

KNOW IT by taking written and verbal reviews to evaluate your learning over the past 15 weeks;

STUDY IT by overviewing Home Study Assignments;

DO IT by leading your Team in making visits;

SHARE IT by celebrating accomplishments this semester or by announcing plans for a FAITH Festival in which the celebration will occur.

IN ADVANCE
- Be prepared to administer the written and verbal reviews.
- Be prepared to explain the process for recognizing Learners and Team Leaders, based on information in the *FAITH Director's Administrative Guide*. See your FAITH Director.
- Consult with the FAITH Director and plan to announce details for the FAITH Festival.
- Be prepared to announce dates for the next semester of training. Give Learners instructions about enlistment contacts to be made.
- Be prepared to point out the four additional weeks of Home Study Assignments, beginning on page 250, to be used between semesters.
- Be prepared to share any special plans for Visitation Time.
- Pray for participants and for Teams as they prepare to visit.
- As Teaching Time begins, direct participants to open their Journals to page 240.

TEAM TIME

CHECK IT (15 MINS.)

If the computer presentation is used, display the agenda for Team Time. Add other points to the agenda as needed.

CHECK IT agenda:
- ✔ FAITH Visit Outline
- ✔ Session 15 Debriefing
- ✔ FAITH Testimony
- ✔ Help for Strengthening a Visit

Leading Team Time

All Team members participate in Team Time. They are primarily responsible for reciting the assigned portion of the FAITH Visit Outline and for discussing other Home Study Assignments.

As you direct this important time of CHECK IT activities with your Team, keep in mind that Learners look to you as a role model, motivator, mentor, and friend. Team Time activities can continue in the car as the Team travels to and from visits.

Lead CHECK IT Activities

✔ *FAITH Visit Outline*
- ❑ Listen while each Learner recites any designated portion of the FAITH Visit Outline. It may be best to ask Learners to recite the segment they seem to have the most difficulty sharing during a visit.
- ❑ A brief time to practice the outline can help Team members confidently approach the verbal review.

✔ *Session 15 Debriefing*
- ❑ Emphasize the importance of each Team member's being available to serve as a Team Leader during future semesters. Review the potential results of choosing not to continue participating in FAITH training.

✔ *FAITH Testimony*
- ❑ Ask participants to turn in their "What FAITH Has Meant to Me" testimonies. Present them to the FAITH Director.

✔ *Help for Strengthening a Visit*
- ❑ Discuss some of the things that have been learned by making evangelistic, ministry, and Opinion Poll visits. Make sure Team members know who will be responsible for taking the lead in making the visits after the written and verbal reviews.

Notes

Actions I Need to Take with Team Members This Week

Write thank-you notes to Team members. Include congratulations for their completion of this semester of training. Indicate your continued support.

Transition to classrooms for written and verbal reviews. (5 mins.)

TEACHING TIME

KNOW IT

Step 1 (5 mins.)

Ask participants to give you the evaluations they completed during the week.

Briefly use "Developing as a Leader" to emphasize the need for participants to continue growing as leaders, particularly through the FAITH Sunday School Evangelism Strategy®. Congratulate participants for their achievement in completing this FAITH Discipleship course and in training Learners this semester. Encourage participants to continue their growth as FAITH leaders by participating in the next semester of FAITH training. Announce plans for a FAITH Festival and any schedule adjustments for this session.

Developing as a Leader

Congratulations! You have completed your training as a leader. Or have you? Obviously, you have completed a FAITH Discipleship course, but is this all there is to becoming the leader God wants you to be? Reread this statement from session 1: "Despite what some people may claim, leaders are not born; rather, they are developed." For spiritual leaders the growth process is never complete as long as you walk this earth. Therefore, you have only come to a pause in your leadership training. You must continue growing because you are not yet where God wants you to be.

Through this course you have learned leadership principles, methods, and skills. Consider the degree to which you have fulfilled the goals of this study that were introduced in session 1.

1. *You understand biblical leadership and have evaluated yourself against those principles.* This semester you have looked at biblical characteristics and skills of leadership, especially as seen in the life of Jesus.
2. *You understand Sunday School as a strategy and have become more effective at carrying it out.* This semester you have discovered more about the connection between FAITH and Sunday School, and you have learned ways you can influence others through the Sunday School strategy.
3. *You have learned how to multiply yourself in your Team, in your Sunday School class, and in other disciples.* This semester you have examined the principles of multiplication and have applied the process of multiplication to several areas. We hope your Learners are excited about becoming—or are at least willing to become—Team Leaders next semester so that they can train others through the FAITH strategy. Maybe you are aware of plans for starting a new Sunday School class, Bible-study group, or church because others have discovered the necessity of multiplying new units. We hope that you recognize the great potential your church and other churches have to advance the kingdom of God as you focus on multiplication rather than addition.
4. *You have developed your skills as a FAITH Team Leader.* This semester you have learned a variety of leadership skills that can strengthen your work with and influence on Team members.

Each goal had a knowledge component—learning what to do. Yet it also had an application component—doing what you learned. To what extent have you put into action the things you have learned? For example, how do your leadership practices and qualities compare with those of Jesus? How well does your Sunday School reflect the purposes of Sunday School? What has been the result of your study of the principle and process of multiplication?

It is likely that you have not fully implemented all the things you have learned this semester. But you now have a foundation on which to build, and you know many ways your leadership can influence your next FAITH Team, your Sunday School class, your church, and the kingdom of God.

Because of the Lord's work in your life, you have become a member of His family. Now you have the privilege of guiding people into His family and leading others farther in their journey of faith. However, many people do not know the Lord and do not follow Him. As a FAITH leader, you are God's instrument to share the message of Christ, to minister to people's needs, and to disciple and multiply other believers, both in your local area and around the world. Take the challenge to accomplish God's will in your life, your church, and His kingdom as you continue growing as a FAITH leader.

Written Review

Consider your growth as a FAITH leader this semester and respond to the following questions.

1. This semester in what ways has your leadership in the following areas been more productive than it was before you began this study?

   A FAITH leader: _____

   _____

   A Sunday School leader: _____

   _____

   A leader in your family and church: _____

   _____

2. Think about the following areas of emphasis this semester. Check the topic that gave you the most insight as a leader.
   - ☐ The Sunday School strategy
   - ☑ Enhancing the ministry of your Sunday School
   - ☐ God's call to ministry
   - ☐ Jesus' leadership qualities
   - ☐ Discovering your leadership qualities
   - ☑ Sharpening your leadership skills
   - ☑ Multiplying new Sunday School units
   - ☐ Multiplying the FAITH Team
   - ☐ The process of multiplication
   - ☐ The principle of multiplication
   - ☑ Growing as a ministry leader
   - ☑ The benefits of leadership
   - ☐ The next steps of leadership

Step 2 (15 mins.)

Instruct participants to complete the written review on pages 241–42 by following the directions in their Journals. State that they will have 15 minutes to complete the review.

[Handwritten notes:]

Session 1
① In which areas should you be able to indicate signs/ways of growth as a leader? (pg 14-16)

② What is a leader? What process is outlined in 2 Tim 2:2? What are the 3 points? (pg 17)

③ Sunday School is a ___² (pg 33)

Session 2
⑤ What are the 5 functions or purposes of the church? (pg 35-36)

Handwritten margin notes:

Session 3
(6) What are some essential steps your class should take to assimilate newcomers? (pg 52-53)

(7) If newcomers have not come to your class in the past month, what do you feel as a teacher or FAITH leader in that class needs to do? (All)

(8) Which is more accurate? Church Growth, Growing The Church when it comes to our Mission-Vision? (All)

Session 5
(9) If we do not stay focused on Jesus in our leadership whether in the world or church it is easy for our ___ to get in the way.

(10) What does EGO stand for?

Session 6
(11) What actions can you take to acquire biblical qualities of a FAITH leader? (pgs 97-101)

(12) What are the FACTS of Multiplication? (pgs 132-133)

Session 9
(13) To cultivate a multiplying ministry a FAITH Team leader needs several types of support from the Group leader, what are they? (pgs 148-149)

---

3. What have you learned this semester that was most beneficial to you in your leadership role(s)?

A leader needs to be willing and able to adapt to the different learning styles of their FAITH learners

4. How has this course changed your view of the FAITH Sunday School Evangelism Strategy®?

Changed No! Enhanced yes!

5. Describe how the focus on multiplication has affected—

your Sunday School class: _____

your church: _____

God's kingdom: _____

6. What is the next step God wants you to take as a FAITH leader?

Verbal Review: FAITH Visit Outline

❏ Preparation

❏ INTRODUCTION
❏ INTERESTS
❏ INVOLVEMENT
❏ **Church Experience/Background**
  ❏ • Ask about the person's church background.
  ❏ • Listen for clues about the person's spiritual involvement.
❏ **Sunday School Testimony**
  ❏ • Tell general benefits of Sunday School.
  ❏ • Tell a current personal experience.
❏ **Evangelistic Testimony**
  ❏ • Tell a little of your preconversion experience.
  ❏ • Say: "I had a life-changing experience."
  ❏ • Tell recent benefits of your conversion.

❏ INQUIRY
❏ **Key Question:** In your personal opinion, what do you understand it takes for a person to go to heaven?
❏ **Possible Answers:** Faith, works, unclear, no opinion
❏ **Transition Statement:** I'd like to share with you how the Bible answers this question, if it is all right. There is a word that can be used to answer this question: FAITH (spell out on fingers).

❏ Presentation

❏ **F is for FORGIVENESS**
❏ We cannot have eternal life and heaven without God's forgiveness.
❏ *"In Him [meaning Jesus] we have redemption through His blood, the forgiveness of sins"* —Ephesians 1:7a, NKJV.

❏ **A is for AVAILABLE**
❏ Forgiveness is available. It is—

  ❏ **AVAILABLE FOR ALL**
  ❏ *"For God so loved the world that He gave His only begotten Son, that whoever believes in Him should not perish but have everlasting life"* —John 3:16, NKJV.

Step 3 (15 mins.)

Ask participants to pair with their accountability partners. (Help form pairs if anyone's partner dropped out during the semester.) Instruct one person to share the FAITH Visit Outline with the partner, who will listen to the presentation and mark incorrect items in the other person's Journal, beginning on page 243. Then the other person in each pair should share the outline. Give partners 15 minutes to recite the outline to each other.

- ❑ **BUT NOT AUTOMATIC**
  - ❑ *"Not everyone who says to Me, 'Lord, Lord,' shall enter the kingdom of heaven"* —Matthew 7:21a, NKJV.

❑ ***I* is for IMPOSSIBLE**
- ❑ It is impossible for God to allow sin into heaven.

  - ❑ **GOD IS—**
    - ❑ • LOVE
      - ❑ *John 3:16, NKJV*
    - ❑ • JUST
      - ❑ *"For judgment is without mercy"* —James 2:13a, NKJV.

  - ❑ **MAN IS SINFUL**
    - ❑ *"For all have sinned and fall short of the glory of God"* —Romans 3:23, NKJV.
    - ❑ **Question:** But how can a sinful person enter heaven, where God allows no sin?

❑ ***T* is for TURN**
  - ❑ **Question:** If you were driving down the road and someone asked you to turn, what would he or she be asking you to do? (change direction)
  - ❑ *Turn* means *repent*.
  - ❑ **TURN** from something—sin and self
  - ❑ *"But unless you repent you will all likewise perish"* —Luke 13:3b, NKJV.
  - ❑ **TURN** to Someone; trust Christ only
  - ❑ (The Bible tells us that) *"Christ died for our sins according to the Scriptures, and that He was buried, and that He rose again the third day according to the Scriptures"* —1 Corinthians 15:3b-4, NKJV.
  - ❑ *"If you confess with your mouth the Lord Jesus and believe in your heart that God has raised Him from the dead, you will be saved"* —Romans 10:9, NKJV.

❑ ***H* is for HEAVEN**
  - ❑ Heaven is eternal life.
  - ❑ **HERE**
  - ❑ *"I have come that they may have life, and that they may have it more abundantly"* —John 10:10b, NKJV.
  - ❑ **HEREAFTER**
  - ❑ *"And if I go and prepare a place for you, I will come again and receive you to Myself; that where I am, there you may be also"* —John 14:3, NKJV.

❑ **HOW**
  ❑ How can a person have God's forgiveness, heaven and eternal life, and Jesus as personal Savior and Lord?
  ❑ Explain based on leaflet picture, FAITH (Forsaking All, I Trust Him), Romans 10:9.

❑ **Invitation**

❑ **INQUIRE**
  ❑ Understanding what we have shared, would you like to receive this forgiveness by trusting in Christ as your personal Savior and Lord?

❑ **INVITE**
  ❑ • Pray to accept Christ.
  ❑ • Pray for commitment/recommitment.
  ❑ • Invite to join Sunday School.

❑ **INSURE**
  ❑ • Use *A Step of Faith* to insure decision.
  ❑ • Personal Acceptance
  ❑ • Sunday School Enrollment
  ❑ • Public Confession

Grade your verbal review. Each item counts one point; the highest possible score is 67. Subtract the number you missed from this total to get your score.

Highest possible score: 67

Number missed: – _____

My score: = _____

Step 4 (5 mins.)

Instruct participants to total the number of incorrect responses their partners have marked in their Journals, then to subtract that total from 67 to get their overall scores.

Step 5 (5 mins.)

Overview the Home Study Assignments for session 16. Remind participants of the four additional weeks of Home Study Assignments, beginning on page 250, which they should use for their personal growth between semesters. Close the session by praying that participants will continue to grow as leaders and witnesses.

Transition to assemble with FAITH Teams to prepare for home visits. (5 mins.)

DO IT (110 MINS.)

SHARE IT (30 MINS.)

Visitation Time

DO IT
1. Your visitation schedule may be altered tonight. Allow for any schedule changes your church has agreed on.
2. Encourage Learners to make the gospel presentation by themselves.
3. Urge your Team members to continue FAITH training next semester and to continue using the FAITH Visit Outline to witness.
4. Encourage Teams to return for a special Celebration Time.

Celebration Time

SHARE IT
1. Ask a Team member to take the lead in sharing reports.
2. Hear reports and testimonies.
3. Complete Evaluation Cards.
4. Complete Participation Cards.
5. Update visitation forms with the results of visits.
6. Allow time for testimonies about what this semester of FAITH has meant to participants and to the persons they have visited.

Home Study Assignments

Day 1: Your Relationship with God

Read Nehemiah 1:1-11. Nehemiah was a significant leader at a crucial time in Israel's history. What is one thing that stands out about him as you read these verses?

_____

Nehemiah was a man of prayer, and this practice made a great difference in his leadership. Your prayer life will likewise make a great difference in your leadership. Mark an X on the line below to indicate the growth in your prayer life over the past 16 weeks.

|—————|—————|—————|—————|—————|—————|—————|—————|
No growth   **Slow growth**   **Moderate growth**   **Significant growth**

What is one thing you will do this week to give greater attention to your communication with God?

_____

Day 2: Your Relationship with Your FAITH Team

Read Acts 15:36. Paul was concerned about people he had influenced in the past, and he felt a responsibility to stay in contact with them. Spiritual leaders don't forget about people they previously mentored. How did a leader encourage you in the weeks following your first semester of FAITH?

_____

Check four ways you will stay in contact with the Learners on your FAITH Team during the next four weeks to continue encouraging them and helping them develop as leaders.
❑ Make a phone call
❑ Visit
❑ Meet for breakfast and prayer
❑ Visit new Sunday School prospects or follow up on previous visits together
❑ Send an e-mail
❑ Write a card
❑ Invite to a meal in your home

Day 3: Your Relationship with Your Sunday School Class

Recall the goal you set after session 1 for growing as a Sunday School leader this semester (see Home Study Assignments, day 3, p. 27). How has your class been strengthened as a result of your leadership over the past 16 weeks?

_____

In what areas does your Sunday School class still need to catch the vision of the FAITH Sunday School strategy? Check all that apply.
❑ Understanding the strategy
❑ Focusing on health instead of growth
❑ Assimilating new people
❑ Working together as a leadership team
❑ Balancing evangelism and ministry
❑ Committing to multiply

Whom in your class can you encourage to join you in FAITH next semester?

_____

How will you begin making contact with them to get them involved?

_____

Day 4: Your Relationship with the Lost

Recall the goal you set after session 1 for growing in your relationship with lost persons this semester (see Home Study Assignments, day 4, p. 27). Did you accomplish your goal?   ❑ Yes   ❑ No

What do you believe is the current spiritual status of the lost person for whom you have prayed over the past 16 weeks?
❑ Believer   ❑ Closer to accepting Christ   ❑ Uncertain

What is your next step with that person if he or she is a—

new believer? _____

spiritual seeker?_____

lost person? _____

Day 5: Your Relationship with Your Family and Your Church

Read Joshua 24:14-15. Joshua's goal was for him and his family to serve the Lord. How do you think he accomplished that goal?

_____

_____

Recall the goal you set after session 1 for growing as a leader in your family and church this semester (see Home Study Assignments, day 5, p. 28). Write it here.

_____

_____

Did you accomplish your goal? ❑ Yes ❑ No

How do you know? _____

_____

_____

How can you give more emphasis to the spiritual leadership of your family over the next four weeks?

_____

_____

SUPPLEMENTAL
Home Study Assignments

It is all-important for a spiritual leader and witness to continue growing. One way to do that is to spend time each day studying God's Word and talking with the Father, as you have done through the Home Study Assignments this semester. Four additional weeks of Home Study Assignments are provided on the following pages. These guided study times will help you bridge the gap between FAITH semesters and will encourage you to maintain a growing relationship with the Lord.

Week 1

Day 1: Your Relationship with God

Read Numbers 20:1-12. Reflect on the leadership of Moses, who was at first reluctant (see Ex. 3:11) but became one of the finest leaders in Israel's history. Though he was a great leader, his sin eventually disqualified from further leadership of the nation.

How could sin affect your spiritual leadership? _____

_____

_____

_____

_____

Spend time today thinking about your relationship with God. Write a confession of any sin that is affecting your relationship with God and that will hinder your spiritual leadership.

_____

_____

_____

_____

_____

_____

_____

_____

Day 2: Your Relationship with Your FAITH Team

Read Hebrews 13:1-2. The fact that the FAITH semester has ended doesn't mean that prospects will stop visiting your church. Check actions your church takes to reach out to these persons between FAITH semesters.

❑ Phone calls
❑ Letters from the pastor
❑ Visits
❑ Nothing
❑ I don't know.
❑ Other: _____

By taking the following steps, your FAITH Team could reach out to guests so that they don't become disinterested before another semester of FAITH visits begins.

1. Contact your church office and ask for the names of two or three prospects who have visited for the first time since the FAITH semester ended.
2. Contact your former Team members and plan a time of visitation during the coming week, perhaps at a different time from your FAITH Visitation Time during the semester. Or contact two members of your Sunday School class who have not been involved in FAITH and ask them to go visiting with you. These may be persons you would like to enlist as Learners next semester.
3. Carry out the visit as if it were a FAITH visitation assignment, sharing testimonies, asking the Key Question, and using the FAITH outline if allowed.

Day 3: Your Relationship with Your Sunday School Class

Get a copy of your Sunday School class's attendance record. Contact all active members and ask them to pray about participating in FAITH next semester.

What benefits of participation in the FAITH ministry will you share with them?

_____

_____

_____

_____

_____

_____

Work with your class leadership to schedule a three-minute testimony about FAITH in your class each Sunday for the next four weeks. Four members of your class could give a testimony, or you may ask someone from another class to share what God has done in his or her life through FAITH.

Day 4: Your Relationship with the Lost

Read Luke 15:11-24. John Kramp, in his book *Out of Their Faces and into Their Shoes*, notes that waiting is often a part of the evangelistic process. Waiting, instead of continuing to talk, after a discussion about faith can give God time to work in the person's heart and can give us time to pray. Waiting also allows our own faith to develop.[1] Based on your experience, do you agree or disagree?
❑ Agree   ❑ Disagree

Think of someone to whom you have witnessed on more than one occasion who has not accepted Christ as Savior and Lord. How can you pray for this person as you wait for God to work in the person's heart? Write your prayer here.

_____
_____
_____
_____
_____
_____
_____
_____
_____
_____
_____
_____
_____
_____

Day 5: Your Relationship with Your Family and Your Church

Read Acts 16:11-15. What evidence does this text provide that Lydia influenced her household to follow the Lord?

_____

_____

What can you do today to influence a member of your family to follow the Lord?

_____

_____

_____

_____

Spend time praying for your family members. If you are single, pray for parents, siblings, or extended family members.

---

[1] John Kramp, *Out of Their Faces and into Their Shoes* (Nashville: Broadman & Holman Publishers, 1995), 157.

Week 2

Day 1: Your Relationship with God

Read Hebrews 12:1-13. What is the race that God has ordained for you?

_____

Check things that hinder you from running the race that is set before you.

❏ Job
❏ Hobbies/leisure activities
❏ Failure to prioritize
❏ Family concerns
❏ Ongoing sin in your life
❏ Other: _____

How do these things interfere with your walk with God and your relationships with others?

_____

_____

_____

_____

How will you deal with this distraction to your calling as a believer?

_____

_____

_____

_____

Day 2: Your Relationship with Your FAITH Team

Read John 17:1-26. Write the verse number beside each of Jesus' requests for His followers.

Protection: _____

Unity: _____

Holiness/sanctification: _____

To recognize God's glory: _____

To commune with God: _____

Influence in the world: _____

Love: _____

To be filled with Christ: _____

Joy: _____

Multiplication: _____

To glorify God: _____

Even though you have spent 16 weeks mentoring the former Learners on your FAITH Team, some of their needs can be met only by God. Use the list above to pray for those you led last semester. Then write notes of encouragement to your former Learners today and let them know that you are praying for them.

Supplemental Home Study Assignments / 257

Day 3: Your Relationship with Your Sunday School Class

Read Proverbs 18:15. How well do persons acquire knowledge through your Sunday School class?

_____

_____

Some teachers say that knowledge is what you learn, while wisdom is what you do with what you learn. If this is the case, you should be balanced in your knowledge and wisdom. If you are, it will be easier to remember what you learned because you put it into practice. Mark an X on the scale to indicate your Sunday School class members' balance between what they know and what they do with what they know.

Knowledge ◁─────────────┼─────────────▷ **Wisdom**

If members need a better balance between learning and doing, how might God want to use you to change the focus of your class leaders and members?

_____

_____

_____

_____

Day 4: Your Relationship with the Lost

List persons you know in the following categories who may not be believers.

Your workplace: _____

_____

A restaurant you frequent: _____

_____

Your school: _____

_____

Your neighborhood: _____

_____

Your family: _____

_____

Beside each name indicate the last time you asked the Key Question and how the person responded.

Pray and ask God to show you ways to connect with unbelievers. Pray about a block party, an ornament party, or a dinner party you could use to lay the groundwork for sharing the gospel.

Supplemental Home Study Assignments / 259

Day 5: Your Relationship with Your Family and Your Church

For the next three days keep a log of the amount of time you spend with your family. If you are single, focus on persons you consider to be like your family. What does the log indicate about your relationships with your family members?

_____

_____

_____

_____

_____

Develop a schedule for the coming month that sets aside time for each member of your family. This can be a date with your spouse, a special time with your children, or focused time with your parent.

Ask the members of your family what their needs are and how you can best meet their needs.

Week 3

Day 1: Your Relationship with God

Read Ephesians 5:1-20. List qualities that should and should not be part of your life.

Should	Should Not
_____	_____
_____	_____
_____	_____
_____	_____
_____	_____
_____	_____
_____	_____
_____	_____

Circle one item in each column that indicates an area of your life in which you want to improve, through God's power, in the coming month.

Pray about these characteristics and ask God to help you imitate Him.

Day 2: Your Relationship with Your FAITH Team

Recall the time after your first semester of FAITH training. Was there a cooling-down period in which you quit sharing your faith, ministering, visiting, or thinking about persons who were not involved in church? ❏ Yes ❏ No
If so, what could someone have done to help you prevent this hiatus?

_____

_____

_____

If not, how did you maintain your fervor for evangelism and ministry?

_____

_____

_____

Plan some time this week to nurture the relationship between you and the former members of your FAITH Team. Write your plan for getting together with them for a time of prayer, encouragement, and accountability so that they and you don't lose zeal for evangelism and ministry.

_____

_____

_____

_____

Day 3: Your Relationship with Your Sunday School Class

List the persons who serve in the following leadership positions in your class.

Teacher: _____

Apprentice teacher: _____

Ministry coordinator: _____

Care-group leaders: _____

Visitation and evangelism coordinator: _____

Fellowship coordinator: _____

Prayer coordinator: _____

Missions coordinator: _____

Your class may not have someone serving in each position, but these areas are important. Draw a plus sign (+) beside the positions that you think are essential for a class. How could the other positions benefit your class?

_____

_____

_____

_____

_____

_____

Day 4: Your Relationship with the Lost

Read Psalm 67. How has God blessed you? _____

_____

_____

_____

_____

_____

How have you made known God's ways and salvation among people of other nations?

_____

_____

_____

_____

_____

Spend time today praising God for what He has done for you and for others. Think about what your life would be like if you had never heard of God or if you did not have a personal relationship with Him. Consider what God is calling you to do so that His salvation is made known throughout the world.

Day 5: Your Relationship with Your Family and Your Church

Read 1 Corinthians 12:12-31. Write the names of 10 persons in your church who seem to be uninvolved in the body of Christ.

_____   _____

_____   _____

_____   _____

_____   _____

_____   _____

Write the names of 10 persons in your church who seem to be overinvolved in the body of Christ.

_____   _____

_____   _____

_____   _____

_____   _____

_____   _____

Pray that each of these persons will discover the ways God has gifted them and the specific places of service He has designated for them. Pray that each of them will do what God wants them to do so that the body of Christ will function as God desires.

Week 4

Day 1: Your Relationship with God

Match each of the following verses with a command God gives to you.

___ 1. 1 Peter 5:8   a. Witness locally and globally.

___ 2. 1 John 2:15   b. Be joyful in trials.

___ 3. Acts 1:8   c. Do not love the things of the world.

___ 4. 1 Corinthians 15:58   d. Obey Christ's commands.

___ 5. James 1:2   e. Fight the good fight of faith.

___ 6. 1 Timothy 6:12   f. Be self-controlled and alert.

___ 7. John 14:15   g. Give yourself completely to God's work.

Day 2: Your Relationship with Your FAITH Team

What needs to change in your life for you to become a FAITH Force Multiplier next semester?

_____

_____

_____

Write the names of the persons you have been praying would become involved with you in FAITH next semester.

_____

_____

What have you shared with them about the FAITH ministry that would encourage them to get involved?

_____

_____

_____

_____

_____

_____

Spend time praying for these persons. Ask God to send them out as laborers in His harvest field.

Day 3: Your Relationship with Your Sunday School Class

On a typical Sunday, how many empty chairs would you estimate are in your Sunday School classroom? _____

This Sunday count the number of empty chairs. How does your space affect the number of members who attend or the number of prospects who can come?

_____

_____

_____

_____

Urge your class leaders to adopt the empty-chair concept as a visual reminder of the need to bring more people into the class.

Day 4: Your Relationship with the Lost

Read 2 Corinthians 5:11-21. What was Paul's motivation for sharing the gospel (see vv. 11,14)?

_____

_____

_____

_____

What is your motivation for sharing the gospel? _____

_____

_____

_____

_____

_____

What is involved in the ministry of reconciliation? _____

_____

_____

_____

_____

If passion for lost people could be measured on a gauge, Paul would no doubt register 100 percent. On the gauge below, indicate how passionate you are to lead lost people to become reconciled to God.

|—————|—————|—————|—————|—————|—————|—————|—————|—————|—————|
10%   20%   30%   40%   50%   60%   70%   80%   90%   100%

Spend time in prayer, asking God to fill you with His passion for reconciling lost people to Himself.

Day 5: Your Relationship with Your Family and Your Church

Read Colossians 3:12-17. How did Paul describe Christians in these verses?

_____

_____

_____

_____

_____

Look at the list of virtues mentioned in this passage.

- ❑ Compassionate
- ❑ Kind
- ❑ Humble
- ❑ Gentle
- ❑ Patient
- ❑ Bearing with one another
- ❑ Forgiving
- ❑ Loving
- ❑ Peaceful
- ❑ Thankful
- ❑ Teaching
- ❑ Admonishing
- ❑ Grateful
- ❑ Doing everything for Christ

Check the virtues that affect your relationship with your family. Underline the virtues that affect your relationship with your church.

Which one quality do you need to express most to have the greatest impact on your family?

_____

Which one quality do you need to express most to have the greatest impact on your church?

_____

Answers to matching activity on page 266: 1. f, 2. c, 3. a, 4. g, 5. b, 6. e, 7. d

Session 1:
Goals of FAITH Discipleship

- To teach you important <u>biblical</u> <u>truths</u>

- To equip you to respond to difficult <u>questions</u>

- To help you develop as a <u>life</u> <u>witness</u> for Christ

- To help you develop as a <u>Team</u> <u>Leader</u> or an <u>Assistant</u> Team Leader

- To suggest ways you can <u>disciple</u> Learners

- To help you lead your Sunday School class to become a <u>reaching</u>, <u>teaching</u>, <u>ministering</u>, <u>multiplying</u> group

Purposes of Growing as a FAITH Leader

You will—

- understand <u>biblical leadership</u> and evaluate yourself against those principles;

- understand <u>Sunday School</u> as a <u>strategy</u> and become more effective at carrying it out;

- learn how to <u>multiply</u> yourself in your Team, in your Sunday School class, and in other disciples;

- develop your skills as a FAITH <u>Team Leader</u>.

Why Do Churches Need Leaders?

From 1996 to 2001, 69 percent of Southern Baptist churches were <u>plateaued</u> or <u>declining</u> in average Sunday School attendance.

While our country's population is rapidly increasing, <u>kingdom growth</u> is not keeping pace.

The problem can be traced to a void in <u>biblical leadership</u>.

What Is a Leader?

Receive (learn): "what you have heard from me."

Repeat (teach): "commit to faithful men."

Reproduce (train): "who will be able to teach others also."

Who Are Leaders?

<u>All</u> <u>Christians</u> are called to be spiritual leaders.

God wants you to join His work of <u>making</u> <u>disciples</u>, who in turn will go and make disciples.

Where Are You to Lead?

Your relationship with <u>God</u>

Your relationship with your <u>FAITH</u> <u>Team</u>

Your relationship with your <u>Sunday</u> <u>School</u> <u>class</u>

Your relationship with the <u>lost</u>

Your relationship with your <u>family</u> and <u>church</u>

When Are You to Lead?

Reproducing leaders is a <u>command</u>.

True biblical leadership is <u>reproducing reproducers</u>.

Delaying obedience is <u>disobedience</u>.

Session 1, Cel 7

How Do You Grow as a Leader?

- Your relationship with <u>God</u>

- Your relationship with your <u>FAITH</u> <u>Team</u>

- Your relationship with your <u>Sunday</u> <u>School</u> <u>class</u>

- Your relationship with the <u>lost</u>

- Your relationship with your <u>family</u> and <u>church</u>

Session 2:
A Quick Review

1. a, c, d, f, g

2. The church is only one generation away from extinction, and a tremendous void of biblical leaders exists in many churches.

Sharpen the Focus of Sunday School

Sunday School is a <u>strategy</u>.

Sunday School leads people to know <u>Jesus</u>.

Sunday School utilizes <u>open</u> Bible-study groups.

Sunday School helps accomplish the work of the <u>church</u>.

Strengthen the FAITH Connection to Your Sunday School

FAITH links <u>evangelism</u> to Sunday School.

FAITH links <u>ministry</u> to Sunday School.

Strengthen the FAITH Connection to Your Church

A church exists for <u>evangelism</u>.

A church exists for <u>discipleship</u>.

A church exists for <u>fellowship</u>.

A church exists for <u>ministry</u>.

A church exists for <u>worship</u>.

Recognize the Importance of Small Groups

- Small groups offer <u>connection</u> <u>points</u>.

- Small groups offer <u>accountability</u> for evangelism.

- Small groups provide <u>effective</u> <u>ministry</u>.

- Small groups enhance <u>spiritual</u> <u>maturity</u>.

- Small groups provide an avenue for <u>service</u>.

Cultivate Open Bible-Study Groups

An <u>open</u> Bible-study group—

- **is an evangelistic group that seeks to include new people, especially unbelievers, at any time;**

- **doesn't require that someone have prior content knowledge or preparation in order to participate;**

- **regularly sees people coming and going—new people coming into the class and others leaving the class to serve somewhere else.**

Cultivate Open Bible-Study Groups

A <u>closed</u> group focuses more on spiritual maturity than on evangelism. A closed group—

- requires people to prepare for the class, and the content progressively builds from session to session;

- usually exists for a limited time, such as for the length of a particular study, then disbands.

It has been estimated that more than half of Adult Sunday School classes in Southern Baptist churches are <u>closed groups</u>.

Session 3: Develop a Healthy Sunday School Class

Make the area of need a matter of <u>prayer</u>.

Discuss the need with <u>FAITH Teams</u>.

Consult with <u>class leaders</u>.

Give Priority to the Sunday School Leadership Meeting

The leadership meeting equips <u>leaders</u>.

The leadership meeting strengthens <u>teamwork</u>.

The leadership meeting promotes <u>communication</u>.

Assimilate New Members

Station a **class** **greeter** at the door.

Wear **name** **tags**.

Enlist **good** **neighbors**.

Assign prospects and new members to **care** **groups**.

Utilize **fellowship**.

Take the **lead**.

Maintain Connections

Assign them to <u>care groups</u>.

Include them in <u>fellowship</u> activities.

Establish a service <u>hall</u> of <u>fame</u>.

Session 4: A Quick Review

1. Pray. Discuss with FAITH Teams. Consult with class leaders.

2. Station a class greeter at the door. Wear name tags. Enlist good neighbors. Assign to care groups. Utilize fellowship. Take the lead.

3. Growth focuses on getting larger; health focuses on staying balanced.

4. FAITH is part of the Sunday School strategy, which builds a healthy church that is balanced in accomplishing evangelism, discipleship, fellowship, ministry, and worship.

Recognize Your Calling

The disciples were all <u>laymen</u>, not paid professionals.

Not all laypersons may know a lot of theology, but they have a <u>love relationship</u> with Jesus Christ that motivates them to <u>obedience</u>.

Understand the Command of God's Call

God has called us not only to <u>salvation</u> but also to <u>service</u>. And that service centers on proclaiming the <u>gospel</u> of <u>Christ</u> so that all people might bring <u>glory</u> to <u>God</u>.

Identify the Characteristics of God's Call

A time of <u>preparation</u> is needed.
<u>God</u> initiates the call.
God's call is first to a <u>relationship</u>.
God does <u>extraordinary</u> things through ordinary people.
God calls us to a life of <u>sacrifice</u>.
God's call and your specific role are <u>unique</u> to you.
God expects instant <u>obedience</u>.

Discover the Purpose of God's Call

Jesus wants us to <u>follow</u> first, then to be His <u>witnesses</u>.

We can't constantly <u>work</u> for God without <u>walking</u> with God.

The purpose of God's call is that all people will come to <u>know</u> Him and <u>glorify</u> Him.

Connect Your Calling

The <u>role</u> we are given

The <u>reason</u> we are called

The <u>reward</u> we will receive

Find Your Place in Ministry

Finding your place in ministry is a process of <u>listening</u> to God and <u>following</u> His direction.

The S.E.R.V.E. Profile

S = <u>spiritual gifts</u>

E = <u>experiences</u>

R = <u>relational style</u> (personality)

V = <u>vocational skills</u>

E = <u>enthusiasm</u> (passion)

Session 5: A Quick Review

1. God calls us first to walk with Him and then to work for Him.

2. God calls every believer to ministry, and He works with us as we work together to lead others to know and love Him.

3. Choices a, c, d, f, g, h, and i are correct.

Follow the Greatest Leader

Jesus remained <u>focused</u> on His purpose regardless of His situation.

- **Jesus recognized that <u>God</u> was with Him.**

- **Jesus did not allow His <u>personal</u> <u>needs</u> to get in the way of God's purpose.**

- **Jesus did not allow other <u>opportunities</u> to distract Him.**

- **Jesus did not allow <u>popular</u> <u>opinion</u> to sway Him.**

Follow the Greatest Leader

Jesus <u>challenged</u> people to move from where they were to where they should have been.

Jesus <u>mentored</u> others so that they could fulfill their potential.

Jesus led by <u>example</u>.

Jesus was <u>balanced</u> in His responses to people.

Jesus <u>prioritized</u> His life and work.

Jesus <u>persevered</u> until His mission was completed.

Session 6:
Look Below

Don't <u>compartmentalize</u>.

Cultivate <u>integrity</u>.

Session 6, Cel 30

Live Low

Resist pride.

Practice humility.

Learn from Jesus.

Let Go

Give God <u>control</u>.

Be filled with the <u>Spirit</u>.

Be willing to <u>grow</u>.

Session 7: A Quick Review

- Don't **compartmentalize**.
- Cultivate **integrity**.
- Resist **pride**.
- Practice **humility**.
- Learn from **Jesus**.
- Give God **control**.
- Be filled with the **Spirit**.
- Be willing to **grow**.

Questions to Be Answered

- How can I help my Learners see the <u>big picture</u> of FAITH?

- How can I manage our <u>time</u> better—each week and for the whole semester?

- How do I <u>encourage</u> my Learners during the week?

- How do I challenge my Learners to give their <u>best</u>?

- How do I deal with <u>personality differences</u> on my Team?

- How can I make sure my Learners have reached appropriate <u>goals</u> by the end of the semester?

Help Learners Catch the Vision

<u>Vision</u> <u>casting</u> is an important skill in leadership, especially for a FAITH Team Leader.

Remind your Learners in every possible way that FAITH is an <u>ongoing</u> <u>strategy</u> rather than a once-a-week activity.

Manage Your Time Wisely

Arrive **early** if possible.

Delegate **previsitation tasks**.

Get to the **car** quickly after Teaching Time.

Focus the Team on the **visit**.

Maximize time between **visits**.

Try one more **door**.

Delegate **postvisitation tasks**.

Encourage Learners

Believe in them.

Praise them for their work.

Contact them during the week.

Let them **practice** the FAITH outline.

Point out areas of concern.

Use Modeling to Teach Skills

Know the **FAITH outline**.

Model effective **time management**.

Discuss **visits**.

Respond to Personality Differences

Pray for Team members.

Focus on strengths.

Embrace differences.

Address problems early.

Session 8:
A Quick Review

1. c, e, f

2. Fill in the blanks:

a. Arrive <u>early</u> if possible.

b. Delegate <u>previsitation tasks</u>.

c. Get to the <u>car</u> quickly after Teaching Time.

d. Focus the Team on the <u>visit</u>.

e. Maximize time between <u>visits</u>.

f. Try one more <u>door</u>.

g. Delegate <u>postvisitation tasks</u>.

Does Your Growth Strategy Add Up?

An addition mentality undermines <u>life change</u>.

An addition mentality thwarts <u>spiritual growth</u>.

An addition mentality impedes <u>church growth</u>.

Multiplication: Do the Math

Receive (learn): "what you have heard from me."

Repeat (teach): "commit to faithful men."

Reproduce (train): "who will be able to teach others also."

Multiplication: Know the FACTS

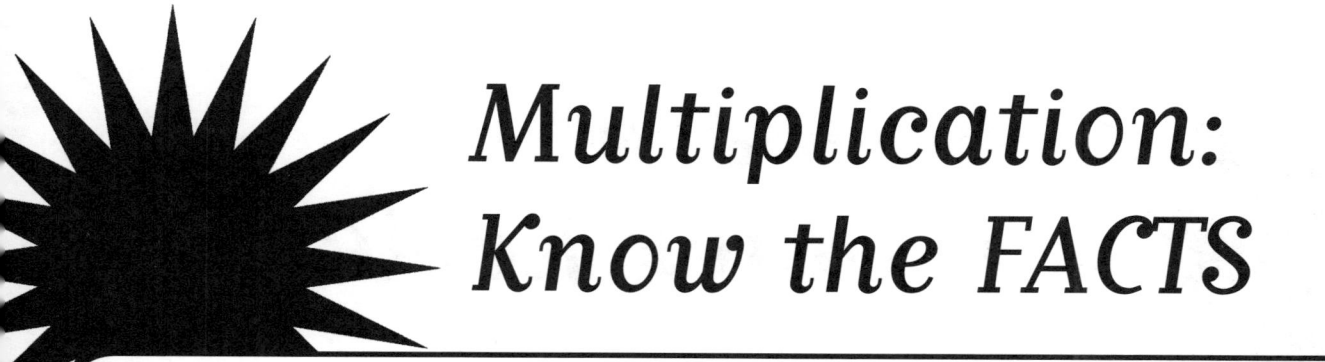

F is for <u>fruitful results</u>.

A is for <u>amazing growth</u>.

C is for <u>continuous action</u>.

T is for <u>time-sensitive</u>.

S is for <u>Spirit-empowered</u>.

Session 9: A Quick Review

1. **Receive:** learn from God's Word through teaching others.

   Repeat: share with others what you've learned.

   Reproduce: guide others to share what they've learned with still others, continuing the process.

2. F is for <u>fruitful results</u>.
   A is for <u>amazing growth</u>.
   C is for <u>continuous action</u>.
   T is for <u>time-sensitive</u>.
   S is for <u>Spirit-empowered</u>.

Recognize Hindrances to Multiplication

The <u>schedule</u> keeps new people from participating.

Church members lack <u>knowledge</u> about FAITH.

New Learners are not <u>enlisted</u>.

Team Leaders do not <u>return</u>.

The FAITH leadership is <u>inconsistent</u>.

Learners are not adequately <u>trained</u> to lead Teams.

Address the Problems

Adjust the <u>schedule</u>.

Share personal <u>testimonies</u>.

Emphasize <u>reenlistment</u> and <u>recruitment</u>.

Encourage <u>quality</u> along with quantity.

Utilize FAITH <u>events</u>.

Remember to <u>pray</u>.

Prepare Your Team to Multiply

Offer constructive <u>evaluation</u>.

Provide increasing <u>ownership</u>.

Confront Learners' <u>apprehensions</u>.

Schedule prearranged <u>visits</u>.

Use some visits for <u>enlistment</u>.

Nurture <u>Assistant</u> Team Leaders.

Look to Your Group Leader for Guidance

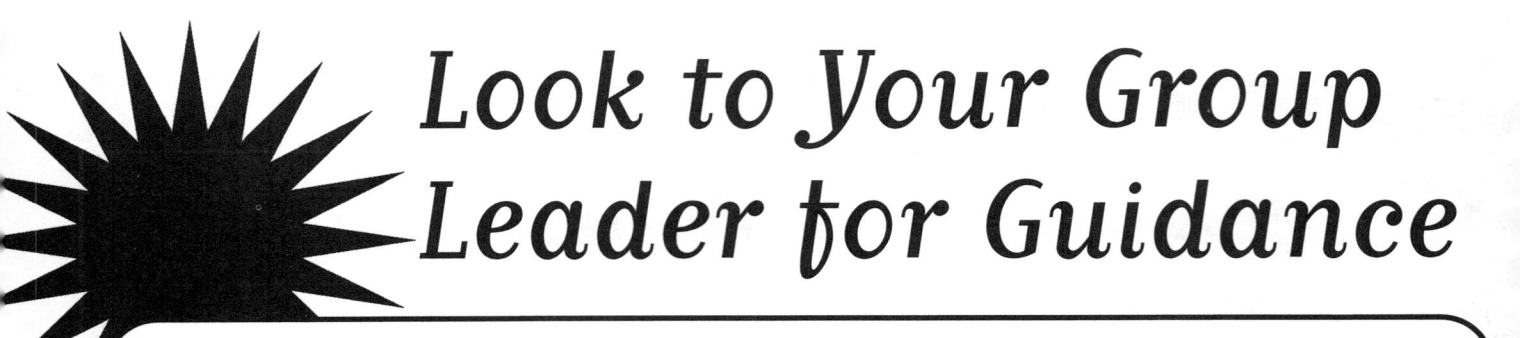

Group Leaders offer <u>accountability</u>.

Group Leaders offer <u>wisdom</u>.

Group Leaders offer <u>encouragement</u>.

Group Leaders offer <u>consistency</u>.

Session 10: A Quick Review

1. Fill in the blanks:

Offer constructive <u>evaluation</u>.

Provide increasing <u>ownership</u>.

Confront Learners' <u>apprehensions</u>.

Schedule prearranged <u>visits</u>.

Use some visits for <u>enlistment</u>.

Nurture <u>Assistant</u> Team Leaders.

2. c, e, f, h

What?

Traditional Sunday School classes

Nontraditional Bible-study groups

New churches

Why?

New units create <u>excitement</u>.

New units are generally more <u>aggressive</u> in evangelism and ministry.

New units make it easier to develop <u>relationships</u>.

New units provide more opportunities for <u>service</u>.

New units generally <u>grow</u> more quickly.

When?

1. A wide <u>age range</u> exists in the class—10 or more years.

2. The class enrollment is between 25 and 40.

3. The meeting place is full of people.

4. <u>Ministry needs</u> are neglected.

5. Many new adults in the community are in the same age group.

6. New church members are being enrolled in other classes.

When?

7. Many active class members have no <u>responsibility</u>.

8. The number of prospects is greater than the number of members.

9. Attendance is less than <u>40</u> percent of enrollment.

10. Too many attend for members to get to know one another.

11. Active members are not missed when they are absent.

12. Class leaders can't <u>recall</u> who attended the previous week.

How?

1. Share the multiplication <u>vision</u> with class members and leaders.

2. Talk with church staff and other leaders.

3. Recast the vision on a regular basis.

4. Seek "missionaries" who will help start a new unit.

5. Allow the missionaries to be <u>apprentices</u> for current leadership positions.

6. Identify the birthday for the new unit.

7. Regularly meet with new class leaders for <u>prayer</u> and <u>coordination</u>.

How?

8. Seek prospects.

9. Plan a <u>fellowship</u> before the new unit begins, inviting all prospects.

10. Visit prospects.

11. Conduct the first meeting of the new unit.

12. Hold regular <u>leadership meetings</u> to evaluate, update, and plan.

13. Keep in touch with the sponsor.

14. Continually pray for God's <u>leadership</u>.

Session 11: A Quick Review

1. Fill in the blanks:

   Traditional Sunday School <u>classes</u>

   Nontraditional Bible-study <u>groups</u>

   New <u>churches</u>

2. The correct order is 6, 10, 5, 7, 11, 13, 1, 8, 4, 9, 12, 14, 3, 2.

Session 11, Cel 56

Focus First on Following

Follow **Jesus**.

Let Jesus make you the **disciple** He wants.

Become a **fisher** of **men**.

Focus First on Following

New believers—
- begin <u>following</u> <u>Christ</u>;
- identify new <u>prospects</u>;
- want to <u>share</u> with others;
- become FAITH <u>Learners</u>.

New Learners—
- want to teach others how to lead people to <u>Christ</u>;
- become new <u>leaders</u> in FAITH.

New leaders mentor <u>new</u> <u>Learners</u> in FAITH, continuing the multiplication process.

Reject Substitutes for Jesus

Don't follow <u>self</u> instead of Jesus.

Don't follow <u>religion</u> instead of Jesus.

Don't follow <u>people</u> instead of Jesus.

Trust Jesus to Do His Part

Jesus' <u>desire</u> is to make believers into multipliers.

Jesus' <u>will</u> is for believers to become multipliers.

Jesus' <u>power</u> enables believers to become multipliers.

Session 13:
A Quick Review

1. b, f, g, h, i

2. To become fishers of men

Minister to Current Class Members

Ministry communicates love to <u>class</u> <u>members</u>.

Ministry demonstrates concern for <u>prospects</u>.

Ministry motivates ministry to <u>others</u>.

Ministry reconnects people to the <u>Lord</u> and His <u>church</u>.

Ministry encourages involvement in <u>FAITH</u>.

Minister to New Members

Use an **assimilation** process.

Involve new members in **Sunday School**.

Encourage participation in **ministry**.

Minister to Your Community

Your class can show caring actions through <u>ministry evangelism</u>.

- Establish a <u>partnership</u> with an adopted school.

- Offer community <u>events</u>.

- Sponsor <u>sports</u> and <u>recreational</u> activities.

- Work with community <u>agencies</u>.

By building bridges through ministry, you can ask the <u>Key</u> <u>Question</u> and perhaps share the FAITH outline.

Emphasize Enrollment

Refer to your class's **ministry list**.

Emphasize that no **risk** is involved.

Get essential **information**.

Remember to **follow through**.

Become a **life minister**.

Session 14:
A Quick Review

1. Evangelism, ministry

2. 1. d, 2. b, 3. e, 4. a, 5. c

Is It Worth the Effort?

The 1 • 5 • 4 principle:

1 driving force:
- The <u>Great</u> <u>Commission</u>

5 essential functions:
- <u>Evangelism</u>
- <u>Discipleship</u>
- <u>Fellowship</u>
- <u>Ministry</u>
- <u>Worship</u>

4 results:
- Numerical <u>growth</u>
- Spiritual <u>transformation</u>
- Ministry <u>expansion</u>
- Kingdom <u>advance</u>

The church can't accomplish its task without <u>leadership</u>.

Discover the Personal Benefits

The satisfaction of—

obeying God's <u>commands</u>;

accomplishing God's <u>will</u>;

influencing another <u>generation</u>;

seeing God work through <u>you</u>;

experiencing spiritual <u>transformation</u>;

seeing <u>growth</u> in others' lives;

seeing <u>humility</u> develop in others' lives;

seeing others gain <u>focus</u>.

Discover the Church Benefits

Numerical growth

Spiritual transformation

Ministry expansion

Kingdom advance

Discover the Kingdom Benefits

The **kingdom** was Jesus' ultimate concern. He knew that the kingdom of God comes when God rules in the **hearts** of people.

As a result of your leadership on a FAITH Team and in your church, you can advance God's **kingdom**.

Session 15: A Quick Review

1. Great Commission; evangelism, discipleship, fellowship, ministry, worship; growth, transformation, expansion, advance

2. The satisfaction of obeying God's commands, accomplishing God's will for your life, influencing another generation, seeing God work through you, experiencing spiritual transformation, seeing growth in others' lives, seeing humility develop in others' lives, seeing others gain focus

Make the Decision

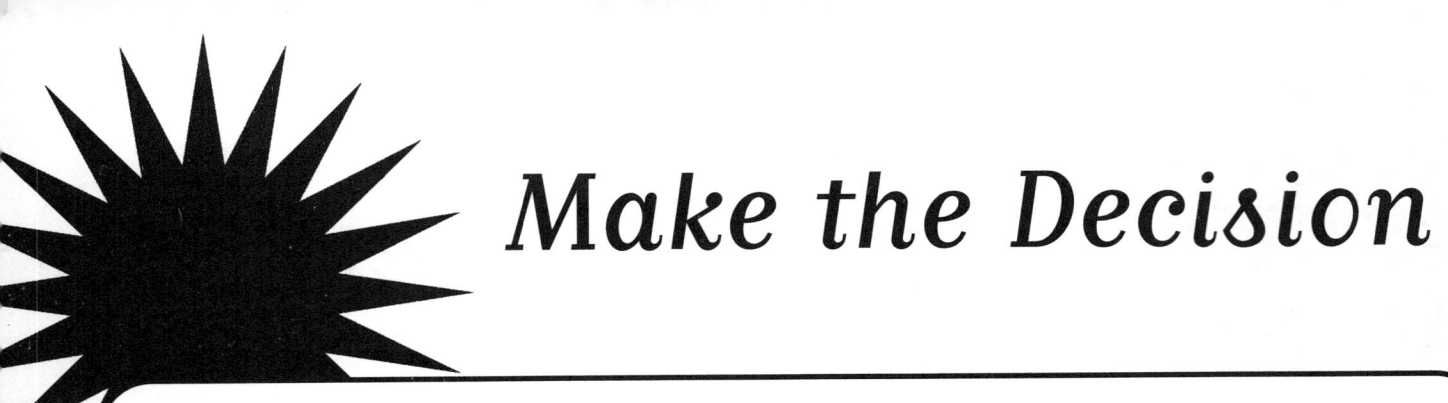

Increase enlistment efforts.

Leave the results to God.

Learn from the past.

Evaluate all of your activities.

Join the FAITH Force

A FAITH Force Multiplier influences <u>individuals</u>.

A FAITH Force Multiplier influences other <u>churches</u>.

A FAITH Force Multiplier influences another <u>state</u> or <u>country</u>.

Using Your CD-ROM

This CD-ROM inside the back cover of this Facilitator Guide provides a FAITH computer presentation and FAITH forms that support *Growing as a FAITH Leader* group sessions.

System Requirements
300 mhz processor, 64 megs of available RAM, Windows 2000, 95, 98, NT, XP, or PowerMac

Using the Computer Presentations
Computer presentations are listed by session in an Adobe® Acrobat® format, a common delivery method for both printable and projectable resources. You very likely have already loaded a free Adobe Acrobat Reader from one of our other CD-ROM products or free from the Acrobat Web site. A copy of Acrobat Reader 5 is included on this disc for your convenience.

It is possible to create a custom opening or closing for each FAITH session that provides your session times, FAITH leaders, and other church information. A PowerPoint® presentation template with the FAITH presentation background is included for this purpose. It allows you to move quickly and seamlessly from your customized introduction to the FAITH presentation and back to a customized closing if you wish.

PowerPoint is required for you to use the template provided, adding your own content. You can include specific times or locations for your sessions. You can introduce your church or church leaders, share photos of Teams, or even include photos of someone being baptized or involved for the first time in Sunday School. You are limited only by your creativity and time. Please read your PowerPoint manual for help in inserting photos and adding special effects.

Running PowerPoint and Acrobat Files
After you have fully developed and tested your custom PowerPoint presentation, practice before your session, using the following guidelines. After a little practice the flow from PowerPoint to Acrobat and back will be almost seamless.

1. Open the PDF folder on the CD-ROM.
2. Click on the session you will be using and drag it to your desktop. (This is not required, but most computers will operate more smoothly running the files on the hard drive rather than from the CD-ROM.)
3. Open Acrobat Reader and select "Preferences/General" under the "Edit" menu. Choose "Full Screen" from the list on the left. Check the box beside "Advance on Any Click." You may also want to experiment with other options in this dialogue. When finished, click "OK."
4. Open the Acrobat session. Make certain that it is in "Full Screen" mode. If it is not, select "Full Screen" from the "View" pulldown menu.
5. Make certain that you are at the page where you wish to begin the FAITH presentation, usually the first slide.
6. Open your prepared PowerPoint introduction.
7. It is best to close all other programs while using your computer for a presentation.
8. Start your PowerPoint presentation.
9. At the time you wish to move to the FAITH presentation, use the keyboard command Alt/Tab (hold the Alt key and press the Tab key one time.) This will shift your screen view to the last program that was up, which should have been your opening slide for the FAITH session.
10. If you wish to return to your PowerPoint presentation at any time, the same key strokes (Alt/Tab) will return to the screen you left.

Using the Forms
Files for key forms used in this course are also provided in Adobe Acrobat and Microsoft Word® formats. Open the files and print copies of the forms for participants' use as needed. Permission is granted for you to print copies of the forms for their intended use only.

- FAITH Catalog and Order Form (Acrobat format only) can be used to order additional FAITH resources.
- FAITH at Work testimonies printed in the Journal and Facilitator Guide are also provided in a computer file. Use them in your church newsletter or other communication pieces to promote FAITH involvement.
- Celebration Time Report is recommended in session 1 for use throughout the course.
- Questions for Evaluating Whether Your Bible-Study Group Is an Open Group is recommended for distribution in session 2.
- Prayer-Partner Commitment Cards should be distributed in session 2 and returned in session 3.
- Leadership-Meeting Plan Sheet can be distributed in session 3 for participants to use in leadership meetings.
- Spiritual-Gifts Worksheet should be distributed in session 4 for participants to complete during the following week.
- Witness-Awareness Quotient (Acrobat format only) can be used in sessions 14–15 of Team Time.
- Preenlistment Card and FAITH Force Multiplier Commitment Card are recommended for use in session 15.
- Course Evaluation should be distributed in session 15 for participants to complete and return in session 16.